State Legislative Innovation

edited by
James A. Robinson

State Legislative Innovation

Case Studies of Washington, Ohio, Florida, Illinois, Wisconsin, and California

PRAEGER SPECIAL STUDIES IN U.S. ECONOMIC, SOCIAL, AND POLITICAL ISSUES

Praeger Publishers   New York   Washington   London

Library of Congress Cataloging in Publication Data

Robinson, James Arthur, 1932-
   State Legislative innovation.

   (Praeger special studies in U. S. economic,
social, and political issues)
   Includes bibliographical references.
   1. Legislative bodies—United States—States—
Case studies.   I. Title.
JK2484. R6   328. 73   73-8172

PRAEGER PUBLISHERS
111 Fourth Avenue, New York, N.Y. 10003, U.S.A.
5, Cromwell Place, London SW7 2JL, England

Published in the United States of America in 1973
by Praeger Publishers, Inc.

Printed in the United States of America

For
Adelaide Ethel

CONTENTS

LIST OF TABLES

xi

EDITOR'S FOREWORD
James A. Robinson

The United States is experiencing a renaissance of public attention to the legislature as an institution of government. From the earliest years of U.S. history until roughly the beginning of the twentieth century, assemblies, councils, houses of burgesses, senates, and other representative bodies usually dominated the other main branches of the state and national governments. To be sure, two and a half centuries of local government, like the first hundred years under the Constitution, were interrupted by occasional brilliant and influential executives. The exceptions to legislative supremacy, however, only served to prove the rule that the popular assembly was the first branch of government.

In the twentieth century, on the other hand, the norm has been radically altered. Governors and presidents have acquired expanded influence in their respective political systems. Executive leadership has come to mean leadership over and within the legislature, expressed through executive budgets, states of the government addresses, special messages, and urgent as well as routine recommendations from the executive for legislative action. Occasional lapses of initiative have encouraged momentary legislative reassertions of their once proud role, but these exceptions have only confirmed the new norm.

After more than a half century of executive dominance, many Americans have taken a lively and renewed interest in legislatures. The late 1960s and early 1970s have been a period for a new look at the balance between these two branches of government in the United States. The revived attention to both Congress and the fifty state legislatures has taken several forms. Legislators themselves have given strength to national associations of representatives and senators. Foundations have encouraged continuing study groups and periodic public forums for discussions of the role of the legislature in contemporary government. Colleges and universities have devoted more research to, and established new courses in, "legislative behavior," "legislative institutions," and "legislative systems."

Among the sources of criticism and commentary, several important agencies deserve mention. The American Assembly has periodically organized national forums and regional panels for appraisal of Congress and state legislatures. The Citizens Conference on State Legislatures has been founded and has produced a series of reports and studies that have attracted widespread public reception. The Eagleton Institute of Politics at Rutgers University has established a graduate program to prepare legislative assistants, organized a staff to study individual legislatures, and acted as liaison in bringing scholars and specialists together with legislators and their staffs. These efforts have often been coordinated with special programs of the Council of State Governments, the American Bar Association, the National Municipal League, and the American Political Science Association. That inimitable figure, Ralph Nader, has given impetus to both national and state appraisals of legislative performance.

Taken together, these developments have altered the agenda of many students, scholars, publicists, and politicians. The consequence of sustained and informed appraisal of legislatures is that <u>legislative processes are now issues of public policy.</u>

It is not readily apparent why legislatures have enjoyed renewed attention just at this moment in national political history. Whatever the whole explanation, multiple causes surely are and have been at work. In some quarters, the motivation for legislative reform was a particular legislature's conflict with a systemwide value orientation, as in the case of most state assemblies' unwillingness to reapportion themselves to reflect shifts in population. In other quarters, the origin of legislative criticism was the search for a power base from which to oppose a particular executive policy, as in the case of congressmen who mobilized the adversaries of President Lyndon Johnson's and President Richard Nixon's Vietnam policies. For others, legislatures have been objects of concern simply as a reaction to the twentieth century's growth of bureaucracies in the executive branch of virtually all governments.

Whatever the motivation for legislative reform, the range of problems for study and action has been, and remains, a long one. The case studies that comprise this volume illustrate some of the major problems associated with legislatures in the fifty states. Some are "structural," some involve "personal" qualities of leadership, others turn on the capacity of analysts and politicians to predict the effects of change, and still others revolve around efforts to popularize the legislature as a political symbol.

It is not the purpose of this brief foreword to summarize each of the cases, nor to review the many ways in which each case is significant for the student of state politics. Despite their diversity, one or two central themes run throughout the several cases. These deserve mention if only in passing.

I believe the reader will soon appreciate that critics and reformers have been drawing on a set of stock alternatives and recommendations for making state government conform to the widely shared goals of the federal system. Theory has had it, to cite one example, that a two-party legislature is more widely representative of and responsive to many segments of the public than a legislature consistently dominated by a single party. Theory has been less than confident, however, about the process by which a competitive or responsible legislature might be created out of a history of domination by one party. Douglas Gatlin's account of Florida's recent experience is, thus, instructive.

The element of personal leadership appears in several of the cases, but with special force in Alan Wyner's study of former Speaker Jesse Unruh's innovations in California. Not only did Unruh initiate change in California, but he popularized similar reforms in other states through lectures, visits, and consultations in a variety of settings.

Despite the stock of organizational and leadership strategies on which critics have drawn, many theorists have maintained an irreverent skepticism about the effectiveness of the very reforms they have advocated. It is valuable to observe whether expected changes actually follow reform. Samuel Gove traces out some of the effects of reorganization in Illinois. James Best monitors some results of reapportionment in Washington. Alan Rosenthal documents the influence of increased reliance on professional staff in Wisconsin. And Thomas Flinn pursues the effect of several changes in Ohio. What emerges is a checkered pattern, indeed; in details, the more things change, the more they sometimes appear to remain the same.

All the cases together may be seen as part of a continuing process of appraisal of state legislatures as arenas for public problem-solving. The persons, situations, and events studied are drawn from a period of ferment about the role of legislatures in the United States, a period of considerable internal dissension and of undiminished external conflict. Representative government in this country means more than regular elections among contending parties. It means, among other things, a balance of roles and responsibilities among major institutions, of which the legislature is but one. Problem-solving, representative government, and checks and balances depend in no small degree on continuing, viligant observation of all governmental institutions.

These essays are the authors' contributions to the continuing reassessment of state legislatures as institutions of creative, responsible government.

1

THE DEVELOPMENT OF
A RESPONSIBLE PARTY SYSTEM
IN THE FLORIDA LEGISLATURE
Douglas S. Gatlin

Three sweeping changes occurred in Florida politics during the
winter of 1966-67. First, Claude R. Kirk, Jr. became the first Republican governor of Florida since Reconstruction as a result of the
November 1966 election, defeating his Democratic opponent with 55
percent of the popular vote. Second, the state legislature was reapportioned by a three-judge federal court on February 8, 1967, after
more than four years of litigation. The "one man, one vote" reapportionment plan adopted by the court moved the locus of electoral
control of the legislature from rural, sparsely populated north Florida
to the rapidly growing cities and towns of the central and southern
areas of the state. Third, the federal court declared invalid the state
legislative elections of the previous November and ordered a new
election to conform to its reapportionment. In this election, held late
in February, a larger number of Republicans were elected to the
Florida legislature than ever before: 42 percent of the Senate and
33 percent of the House of Representatives were Republicans, as
compared with previous highs of 5 percent and 20 percent respectively.
Thus, within four months, the rural, one-party domination of Florida
government that had continued for almost a century came to an end.
Rarely in recent U.S. history has a state political system undergone
so rapid and thorough a transformation.

The legislature that convened in the spring of 1967 was very
different from any in the past with respect to the party membership
and constituency background of legislators. As Table 1.1 shows, the
balance of numerical strength in the 1965 legislature heavily favored
the Democrats and the rural and small town areas of the state, as
had been the case for many generations. In 1967, the Democrats
remained in the majority in both houses. However, the twenty-eight
Senate Democrats did not constitute the two-thirds vote necessary to

TABLE 1.1

Membership of Florida Legislature, 1965 and 1967,
by Political Party and Urban-Rural Constituency

| | Party Membership | | | | Urban-Rural Membership as a Percent of Total Membership | |
| | Republicans | | Democrats | | | |
	1965	1967	1965	1967	1965	1967
Senate						
Urban	1	11	10	14	25	52
Mixed	1	7	14	7	34	29
Rural	0	2	18	7	41	19
Total	2	20	42	28		
Percent of total membership	5	42	95	58	100	100
House of Representatives						
Urban	7	17	37	37	39	45
Mixed	2	21	38	35	36	47
Rural	1	1	27	8	25	8
Total	10	39	102	80		
Percent of total membership	9	33	91	67	100	100

Source: Compiled by the author.

override gubernatorial vetoes. In the House, the eighty Democrats numbered exactly the two-thirds vote needed to override; only one Democratic defector in the House would serve to uphold a veto assuming Republican cohesion. Further, the Democratic membership in both houses in 1967 shifted away from its traditional rural base in an urban direction—a particularly notable change because the rural and usually conservative "pork choppers" who had dominated the legislature for many years were now reduced to small minorities in each house. Indeed, in both parties, urban power seemed to be in the ascendance.

Despite the hopes and fears generated by the events of the winter, however, the actual effects that reapportionment and two-party politics might have on the workings of the legislature were by no means clear. All that had been determined was that the party and regional characteristics of the legislative membership had changed, but the further effects of these changes upon the group structure of the legislature, its formal processes and policy output, were problematic. The fact that there were significant Republican minorities did not necessarily imply that they would cohere as a party or that their relationships with the governor were as yet well formed. Nor was it clear that the Democratic majorities would unify solidly against the Republicans, for the majority party still included members from a wide ecological range of constituencies. Further, the legislature elected in 1967 included many who had little or no previous legislative experience. As Table 1.2 shows, 17 percent of the total membership of the Senate and 46 percent of the House had been elected first in November 1966, but had served only in a brief special session devoted to legislative reapportionment. About another 18 percent in each House had no previous legislative experience whatsoever. The Republican membership of both houses was lower in experience than the Democrats. The rate of turnover in 1967 was less than in previous years;[1] nevertheless, a considerable number of legislators were inexperienced in legislative processes and largely unknown to each other. Finally, a number of veteran legislative leaders retired from office in 1967, voluntarily or otherwise, and their expert knowledge of the complexities of Florida government was matched by only a few who were reelected. Leaders of the 1967 legislature faced not only the novelty of a two-party system but also a lack of familiarity with many of their rank-and-file members. The leadership could have little basis for predicting the future of the legislative process with much confidence, for as the familiar faces and factions had disappeared, so the legislative norms and behavioral expectations of the past were of doubtful relevance. Therefore, as the Florida Senate and House convened in April 1967, the political scientist had the opportunity to observe the birth of what amounted to a new legislative system.

3

TABLE 1.2

Previous Legislative Service of Florida
Legislators, 1967 Session*

	Year of First Election to Either House			
	1965 or Before	1966	1967	Total
Senate				
Republicans	40% (8)	20% (4)	40% (8)	100% (20)
Democrats	82% (23)	14% (4)	4% (1)	100% (28)
Totals	65% (31)	17% (8)	19% (9)	100% (48)
House of Representatives				
Republicans	25% (10)	31% (12)	44% (17)	100% (39)
Democrats	40% (32)	54% (43)	6% (5)	100% (80)
Totals	35% (42)	46% (55)	18% (22)	100% (119)

*Previous legislative service is defined as experience in either house, not necessarily the house in which legislators served in 1967. Percentages sometimes do not add to 100 percent because of rounding.

Source: Compiled by the author.

The purpose of this case study is to trace the forces that encouraged, or impeded, the growth of a more responsible party system in the Florida legislature in its regular session of 1967 and the two special sessions that followed and continued its work in 1967 and 1968. Evidence was obtained from five types of sources. First, the writer conducted interviews with formal leaders in both legislative parties and also with selected legislators who did not hold such positions but who had been in the legislature for several terms previous to 1967, in order to better assess the nature of changes in the system. A total of ten interviews were conducted, some lasting for more than two hours. Second, the Journals of the Florida Senate and House of Representatives were the sources for analyzing roll-call votes, committee memberships, and occasional comments by legislators. Third, subscriptions to five Florida newspapers during the regular and special sessions revealed much of the strategies of party politics, supplementing the interviews and Journals. Fourth, a master's thesis, supervised by the writer, contained valuable analyses of communication patterns in the House in 1967, both within and across party lines, based upon mail questionnaires.[2] The preceding sources primarily reveal data and interpretations on party development within the 1967-68 regular and special sessions. Fifth, analyses of the pre-1967 Florida legislature, condensed from the work of several authors, will provide data for longer-run comparisons before and after the appearance of a sizable minority party. Thus, our methodology is eclectic, mixing narrative, systematic data analysis, and interpretation to provide the broadest perspective on the development of legislative party politics.

OPERATIONAL CRITERIA OF A RESPONSIBLE PARTY SYSTEM

The goal is to portray the major outlines of change that occurred in the internal structure and style of the legislature subsequent to the appearance of a significant minority party. In order to appraise such changes, we may imagine a continuum ranging from a responsible two-party system to a single-party system without stable factions. Research should enable us to estimate roughly ordinal locations of empirical party systems along the scale and to gauge their temporal movement along it. By comparing the attributes of party systems along the scale at different points in time, we might then hypothesize the factors causing temporal changes. The Florida legislature is a particularly useful case for research on factors associated with changes in party systems. We can describe its approximate position before the appearance of a large minority in the winter of 1966-67, and trace the forces in the subsequent year that seemed to promote or inhibit the development of the Florida legislature in the direction of a more responsible party system.

Without discussing the virtues or vices of the responsible party system, it can be used as a descriptive archetype or empirical model entailing explicit behavioral and structural conditions. Under given empirical conditions a responsible party system exists, whatever its normative value. A necessary condition of a responsible party system is the presence in the legislature of two sets of legislators distinguishable by party labels, but it is clearly not a sufficient condition. Certain role expectations and role behaviors, and certain structures for the flow of communication and influence within parties, would be necessary to render the model operational. For the purpose of this study, the focus of attention is restricted to factors within the legislative system affecting party responsibility. Thus, we may ignore factors such as extralegislative party organization, nominating conventions and platforms, candidate slates, and electoral behavior that are treated in the broader conception of responsible party systems.[3]

The model requires two legislative parties acting cohesively in pursuit of alternative goals on major issues of public policy. To this end, rank-and-file legislators would subordinate their personal ideologies and their perception of constituency interests to the party's position on legislative issues. In voting on bills, the individual legislator would accede to his party's position, accepting the party leadership as the principal guides in formulating the party position and as the field commanders in legislative strategy and tactics. The party leaders, in turn, would be expected to promote the establishment of party policy on major legislative issues in consultation with the rank-and-file. Once the party position was decided, the leaders would apply sanctions against deviant members. The majority party leaders would control the legislative calendar and appoint committee chairmen on the basis of their commitment to uphold the party's position. Organizationally, the model seems to require frequent party caucuses to discuss pending legislation and to reach binding votes on party policy. Between caucuses, a communications network would link the leaders and followers, transmitting information and directives on the immediate business before the legislature. The model does not assume that all legislative issues will stimulate conflicting party positions; interparty consensus may exist on many measures, and others of relatively minor or local import may be nonpartisan in that the parties do not declare a position. Nevertheless, major issues of public policy will be the subject of contrasting proposals by the two parties, and a high degree of intraparty cohesion on these issues is required by the model. Thus, the party system would be responsible in that it offers a choice to the electorate of two parties advocating distinguishable alternative programs on major issues.

The role behaviors of the chief executive and legislative party vis-à-vis each other are not clear in the literature on responsible party systems. The original prescriptive model calls for a "sensible give and take" between the two in formulating party positions on public policy.[4] The executive should not be "the exclusive leader in legislation" yet he should occupy "a central place" in the party organization, and he presumably articulates the interests of a somewhat different constituency than the legislative party.[5] On balance, the original model seems to envision a bargaining relationship between the executive and his legislative party. However, at least one advocate of the concept of party responsibility would prefer that the executive have hierarchical superiority, apparently on the assumption that the likelihood of achieving party unity would be greater under conditions of hierarchy.[6] It is clear enough that intransigence between the executive and the legislative party would defeat the central purpose of the normative model—to present a unified front as a party to the electorate. On purely logical grounds, however, unity could be achieved by executive domination, by bargaining, or by legislative superiority. Arbitrarily, one may escape the dilemma by invoking the principle that "the party in power itself, rather than particular individuals . . . is responsible for its record of legislative and executive action."[7] This principle suggests bargaining as the typical mode of resolving conflict within a party, though it makes no reference to the relative weight of the actors in the bargaining process. These issues are stressed because, as we shall see, the conflict between hierarchy and bargaining became a very real and vexing problem for the Republican party in the Florida legislature of 1967-68 and, in fact, it eventually led to the collapse of unity within the party.

The polar model of a one-party system without stable factions is quite clearly one of bargaining in a many-person game. It would contain multiple centers of power, based upon such factors as the occupancy of committee chairmanships as well as personal prestige and expertise. Legislators would vote according to constituency interests or personal conviction. Leaders would influence, check, and balance each other in free-forming and evanescent transactions. Legislative leaders would be selected on the basis of personal prestige, experience, and promises to supporters. Organizationally, caucuses would be unknown or at most ad hoc and informal. Leaders might have coteries of lieutenants, but the latter would act more as personal emissaries on bargaining missions, rather than as links in a hierarchical chain. A governor, likewise, would depend upon his personal skills as a legislative leader, buttressed by whatever sanctions and favors he could wield by virtue of his formal position, but unaided by any lasting loyalties to a common political organization. In elections, voters would evaluate the past records or future promises of candidates as individuals, since it would be virtually impossible to identify them as members of stable factional or partisan groups.

Probably no existing U.S. legislative body could be located at the extremes of this hypothetical continuum. However, political scientists have accumulated some evidence that state legislative party systems occupy positions across a considerable portion of it. Some systematic, quantitative research helps to shed light upon factors tending to promote or discourage party responsibility in state legislatures. Thomas Flinn tests a number of hypotheses about variables affecting party loyalty on roll-call votes in the Ohio legislature.[8] He finds little or no relationship between support for party on roll calls and such factors as the margin of victory of legislators in elections, seniority or the holding of leadership positions in the legislature, or political ideology. The only significant factor associated with party support found in Flinn's study was an aspect of constituencies:

7

members from districts typical of their party (as measured by several socioeconomic indicators) tended to support their party more often than others. In our study of the Florida legislature, it will be possible to retest the impact of some of these factors on the party loyalty of individual legislators and on the overall cohesion of the parties on roll-call votes. However, it must be stressed that high party loyalty and cohesion, as measured by objective data, are necessary but not sufficient conditions for party responsibility. For the model to be fully realized, the additional institutional and behavioral characteristics of legislative parties that were mentioned previously must also be in evidence. In a responsible party system, high degrees of party loyalty and cohesion are the result of a particular configuration of motivations, role behaviors, and institutional processes, and it is with these factors that this study is concerned.

A case study of a single legislature is especially useful for investigating the group dynamics, institutional characteristics, and processes within legislative parties, since comparative data on such factors for a number of states are so difficult to obtain. A case study cannot lead to confident generalizations about factors inhibiting or encouraging party responsibility, but as an intensive study it may provide a greater range of hypotheses for more systematic testing in the future. Therefore, we turn to a brief characterization of the Florida legislature before 1967, followed by a more detailed analysis of the 1967-68 sessions, to try to understand the distance traveled and the moving forces.

THE FLORIDA LEGISLATURE BEFORE 1967

For generations before 1967, the Florida legislature was a one-party system whose membership was weighted in favor of rural interests. As Loren Beth and William Havard have argued, the absence of party competition in most state legislative elections produced a body of instructed delegates from local constituencies.[9] The handful of Republican legislators who appeared in the 1960s (never more than twenty in either house) hardly comprised a sufficient number to offer serious opposition as a group to the overwhelmingly large Democratic majority. Further, as bifactional rivalry made its appearance within the majority party, the few Republicans could do little but choose between policy alternatives as defined by the majority factions. Democratic bifactionalism first appeared in the mid-1950s.[10] It was sparked primarily by the clash of urban and rural interests over reapportionment, but the related issues of taxation and the distribution of state benefits to counties also divided the two groups. By the late 1950s, majority factionalism had become institutionalized. The

8

rural group took on nominal identity as the "pork choppers" and the urban group as "lamb choppers." Separate caucuses were sometimes held, fairly stable factional communications networks were organized, and factional divisions on roll-call votes in the Senate were frequent and clear. Still, the scope of influence of the lamb choppers was limited by the greater size of the pork chop group and the latter's domination of all major committees and positions of formal legislative leadership. In effect, the legislative process until the mid-1950s was characterized by complex bargaining in a many-person game, but from this period until 1967, the one-party legislature resembled a two-person game with one faction favorably weighted.

Florida governors have been weak both constitutionally and politically. Constitutionally, the governor has an item veto on appropriations bills and the usual power of summoning the legislature into special sessions, but prior to the governmental reorganization of 1969, governors could not hold two successive four-year terms in office. Until 1964, gubernatorial elections continued to be conducted as V.O. Key had characterized them in 1948—"every man for himself."[11] There were no strong statewide party organizations and no party platforms to encourage cohesion between gubernatorial and legislative candidates. Politically, therefore, the governor could not claim legislative leadership as the head of a party. Further, the governor's influence in legislation was perhaps matched by that of the elected cabinet of five department heads, who could and usually did remain in office for several successive four-year terms. These five cabinet officers shared collegial powers with the governor as the State Budget Commission and as numerous other executive boards and commissions. The governor, having no integrated administrative control and with little or no political organization in the legislature, was in a relatively weak position of influence on public policy compared to the cabinet. The cabinet officials, on the other hand, derived considerable legislative influence from their established clienteles throughout the state and their departmental storehouses of information and expertise. Up to 1967, the cabinet officials usually could marshall at least as much influence in the legislature as the governor.

Within the legislature, leadership was concentrated in the president of the Senate and the speaker of the House of Representatives. Both presiding officers had the power to appoint all members and chairmen of committees and considerable discretion in the assignment of bills to committees. The speaker and president were elected by their respective houses by virtue of gaining pledges of votes from legislators in exchange for promises of desirable committee assignments and support for pet bills. It was a rarity for an urban legislator to occupy either the presiding officer's chair or an important committee chairmanship prior to the 1967 reapportionment. Up to

1965, the power of the predominantly rural committee chairmen was enhanced by the practice of proxy voting in committees; not unusually, the chairmen held a number of proxies and cast them until the member returned to the committee in person.

Further, the selection of presiding officers and committee chairmen was largely insulated from gubernatorial influence. The presiding officers were elected in each house two years before their assumption of office, and, in fact, they began collecting pledges of support four years in advance. Thus, a governor took office along with presiding officers and committee chairmen elected two years previously. True, the governor served a four-year term encompassing two biennial sessions of the legislature, but even in the second session the leadership had been selected two years or more beforehand. Thus, access to legislative leadership was restricted to those acceptable to the pork choppers and was virtually insulated from gubernatorial influence. The governor had few political bridges across the constitutional separation of powers.[12]

On our hypothetical scale of legislative party systems, the Florida legislature was not far removed from the atomized one-party model before 1955. The advent of bifactionalism constituted a movement away from it, but the sudden increase in Republican numbers in 1967 provided the minimum necessary conditions for further movement toward the responsible party end of the scale. Whether the other necessary behavioral and structural requisites of a responsible party system would emerge is the subject of the remaining sections of this chapter.

PARTY LEADERSHIP AND ORGANIZATION

The presiding officers of the 1967 legislature had been elected by the one-party Democratic legislature of 1965. They had achieved their leadership posts in a context of bifactional rivalry owing to their personal acceptability to a majority composed of pork choppers, lamb choppers, and a few legislators who stood on the fence. They were not chosen to guide in the formulation of a party program of legislation, and whether they were the leaders who would have been chosen by the 1967 Democratic membership is uncertain.

The Senate president was Verle A. Pope, a senator since 1948, and, since reapportionment, a delegate from a district including urban Jacksonville. Some considered Pope a maverick; he had sometimes supported one faction, sometimes the other, but withal had maintained a reputation for integrity and personal charm among his colleagues. The speaker of the House was Ralph Turlington, a representative from a mixed urban-rural district including Gainesville, the site of the University of Florida, and with fifteen years of service in the lower House. Like Pope, Turlington was considered moderately liberal and both had received considerable urban support in achieving legislative leadership. Minority leaders also had been elected by the small Republican contingents in the 1965 session. The Senate minority leader was William C. Young of St. Petersburg; he had served in the upper House since 1960, and in one session he had been the only Republican in the Senate. Young had cultivated expertise in the fields of transportation and public safety and, in spite of his party membership, had been an effective and respected senator in the one-party era. The House minority leader, Donald Reed of Boca Raton, had represented Palm Beach County since 1963 and had become especially knowledgeable in legislation affecting higher education. Both Young and Reed identified themselves as conservatives, but they had often cooperated with urban Democrats on measures designed to benefit cities. Thus, the four leaders could be characterized as moderates within their parties, sensitive to the norms of a one-party bifactional system, and skilled in bargaining and compromise.

Interviews with members of both parties in the 1967 legislature indicated that, in the first days of the new session, party was not generally conceived as the paramount focus of loyalty among either Republicans or Democrats. As in the past, most legislators felt that they had won office largely because of their individual campaign efforts and personal pledges to constituents. Indeed, there were in existence no state party platforms or powerful statewide organizations to divert the legislators from constituency orientations. And as events were to show, within each party there were important differences of interest among constituencies (particularly regarding ad valorem taxation), tending to discourage party cohesion.

While neither party in the legislature displayed a keen sense of mission as a party, the Republicans were more conscious of a common identification than the Democrats. In both houses, the minority quickly organized a more-or-less formal communications net; whips and assistant whips were elected in both Republican caucuses to link the rank and file with the minority leaders. On the other hand, the majority party did not immediately perceive a need for legislative party organization. In fact, not until the session had progressed into its second week did the Senate Democrats hold their first caucus. They began to organize only after the governor assumed a partisan role as "chief legislator." The stimulus to Democratic organization stemmed less from internal cohesion than from external threat; further discussion of this conclusion will appear presently.

Senate President Pope was not selected as leader of the Democratic caucus in the upper house; the reasons for this were variously attributed to his poor health, his maverick reputation, and his alleged

lack of talent for organization. Pope reportedly contributed heavily
to caucus discussions, but the chairman was Dempsey Barron, a
senator from a predominantly rural North Florida district, with
seven years' seniority and president pro tem of the Senate. The
Democratic caucus never formally selected whips; several different
senators informally performed this function from time to time.
Much the same informality characterized the House Democratic
caucus. Speaker Turlington normally chaired the caucus, but whips
were not formally selected. Speakers had traditionally used their
appointed Rules Committee chairman as floor leader; Turlington
followed this precedent at first but, because of a split with the Rules
chairman to be explained presently, he later informally appointed a
different set of lieutenants. Thus, Democratic party organization
was more informal than that of the Republicans in both houses and
also was more weakened by internal dissension. Nevertheless, the
fact that Democratic organizations appeared at all must be counted
as a novel departure from past practice.

  The Democratic and Republican caucuses in both houses attempted to obtain binding votes on policy issues during the earliest
days of the session. The House Republicans did so apparently somewhat longer than the other caucuses, but all had abandoned the attempt
before the close of the session. The Democrats were first to "release"
dissident members from support of party positions on public policy.
Mail questionnaires to members of the House of Representatives
revealed that the Republican party caucus was an important source
of voting cues to its members, while the Democrats ascribed little
such influence to their caucus.[13] Policy preferences aside, however,
several Democratic legislators revealed in personal interviews that
they resented the notion of an obligation to support a party position.
The Republicans who were interviewed usually expressed the belief
that they owed support to their party "whenever possible," but none
viewed parties as pernicious, as a few Democrats did. Some (though
certainly not all) Democrats who had been socialized to the older
ways of the Florida legislature expressed genuine nostalgia for its
more individualistic and, to them, more democratic character. More
than once, a senior Democrat rose in party caucus to defend the
legislator's obligation to exercise his independent judgment. The
legislative leaders of both parties professed respect for their dis-
senting colleagues, and there is no convincing evidence that sanctions
were levied against dissenters. While efforts to reach binding party
decisions were dropped, caucuses continued to be held throughout the
1967-68 sessions by both parties in both houses for the purpose of
exchanging information and nurturing consensus insofar as possible.

STANDING COMMITTEES

The absence of intense party orientations in early 1967, as reported in the interviews, tends to be substantiated by evidence on committee appointments. All appointments were made formally by the Democratic presiding officers. Before making their committee appointments, both the Senate president and the speaker sought the advice of the minority leaders about the assignment of Republicans to committees. The minority leaders said that their recommendations were followed in most cases, and the press reported that the Republican legislators were usually satisfied by their appointments. The minority leaders themselves were appointed to the Rules and Calendar committees in their respective houses. In the House, several committees were awarded Republican vice-chairmen, and in the Senate two senior Republicans were named committee chairmen. These two committees were not among the most influential in the Senate (Retirement and Claims, Transportation and Safety); however, considering that the Senate president had unlimited appointment powers, the Republican appointments did not suggest as strong a partisan perspective as would be expected in a responsible two-party legislature.

Table 1.3 shows the new urban orientation of the key committees in the 1967 legislature. The number of urban legislators on these committees is in striking contrast to the heavy rural weighting of key committees in the previous decade that was found by Havard and Beth.[14] Even where the rural Democratic committee membership was largest, in the Appropriations and the Rules and Calendar committees, it constituted less than 30 percent of the total. The Senate president's appointment of these rural committeemen was attributed to his desire to placate the remnants of the pork chop group and thereby to encourage intraparty harmony. Nevertheless, three of the critically important Senate committees had urban chairmen. This, together with the preponderant voting power of the urban and mixed constituencies, evident in Table 1.3, reflects a fundamental change from the halcyon days of pork chop power.

In the House of Representatives, the urban weight in the composition of key committees is even more apparent than in the Senate. Three committees had clear urban majorities (Ad Valorem Taxation, Appropriations, Rules and Calendar) and two of these also had urban chairmen. Only one committee (Public School Education) was balanced with respect to the types of constituencies represented by its members.

Table 1.4 adds further evidence of the power of urban Democrats in the 1967 session. In each House, it was the urban Democrats who held more "interlocking directorships," i.e., memberships on two or more of the key committees. In each House, membership on

TABLE 1.3

Membership of Key Committees in Florida Senate and House, 1967, by Party and Urban-Rural Constituency

	Republicans			Democrats		
	Rural	Mixed	Urban	Rural	Mixed	Urban
Senate						
Committee						
Appropriations	0	2	1	5	5	5*
Education: Higher Learning	2	2	1	2	3	4*
Education: Public Schools and Junior Colleges	0	3	2	0	4*	5
Finance and Taxation	1	3	3	1	4*	7
Rules and Calendar	0	2	2	5	4	5*
Total seats in Senate	2	10	8	6	9	13
House of Representatives						
Committee						
Ad Valorem Taxation	1	3	5	3	3	9*
Appropriations	0	2	3	4	4	11*
Finance and Taxation	0	4	2	0	11*	9
Higher Education	0	4	3	2	6	7*
Public School Education	0	4	4	3*	4	7
Rules and Calendar	0	1	2	1	10*	10
Total seats in House	1	21	17	8	35	37

*Asterisk indicates constituency of committee chairman.

Source: Compiled by the author.

TABLE 1.4

Numbers of Democratic Legislators with More Than
Two Key Committee Assignments, by Urban-Rural
Constituency

	Rural	Mixed	Urban
Senate			
Number of Key Committee Assignments			
Four	0	0	2
Three	2	4	2
Two	2	2	2
Total	4	6	6
House of Representatives			
Number of Key Committee Assignments			
Four	0	0	3
Three	1	1	6
Two	4	13	7
Total	5	14	16

Source: Compiled by the author.

as many as four key committees was awarded only to urban Democrats. Rural Democrats with overlapping key assignments were
heavily outnumbered by their colleagues from mixed and urban areas,
in striking contrast to Havard and Beth's observations on committee
membership in previous years.[15]
 In summary, the committee appointments made by the presiding
officers signified important changes in the internal structure of the
legislature since the days of one-party, rural dominance. For one
thing, the movement toward an urban electoral base in the Democratic
party was carried through to the legislative system by the appointment of urban Democrats to dominant positions of key committees.
Nevertheless, the remaining members of the old ruling clique from
rural Florida—six in the Senate and eight in the House—were retained

in important committee positions disproportionate to their total number, both because of their past experience in the legislature and to promote opportunities for bargaining. Republicans, moreover, were appointed to committees by the Democratic presiding officers in an apparent spirit of conciliation. Thus, committee appointments were distributed more for the purpose of encouraging bargaining and compromise, both within the majority party and between the two parties, than for the purpose of promoting intraparty consistency and interparty contrast. The effect of the committee appointments was to structure the legislature to allow a flow of pluralistic exchanges rather than to draw rigid partisan boundaries.

So far, our purpose has been to portray the background and structure of the 1967 legislature as it began its deliberations. The characteristics of the legislature in its first days hardly served to encourage party responsibility. The bipartisan and bifactional composition of major committees, the socialization of legislative leaders in a one-party system, the tendency of legislators to minimize partisan differences, the mixture of constituency backgrounds within each party all would tend to block the rise of a responsible party system. Nevertheless, as the regular and special sessions of 1967-68 progressed, party caucuses became institutionalized, intraparty cohesion on roll-call votes increased, party loyalty became an important motive in legislators' voting decisions, and party positions on major legislative issues were fashioned. Thus, in spite of initial conditions unfavorable to party responsibility, the latter developed to a marked degree. The task remaining is to try to isolate the causal factors underlying this major innovation in the Florida legislative system.

THE PARTIES AND THE ISSUES

Shortly before the session convened, the new Republican governor clashed with the Senate president and House speaker over the issues that should be given priority in the legislature. Kirk had repeatedly stressed in his election campaign his opposition to new taxes of any kind. The governor wished the legislature to concentrate on constitutional revision and, particularly, upon augmenting gubernatorial power by abolishing the independent elective status of the cabinet and by making the latter appointive. However, Pope and Turlington said publicly that constitutional revision should not be thrust upon an inexperienced legislature, and they privately feared the possible effects of constitutional changes on party fortunes. They preferred to devote the regular session to ad valorem tax relief and educational financing, postponing constitutional revision for a possible special session. Constituency and group pressures for tax relief and increased educational appropriations were very strong in the eyes of many legislators, but they saw no ground swell of public opinion for constitutional reform.

The issues of public school finance and teachers' salaries were to be the most divisive in the 1967-68 regular and special sessions. These issues provided the leaven for the rise of party conflict in the legislature. In effect, the issues were thrust upon the legislature by the growing militancy of the Florida Education Association (FEA). For some time prior to the convening of the 1967 session, the FEA had been campaigning for increases in public school expenditures and teacher salaries amounting to $500 million. It charged that the legislature had not increased educational spending significantly in the past decade in spite of rising costs and a soaring school-age population. In regional and county meetings across the state, the 55,000 members of the FEA had been mobilized to the point that the organization's leaders felt confident in threatening a possible walkout of teachers, as well as other sanctions, unless its demands were met. The FEA leaders also believed that the new urban orientation of the legislature would contribute to the teachers' benefit, for educational needs had risen fastest in the areas of growing urbanization. However, while some legislators in both parties agreed that increased educational expenditures were necessary, virtually none wished to raise taxes to the extent that would satisfy the FEA's spending proposals. Indeed, the major concern of a number of urban legislators was to lower ad valorem taxes, the primary source of local support for public schools. And if local support was to be reduced, then additional state support would be required to maintain or improve existing programs and facilities of public education.

Thus, four specific issues converged around public school policy. First, the "no new taxes" pledge of the governor was supported by most Republicans as well as some Democrats, though the Democratic leadership had publicly proposed higher expenditures for public education. Second, the issue of constitutional reform was part of the more general problem because the status of the state superintendent of public instruction as an independently elected cabinet official was opposed by the governor, again with the support of his legislative party. No Democrats announced themselves against constitutional reform in principle, but there was understandable reluctance by some of them to jeopardize what so far had been a safe Democratic seat. Gubernatorial control of administrative posts is a favorite proposal of reformists, but at least in Florida it could not be divorced realistically from considerations of partisan advantage. Third, on the issue of ad valorem taxation both legislative parties were divided. The property tax was the major source of local support for schools. Assessed property valuation in some urban counties was already considered high, and legislators from these areas strongly favored millage reduction; Democrats from Duval County (Jacksonville) especially insisted on lowering millage. On the other hand, property was assessed at a lower rate by officials in some urban counties and here there was little pressure for millage reduction; in fact, a referendum in urban Pinellas County (St. Petersburg and Clearwater) had raised the millage in order to provide more support for public schools. Thus, the initial policy divisions clearly followed party lines only on the issue of constitutional revision. The remaining issues cut across both party labels and constituency types.

ROLE CONFLICTS AND THE REPUBLICAN PARTY

Previous governors of Florida had tried to influence the legislature on major issues of public policy, but they had been unable to play the role of party leader in these efforts. That Kirk regarded himself as the central figure in his party on legislative issues was manifested in a speech to a caucus of Senate and House Republicans about two weeks after his budget address. The governor demanded that the Republicans commit themselves "100 percent" to sustaining any gubernatorial veto and admonishing them that "they are not loyal to the party if they refuse." He argued further that the Republican legislators had ridden into office on his coattails and that it would be politically unwise for them to oppose his legislative proposals.[16] Some Republicans in both houses reportedly were offended at the bluntness of Kirk's remarks. Following Kirk's address, William C. Young, the Senate minority leader, stressed the opposite view in a speech to the assembled Republicans. Young praised his colleagues for their individual campaign efforts and emphasized the independence and equality of the legislative and executive branches, while assuring the governor of legislative support whenever possible. The House minority leader, Donald H. Reed, pledged support for the governor but admitted that some members of the lower house were not so committed. Thus, a conflict of roles between the governor and many members of his legislative party developed early in the session. Interviews with senators in both parties revealed that Young continued to perceive himself not as "the governor's man" but as leader of a group in equal partnership with the governor. On the other hand, House minority leader Reed felt that the long-run growth of Florida Republicanism would be fostered by a united front between the governor and the legislative party, and he continued to support Kirk throughout the session even at the cost of frequent personal frustrations. The governor was never to abandon his self-proclaimed role as the dominant figure in the party and would continue to insist upon his party's support, sometimes belligerently so in the opinion of some Republican legislators. Thus, the conflict between the opposing principles of party solidarity across the bridge between separation of powers and legislative independence—perhaps endemic to the American political culture—was manifested early in the session and was never to be fully resolved.

STRATEGIES OF PARTY CONFLICT

The strategies employed by parties in the legislative process can be revealing indicators of their nature as parties, for strategies can be fashioned to realize at least two different political goals. First, it is taken for granted that a party's legislative strategies would be designed to try to enact its policy positions into law, and no doubt this is usually the case. Second, however, a party may adopt a legislative strategy purely to place the opposite party in an embarrassing light, to try to force it to defend a position that it would prefer to avoid. In pursuing such a strategy, a party may subordinate its policy goals to a desire to defeat the opposite party and to gain victory for its own sake. Rationally, it might adopt whatever policy that seems appropriate for placing its adversary in an untenable strategic position. Figuratively, the legislative struggle may be not only a "policy game" but also a "party game" in which winning or losing per se are major stakes. Party itself can take on characteristics of an interest group, concerned with a favorable public image and with long-run electoral success beyond the particular and perhaps transient policy issues of the moment. Thus, rational strategies for parties conceived as interest groups may be somewhat different from strategies that would be followed under the assumption that parties mechanically aggregate social demands and try to convert them into public policy. Moreover, a legislative party is a human group as defined by the psychological commitment of its members to a common political identity. Party identifications are apt to be strong among legislators, and they may show signs of "team spirit" and the emotional stresses characteristic of groups in conflict.[17] Therefore, because of both rational calculations of winning strategies and sociopsychological aspects of group conflict, a party may abandon policy positions rather than continue defending them at the risk of losing security and prestige. The whole thrust of the responsible party model is to produce policy-oriented parties. Insofar as parties pursue victory for their own sake, apart from programmatic goals, they do not meet the conditions of the model. The strategies pursued by the parties in the Florida legislature initially reveal strong policy orientations, but subsequently the abandonment of the latter in favor of strategies to defend party as interest group.

The State Budget Commission, a subgroup of the cabinet that includes the governor, had recommended a total budget of $1.36 billion for the biennium. In a surprising move, Governor Kirk proposed in his budget message to reduce this figure by $66 million, and the greatest cuts recommended were in public school programs. Kirk did recommend a $1,050 average salary increase for teachers, but proposed deep cuts in the school lunch program, the free textbook program, and in support for kindergartens and school libraries. Swift negative reactions came from the FEA, from the Democratic leaders in the legislature, and from State Superintendent of Education Floyd Christian, a Democrat and a cabinet member. They protested that Kirk had promised a $5,000 salary increase in his campaign and that his proposed cuts would play havoc with already weak programs.

Kirk's budget proposals seriously divided the legislature on party lines for the first time. It was at this juncture that the Democrats began caucusing to discuss policy and strategy and organized a communications network as mentioned previously. Some conservative Democrats were pleased with the governor's proposals, but the Democratic leadership as well as a majority of the rank and file perceived increased educational spending as necessary, either for reasons of sound policy or in hopes of gaining political credit from teachers and their allies. Further, the governor had placed himself squarely in opposition to Democratic School Superintendent Christian, not only because of the issue of constitutional revision but also because Christian had publicly appealed to the legislature for increased educational spending. From this point onward, Christian was in almost day-to-day contact with the Democratic leadership of the legislature in attempting to consolidate the party's position on bills related to public education. In fact, Christian moved into a small office near the legislative chambers to facilitate immediate communication with fellow Democrats in the Senate and House.[18] Thus, in the view of both legislators and the press, Kirk's proposed reductions in educational spending were so extreme as to awaken the Democrats into activation as a party. Up to this point, relationships between the two parties in the legislature had been structured to encourage interparty bargaining and compromise, and party identification, while certainly present, had not been urged upon the legislators as the primary focus of their loyalties. And while some legislators in both parties resented the appeal to party loyalty above other orientations, the governor's action separated the two parties on a dramatic legislative issue for the first time and thus raised the question of party loyalty to a new importance. Whether clear, definitive party programs would have originated within the legislature itself, without external stimulus, can only be speculated, but at least there were no party programs in sight before the governor's speech.

Governor Kirk's budget proposals were introduced by a Republican senator and duly referred to the Appropriations Committee. About two weeks later, the committee reported what was, in effect, a Democratic bill for a record $1.335 billion budget, about $40 million more than the governor's proposal. The committee bill more than restored the cuts proposed by the governor for public school programs but it included no recommendations on teacher salaries. The Democratic strategy was to recommend salary increases in a separate bill in order to dramatize the party's support for teacher pay raises. Moreover, since pay raises would require new revenues, the separate bill also would call the governor's hand on his "no new taxes" pledge; to carry out his pledge, he would have to veto the bill and this presumably would direct the teachers' ire against him.

On the Senate floor the Republicans tried to amend the committee bill to incorporate Kirk's proposed teacher pay raises and to reduce or eliminate about a dozen line-item appropriations. The bill passed, however, and both parties maintained perfect cohesion in the final roll-call vote on passage of the bill. A few days later the Senate Appropriations Committee reported a bill raising the salaries of public school and junior college teachers by $227 million. The Republicans fought for two days on the Senate floor to merge this bill with the general appropriations bill but were unsuccessful. Again, on the critical roll calls the Senate Democrats voted unanimously, while one Republican from an urban district voted with them.

So far, both parties in the Senate were impressively cohesive in the pursuit of alternative educational policies. However, the Democrats in the House of Representatives were seriously divided. Conservative House Democrats argued in the party caucus that the proposed expenditures were $40 billion more than anticipated revenues for the biennium. In spite of strong appeals for unity from the party leadership in the House, most of the Democratic conservatives refused to support the appropriations. The basis for the Democratic split will be explored further in the next section. At this point, it is sufficient to report that a former Democratic Speaker of the House successfully sponsored an amendment to the Senate bill to merge the appropriations and pay raise bills, thus contradicting the strategy adopted from the Senate by Speaker Turlington. The Senate Democrats, faced with an impasse in the House, agreed to the single-package appropriations bill as passed in the lower chamber, but still held out hopes of passing supplemental pay raise bills in the future.

The governor vetoed the entire appropriations bill nine days after its passage. In the House, a motion to override failed. Less than ten minutes later, the Democrat-dominated House Appropriations Committee reported a so-called governor's bill, patterned after Kirk's original budget proposals, and with unprecedented speed the bill also

cleared the Senate Appropriations Committee. The Democratic strategy
was to give the governor almost exactly the appropriations he had
proposed for educational salaries and programs, and hopefully to pass
supplemental spending bills that Kirk would be forced to veto to uphold his repeatedly announced stand on no new taxes. Republican
leaders angrily labeled this as a "spite bill"; the minority party wished
to increase certain items in the bill to correct glaring errors in the
governor's original financial calculations (retained in the Democrat-
sponsored bill), and wished to avert the Democratic strategy of forcing
a possibly damaging choice upon the governor. Nevertheless, the
"governor's bill" passed the Senate by a strict party-line vote. In the
House, seven Democrats voted with the solidly cohesive Republicans
but the bill passed by a margin of sixty-six to forty-four.

The governor used his line-item veto power to cut over $150
million from the public and higher education spending bill. The motions
to override the line items rose in the Senate. The Republicans maintained strict party cohesion on all but one of the thirty-three roll calls
to override various vetoes, as did the Democrats. Thus, by the nar-
rowest of margins, the vetoes were sustained.

Initially, therefore, a majority of Democrats in both houses had
supported the party policy of increased educational appropriations
and a majority of Republicans had championed the governor's budget
proposals. Following the veto of the first general appropriations bill,
however, the Democrats abandoned their policy position in introducing
the "spite bill." True, the Democrats also introduced supplemental
bills providing for teacher pay raises, but it was privately admitted
that they had little chance of enactment into law in view of the division
in the House Democratic ranks. At no time did the Democrats attempt
to rationalize their bill as being in the public interest. Their strategy
was admittedly one having partisan advantage at stake. Yet the Democrats also seem to have acted partly out of frustration. During this
period the Florida Education Association's executive board had voted
to censure the governor for his "lack of leadership in education,"
and to notify formally the National Education Association that Florida
was an unsatisfactory state in which to teach. Democratic Senators
Dubbin and Pope had appeared before the board, had pleaded for re-
straint and reminded the organization of the party's efforts in the
teachers' behalf, but the FEA passed the resolutions and threatened
further sanctions. Thus, the Democrats were caught between the
demands of the FEA and the obduracy of the governor. Their strategy
of introducing the "spite bill" was rationally motivated by considerations of partisan advantage and in part an emotional release from
tensions caused by the conflicting demands of the governor and the
FEA. To have continued defending increased educational appropriations would have been a futile gesture, almost certainly doomed to

defeat. Thus, if the Democratic strategy violated the concept of party responsibility for a policy position, perhaps it was understandable from the viewpoint of party as interest group.

THE MANAGEMENT OF INTERNAL CONFLICT
IN THE DEMOCRATIC PARTY

In the Senate, each party was impressively cohesive on roll-call votes taken on the measures discussed in the preceding section. On thirty-six motions to pass, amend, or override vetoes on these bills, the mean Rice index of cohesion* for the Senate Democrats was 95.4 and that for the Republicans was 96.4. In the House of Representatives, the index of cohesion for the Republicans was 97.6 but it fell to 67.8 for the Democrats. In this section, we explore factors accounting for the dissension among the House Democrats.

When the first Democrat-sponsored appropriations bills reached the House, minority leader Reed opposed them with active support from several Democrats including two former speakers of the House: William V. Chappell, Jr., and E. C. Rowell; the latter was also currently chairman of the House Rules and Calendar Committee. It was Chappell who successfully sponsored an amendment to merge the general appropriations bill with the teacher pay raise bills. Speaker Turlington, together with Appropriations Committee Chairman Henry Land, worked assiduously with several other senior Democrats to hold the party line but with only moderate success. An analysis of the six roll calls on the appropriations bill in the House showed no clear constituency patterns of Democratic support for, or opposition to, the party position. If "defector" is defined as one who voted against his party on four or more of these six roll calls, there was a slight tendency for the eighteen defectors to come from mixed or rural areas, but more representatives from the latter constituency types supported than opposed the party position. Likewise, while the defectors were largely senior representatives schooled in the nonpartisan ways of the past, the overwhelming majority of senior Democrats supported the party. Six of the eighteen defectors were from Duval County (Jacksonville); their written explanations of their opposition to the bills, entered in the House Journal, stated their antipathy to tax increases that the bills would entail. Thus, defection on these bills was not purely and simply a continuation of the past pattern of bifactionalism in the Democratic party. According to all informants, opposition within the

----

*See p. 32 for an explanation of the Rice index of cohesion.

Democratic ranks was rooted in an economic conservatism that transcended constituency backgrounds.

The Democratic defectors totaled only about 20 percent of the majority party, but the intensity of their feeling was high and they included important segments of the party leadership. The chairman of the Rules Committee had traditionally functioned as the speaker's floor leader and confidant, but the present chairman, E. C. Rowell, had actively opposed the appropriations backed by Turlington. Rowell had been endorsed for reelection by Kirk and relations between the two were marked by frequent, mutually complimentary public statements. Rowell had been appointed as Rules chairman by Turlington in an attempt to build harmony between the conservative and liberal wings of the Democratic party, but his effort was now seen to be of no avail. During one closed-door caucus, Rowell was reported almost at blows with a liberal Dade County representative and there were exchanges of bitter name-calling. So acute was the breach in the party that Speaker Turlington was advised by some of his supporters to pack the Rules Committee and the Finance and Taxation Committee with more liberal party loyalists. Turlington decided otherwise, for to take this course of action probably would have caused the resignation of the two former speakers from their committee chairmanships, followed by other experienced leaders, thus deepening the animosity of the defecting group. However, Turlington did appoint as his informal floor leaders three urban representatives from Pensacola, Jacksonville, and Miami, thus strengthening the leadership of the moderate and liberal wing of the party in the House without publicly denouncing the conservative wing. By this action, Turlington also improved his image among the party regulars. As one Democrat said, "Before this event nobody on the floor could speak with authority," given the ideologically divided party leadership.[19]

The House Republican leaders made gestures toward a more permanent alliance with the conservative Democrats. Reed reported a number of discussions with the latter on the kinds of measures that such a coalition might support and the number of votes it might muster. However, former Speaker Rowell and other conservative Democrats reportedly preferred to avoid a formal, institutionalized coalition in order to retain a more independent role in the House. Thus, for example, Rowell gave the Republicans the one Democratic vote they needed to sustain a veto of a bill extending the hours in which polls were to be open, but two days later he introduced a resolution commending Speaker Turlington's leadership of the House and moved it through to passage. Therefore, Reed's efforts toward a more permanent alliance with the conservative Democrats failed although he continued to find frequent support from them on roll calls.

Party cohesion was very high in each of the legislative parties save for the House Democrats. Here, Speaker Turlington's hope of building party unity through committee appointments to all segments of the party came to naught. The serious breach in House Democratic leadership did not result in sanctions against the dissenters. Though some House Democrats urged punitive measures against those disloyal to the party, the speaker's decision not to impose sanctions was designed to avoid what would have been an irrevocable and bitter intraparty factionalism. Nevertheless, the defection of the conservative Democrats on these issues resulted in a restructuring of the caucus leadership to strengthen the loyalist Democrats. Therefore, if the Speaker's decision was not fully in accord with the assumptions of the responsible party model, at least it was motivated by considerations of party welfare. In brief, both the strategies of interparty conflict and the management of intraparty dissension are evidence of considerable change from the pre-1967 legislative system in the direction of a more responsible party system.

THE BEGINNINGS OF BIPARTISAN COMPROMISE

There was considerable displeasure within both parties especially with regard to appropriations for the state's twenty-two junior colleges because certain errors in calculations had produced abnormally severe cuts in their projected operating expenditures. The legislature recessed for three days to allow a bipartisan group to write a compromise bill on junior college spending. The group was composed of Reuben Askew and Henry Land, Democratic chairmen of the Appropriations Committees in the Senate and House respectively, together with the minority leaders in the two houses and Wade Hopping, the governor's legislative aide. The bill proposed by the committee compromised the $26 million figure advanced by the Democratic leadership and the $18 million desired by Kirk. The bill was passed by a majority of both parties in the House and the Senate. However, on the last statutory day of the session, the governor vetoed the bill in its entirety, insisting that junior college expenditures not exceed $18 million. A frantic effort to write a bill that would meet the governor's approval failed to get out of committee before the statutory deadline of the session.

The junior college appropriations bill is notable as the first attempt to write a bipartisan bill on a major legislative issue. True, the bipartisan effort was undertaken partly because of the pressure of time: statutory adjournment was only days away and a bipartisan approach was perhaps seen as simply the most efficient means of writing a bill that could pass in short order. But if conservation of

effort was a spur to party cooperation, an equally important influence
was the breakdown of communication between the governor and his
legislative party, as will be explained.

As the regular session continued, communications in the legislative system took on a characteristic pattern. When the education
issues first arose, communications between the legislative parties
were largely adversary rather than bargaining in nature. However,
after the governor delivered a total of forty-eight vetoes (including
line-item vetoes of appropriations), interparty communications in the
legislature assumed more of a bargaining character. Indeed, the
Republican Senate leaders initiated a number of the interparty conferences held in the last days of the session.

Yet the Republican leaders in the legislature sometimes were
handicapped in these attempts to compromise by a lack of clear understanding of the governor's position on bills. The junior college appropriations bill, for example, had been written and passed by a bipartisan legislative effort, and while frequent consultations had occurred between Kirk and various minority legislators, the latter came
away unsure of the maximum appropriation that Kirk would accept.
Repeatedly, Kirk remained noncommittal until a bill was laid on his
desk. Interviews with Republican legislators and newspaper reports
both indicated the governor's frequent unwillingness to reveal his
plans in advance and his public pronouncements often came as a surprise to his own party. Republican legislators also pointed out that
the governor's staff included no one who had served in the legislature,
and they increasingly felt that the governor had little appreciation of
their problems as legislators and of their efforts to support him.
They often lacked information about his positions on issues. Some
speculated that the governor wished to create a public image as a
dramatic figure, the central object of political attention and a firm
and strong decisionmaker, in hopes of gaining national publicity as a
possible vice-presidential choice in 1968. The governor's actions
clearly reveal his self-perception as "chief legislator," and he repeatedly demanded his party's support, but his communications with
the legislative party increasingly deteriorated as the session progressed.

Further, on occasions when the governor did make known his
views on pending bills, he was obdurate in refusing to compromise
with his legislative party. In effect, therefore, Kirk often pitted himself against bipartisan combinations, particularly in the Senate.
Senate minority leader Young had never committed himself to complete support of the governor, and as motions to override vetoes began
to flood the Senate calendar, Young often instigated efforts to produce
bipartisan compromises. As the session lengthened, Kirk increasingly
turned to Senator L. A. Bafalis of Palm Beach County as his chief

Senate spokesman and supporter—and there was growing enmity between Young and Bafalis. House minority leader Reed continued as a supporter and confidant of the governor. Again, however, even Kirk's strongest supporters were sometimes unsure of his intentions.

The new pattern of bipartisan consultation in the legislature, together with a lack of complete and straightforward communication between the governor and his legislative party, reappeared in a special three-day session on junior college appropriations held a few days after the regular session. Both houses quickly passed bills totaling $21 million for the junior colleges. In the House, the Republicans solidly opposed the appropriations, with an assist from three or four conservative Democrats who absented themselves or voted with the minority on critical roll calls. Twelve of the twenty Republican Senators, including Young, voted with the cohesive Democrats in passing the bill. The governor vetoed the appropriations bill on the day following its passage, and the Senate Republicans reverted to complete cohesion in sustaining his veto. On the same day, the Appropriations Committees in both houses approved bills providing for $18.1 million in junior college appropriations with solid Republican support. The bills passed in both houses with token opposition in both parties and were approved by the governor.

In the special three-day session, the governor had announced his position on junior college appropriations publicly and in advance. Since he could be fairly certain of House support for his veto of the $21 million bill, he evidently saw little need to compromise with the more liberal, bipartisan Senate coalition. Yet his actions on this occasion are an example of his typical style of gubernatorial leadership. On this bill as on many others, Kirk apparently saw his leadership as paramount vis-à-vis the legislative party, in contrast to a role as equal partner attempting to build a more comprehensive party position through bilateral negotiation. The governor's style tended to be personalistic and not notably oriented toward achieving positions of consensus within the party.

THE COLLAPSE OF REPUBLICAN COHESION

The leaders of the Florida Education Association were distressed at the failure of the legislature to increase public school funding significantly. Through the summer and fall of 1967, the FEA leaders planned a campaign to bring about a special session of the legislature on education. They redoubled efforts to gain undated resignations from the 55,000 members of the organization, with apparent success, and claimed that the resignations could be activated within three hours by a prearranged telephone network. Appeals to public opinion were

27

made in local meetings and on television, and telegrams were sent to all legislators urging them to call themselves into session. In early October, great majorities of teachers walked out of their classrooms in Broward and Pinellas counties over local contractual issues; these walkouts apparently were not engineered by the state FEA, but they revealed an unprecedented militancy among teachers and underscored the FEA threat of a statewide walkout.

After much hesitation, the governor agreed to call a special session in January 1968. The legislature, he said, should consider a report of the Quality Education Commission, an ad hoc, bipartisan group appointed by Kirk several months previously to consider the broad-range problems and needs of the Florida public school system. The commission's report recommended $400 million in new funds for education. Repeatedly, however, the governor insisted that any new taxes be the subject of statewide referenda. He hinted that he would campaign for such taxes if they were attached to a measure abolishing the elected status of the state superintendent of education and creating an appointed commissioner of education. Thus, public school appropriations, taxation, and now structural reform of the school system were the major issues around which the party system took shape in the remainder of the 1967-68 legislature.

Governor Kirk surprised both parties in his opening speech to the second special session by abandoning his insistence on no new taxes. He proposed a sales tax increase of 2 percent and an additional cigarette tax of five cents per package to provide for educational spending. However, he also proposed a referendum on changing the status of the state superintendent of education from an elective to an appointive office. And further, if the voters rejected this structural change in a referendum, any new taxes were to be nullified automatically thereby.

Attorneys in both parties in the legislature expressed doubt about the constitutionality of making a tax contingent upon a structural change in a referendum. At the moment, however, the political question forced on the Democrats was whether to agree to the referendum on the structural change, thus jeopardizing what had been a safe cabinet seat for the party, in order to obtain increased educational appropriations. The Democrats were unanimous in rejecting the structural change. Moreover, Senator Young said publicly that the Republicans might not support the governor's insistence on coupling the two issues in a referendum. A number of Senate Republicans had recently become even more alienated from the governor because they were passed over for certain judicial appointments, had not been granted patronage that they had expected, and suspected the governor of supporting opponents in the party primaries to be held in the spring.[20] Thus, Young and other Senate Republicans discussed a compromise with the Democrats on the referendum issue in spite of the governor's position. House minority leader Reed still pledged Kirk the support of Republican Representatives. However, he admitted that he and Speaker Turlington had agreed to stay in close consultation and, for the first time, the leaders of each party in the House addressed a caucus of the other party to explain their policy intentions.[21]

In a surprising move on the day following the governor's address, State Superintendent of Education Floyd Christian gained permission to address a joint session of the legislature and announced his support for a referendum on an appointive superintendent. While some Republicans doubted Christian's sincerity, the possibility for bipartisan agreement was now much greater. Kirk was still believed to be adamant that any new taxes be submitted to a referendum, but his legislative support appeared even more weakened in the light of Christian's gesture.

Democratic leaders consulted with their Republican counterparts almost hourly during the first week of the second special session to try to reach a mutually acceptable set of bills on appropriations, structural changes in education, and on the issue of submitting these matters to a referendum. As reflected in a number of proposals, the Democrats tended to prefer higher appropriations and new taxes without a referendum and, following the Christian speech, they agreed to structural changes; the latter, as a constitutional matter, would have to be achieved by a referendum. The Republicans tended to prefer more moderate increases in appropriations, with new taxes contingent on their approval in a referendum and, of course, structural changes in the administration of public education. The chief points of contention were whether to hold a referendum on new taxes and the precise character of the structural changes. Senator Young concluded a "handshake agreement" with the Democratic leaders to support new taxes to be imposed by the legislature itself in exchange for the Democrats' support of a referendum allowing the governor to appoint the state's chief educational administrator. But Young could not obtain the support of the Senate Republicans on this compromise. Indeed, Young reported that the Republican caucus objected to giving governors such a direct and complete control of education—even Republican governors.

The failure of the Young compromise momentarily angered the Senate Democrats and disrupted the bipartisan negotiations that had become customary. They attempted to push through their own appropriations bill but withdrew it when Young protested angrily in floor debate that the bill would ruin chances for bipartisan agreement; the presiding officer, Senator Pope, permitted Young to block a vote on the bill through a point of order. The brief flare-up of tempers subsided and the bipartisan consultations were resumed.

29

House minority leader Reed stated to the press that "most"
Republican representatives would stand firm in favor of Kirk's demand
that any new tax proposals be submitted to the electorate.[22] However,
some House Republicans now were becoming restive and threatened
to desert the governor. Also, Reed, Speaker Turlington, and other
House leaders began meeting in private conferences to try to reach
agreement on the major legislative issues. Thus, for the first time
in the House of Representatives, there were suggestions of a break
in Republican ranks and a possibility of compromise with the majority
party's position.

The governor had been campaigning in the New Hampshire
presidential primary for several days (to the extreme annoyance of
his legislative party), but flew back to Tallahassee upon hearing of
the growing bipartisan spirit. He quickly called the Republican Senate
and House members to a meeting in the executive mansion. Those
who attended reported that Kirk "really raised hell" in demanding a
referendum on any new taxes and that he threatened to veto any bills
to the contrary. But the senators who had participated in the compromise refused to back down, affirming that they would vote to override any such veto. One senator said that the meeting finally had
established the independence of the Republican caucus. Another
declared that "Kirk learned he can't run roughshod over legislators";
he added that the Republicans had "really bled" for the governor but
that "little appreciation was ever expressed" for their trials.[23] The
Senate caucus had declared its independence although House minority
leader Reed still claimed enough votes to sustain a veto.

A twelve-man bipartisan conference committee met in secret
for two days to try to reach a compromise acceptable to the parties
in both houses. It recommended a total of $267 million for public
education in a series of nine bills. It was on these nine bills that
Republican cohesion on educational appropriations finally melted.
The Rice index of cohesion on educational appropriations had a mean
value of 87.9 in the 1967-68 session up to this point, but on these
nine bills it dropped to 25.5. On the Democratic side, cohesion on
educational appropriations had a mean value of 78.7 in the sessions
up to this time, but now increased to 96.5.* The Democratic defectors

---

*There is obvious danger in comparing indexes based on very
different N's, as between some forty-three roll calls up to this time
and only nine on the committee reports. At least, however, the indexes
of cohesion for these nine bills are strikingly different between the
two parties, and the mean values for the previous periods may be
taken as suggestive of the temporal change.

from the party position again were primarily Duval County representatives who had voted with the Republicans rather consistently throughout the sessions. The major Republican defections were from Pinellas and Brevard counties; the personal influence of Senate minority leader Young, from Pinellas, encouraged representatives from these counties to vote independently.

A compromise between the two Senate caucuses resulted in Republican support for a revised appropriations bill and Democratic support for a referendum on the abolition of the elective status of the school superintendent. Moreover, half of the Senate Republicans, including the minority leader, agreed to support new sales and excise taxes without a referendum—placing themselves in open defiance of the governor for the first time. Kirk's legislative aides tried vigorously to hold the Senate Republicans to the governor's position but to little avail. Less than half of them supported a move by Senator Bafalis to tie a referendum to the new taxes. Representative Reed angrily denounced the Senate Republican compromise as a "sell-out" and claimed enough votes in the House to "sustain anything I want."[24] However, the Republican state party chairman as well as other high officials of the organization were quietly encouraging support of the bipartisan agreement between Young and the Democratic leaders.

The party caucus discussions leading to the Senate compromise had been held in strict secrecy, aides guarding the doors, and with emissaries of the two groups meeting as necessary. But secret caucus meetings had not always been the case. Journalists, lobbyists, and constituents had been admitted to at least some Senate caucuses of both parties in the past. However, as party loyalty had become an ever more sensitive issue, and as interparty agreements began to be discussed, the Senate caucuses began to close their doors. In the House, the Republican caucus was well unified, at least publicly, and the minority leader continued to invite reporters to attend its meetings. Perhaps as a consequence of the open party caucuses, Republican representatives from Pinellas County, and also from the lower east coast counties, had often held subcaucuses with secret meetings, and the more difficult points of party policy were negotiated through private contacts.[25] The House Democrats had also held open meetings frequently but had found it increasingly difficult to discuss issues and strategies candidly and to mold a party position in the presence of constituency and organizational spokesmen. They also had held subcaucuses. In the second special session, even the location of caucus meetings was kept secret as the parties faced internal factionalism and as interparty bargaining increased. Thus, private caucuses were not manifestations of any early waves of enthusiasm for building party solidarity around substantive programs. Rather, they were begun somewhat reluctantly, months after the legislature had first convened.

Primarily, they stemmed from frustrations felt in both parties as a
result of the governor's forceful leadership. Their purpose was to
discover grounds for bipartisan agreement about as often as it was
to nurture partisan distinctiveness and solidarity.

The legislature adjourned its second special session with the
threat of a teacher walkout still imminent. The FEA leaders complained that the final appropriations bills were deceptive because they
required counties to use part of their new state monies to roll back
their school millage. They called for a veto of the bills and a new
session. The governor had about two weeks in which he could veto
all or part of the bills; he was reported to be polling the Republican
legislators about their willingness to sustain his vetoes and to have
received overwhelmingly negative replies. Democratic Senator Barrow
called for the legislators to assemble themselves in a "self-starter"
session to override vetoes if they occurred. The FEA leaders called
a walkout of teachers that was temporarily successful, but as it became
apparent that neither party favored further increases in appropriations, the teachers gradually drifted back to work in the spring. The
governor allowed the bills to become law without his signature while
his legislative support for vetoes virtually disappeared.

ANALYSES OF ROLL-CALL VOTING

The Rice index of cohesion is a measure of the solidarity of
any set of legislators in voting on bills, where yea and nay votes are
recorded for each legislator. It can vary between 100.0, indicating
perfect unity in voting, and 0.0, indicating a division of 50 percent
yeas and 50 percent nays.[26] The theory of responsible party systems
implies that, for each party, the Rice index of cohesion should approach
very nearly 100.0 to satisfy the conditions of the model. But even if
we should observe a high degree of voting cohesion among members
of a legislative party, we cannot be sure that it is motivated by party
loyalty. For similar constituency interests of members, similar
ideologies, or other factors conceivably could produce a high degree
of observed cohesion, unrelated to any concern for party. While a
low degree of cohesion certainly indicates the absence of the motivations required by the model, a high degree does not necessarily indicate its presence. Nevertheless, as Rice indexes of cohesion for a
legislative party increase, especially on bills shown by independent
evidence to be party issues, there may be increasing confidence that
the indexes reflect party loyalty as a cause of solidarity in voting.

We may begin by asking how much change in party cohesion
occurred after the rise of a significantly large minority party in
comparison with party cohesion in previous years. To measure

temporal change, it will be necessary to ignore the usual stipulation
that bills selected for measuring party cohesion be only those for
which the parties have announced positions, for indeed there were no
attempts to mold a party position on bills in the faction-ridden, one-
party legislature of the pre-1967 era. Also, in the two-party 1967-68
sessions, the randomly selected roll calls used as a basis for calcu-
lating the indexes include many for which there were no announced
party positions; therefore, in these sessions there is no reason to
expect that the observed levels of party cohesion would approach those
required by the responsible party model. Thus, Table 1.5 presents
rather gross measures of intraparty cohesion over six sessions, but
in broad terms it suggests the difference that may be made by the
appearance of a strong minority party in a previously one-party
legislature.

The 1966 special session is included in Table 1.5 because it was
the first session with a substantial number of Republicans (twenty) in
the House of Representatives. But as the table shows, the mere presence of a minority party in the House did not produce a higher degree
of overall party cohesion than existed in the previous, one-party
sessions. The low cohesion in both parties in 1966 evidently followed
from the type of legislation considered in the special session. The
session was called to consider reapportionment of the state legislature, and an inspection of roll calls showed that divisions tended to
fall on urban-rural lines in each party. On reapportionment bills,
constituency interests were clearly superior to party unity.

The notable increase in party cohesion occurred with the advent
of the two-party system in the 1967 regular session. The indexes
for this session do not approach the level of cohesion required by the
responsible party model—but again, these measures are based on a
random selection of roll calls, not necessarily on bills for which there
was a deliberate attempt to bring about party unity. Nevertheless,
there was a significant change in party cohesion in 1967, and our
analysis of the legislature up to this point strongly suggests that it
was caused, at least partly, by considerations of party loyalty.

Republican support for a distinctive party position on roll calls
declined after the 1967 regular session. Republican cohesion in the
Senate reached 79.1 in the second special session but this figure is
somewhat misleading because most Republican senators voted in
support of positions endorsed by the Democratic leadership rather
than in opposition to them. (A few Republican senators joined with
conservative Democrats in the Senate to constitute a minority of at
least 10 percent on these roll calls.) Therefore, the Republican
senators moved from a moderately high degree of cohesion against
the Democrats in the regular session, to a lower level of cohesion
in the first special session, to substantial unity with about half the

TABLE 1.5

Mean Rice Indexes of Party Cohesion
in Six Sessions of the Florida Legislature, 1963-67

	1963 Regular[a]	1965 Regular[a]	1966 Special	1967 Regular	1967 First Special	1968 Second Special
House of Representatives						
Republican	b	b	52.5	75.0	69.3	56.0
Democratic	58.7	56.6	49.4	67.1	59.1	50.7
Senate						
Republican	b	b	b	64.0	61.5	79.1
Democratic	59.5	62.8	52.5	65.5	69.0	46.6

[a]One hundred roll calls were selected randomly for the 1963 and 1965 regular sessions, with the stipulation that at least 10 percent of the members voted in the minority on any roll call. In the brief 1966 special session, all seven of the divisions meeting the latter qualification were analyzed. For the combined regular and special sessions of 1967-68, 198 roll calls with at least a 10 percent minority vote were selected randomly.

[b]In these cases the minority party was less than 10 percent of the given house; thus, the minority was too small to supply the 10 percent division stipulated above for the selection of roll calls.

Source: Compiled by the author.

in the second special session. Meanwhile, the Republican representatives' party cohesion declined steadily. Judging from these data, it seems improbable that the House Republicans would have sustained a gubernatorial veto by the time of the second special session.

Democratic cohesion increased in both houses in the 1967 regular session but thereafter fell to the low levels of the pre-1967 era. As subsequent analysis will show, while the internal stresses within each party grew, the majority position on roll calls tended to consist of a bipartisan group of legislators from urban or mixed urban-rural districts, in opposition to a somewhat heterogeneous minority made up of conservative Democrats and a few Republicans from all types of constituencies who continued to support the governor.

Rice indexes of party cohesion were also calculated for roll-call votes on each of the three major party-related issues in the 1967-68 sessions; educational appropriations, taxation, and motions to override vetoes. The discussion so far has suggested that party was a particularly important consideration on these issues, and we might expect higher party cohesion here than on a random sample of roll calls. Further, since these were "party sensitive" issues, they constitute a more appropriate basis for analyzing intraparty factionalism in the 1967-68 sessions.

Table 1.6 indicates that cohesion in both parties on tax measures tended to be lower than on the other two types of issues. A cluster-bloc analysis of voting on the tax bills (not presented here because of space considerations) failed to indicate any consistent urban-rural split in either party. Urban-rural divisions cutting across party lines were discernable on several bills proposing to increase the allocation of state revenues to urban counties at the expense of rural areas. However, no such division appeared on bills affecting property taxation. As mentioned previously, factional voting on ad valorem tax bills was related to peculiarities of local tax administration, not to any more fundamental socioeconomic cleavages. Factionalism did exist, however, and the low indexes of cohesion at least show that constituency interests prevailed over party solidarity on taxation, perhaps the most sensitive of local issues.

But cohesion in both parties was considerably higher on educational appropriations and on motions to override vetoes. In the Senate, Democratic cohesion is remarkably high in comparison to the factionalism of the previous era. Cohesion approaches the level required by the responsible party model on these two types of bills in the regular session, but thereafter it declines. The collapse of Senate Republican cohesion by the second special session is strikingly evident in Table 1.6. In the House, the Republicans initially had a very high degree of solidarity on motions to override vetoes. While there were no House roll calls on such motions in the special sessions, the decline of Republican cohesion on educational appropriations again raises doubt that vetoes could have been sustained by the time of the second special session. Still, the pressures for Republican party unity in the House remained more effective than in the Senate; much of this difference appears to be the product of contrasting leadership orientations of the House and Senate minority leaders, as explained previously.

TABLE 1.6

Mean Rice Indexes of Party Cohesion on Three Policy Issues,
Florida Legislature, 1967-68

	Regular Session			First Special Session			Second Special Session		
	Dems.	Reps.	(N)	Dems.	Reps.	(N)	Dems.	Reps.	(N)
Senate									
Educational appropriations	90.8	84.0	(48)	71.1	69.1	(2)	64.5	61.9	(8)
Motions to override vetoes	81.0	97.9	(6)	–	–	(0)	–	–	(0)
Tax bills	53.0	69.5	(15)	61.5	80.0	(3)	52.4	49.8	(10)
House of Representatives									
Educational appropriations	96.1	84.3	(40)	83.3	66.6	(2)	97.1	31.9	(8)
Motions to override vetoes	99.5	93.6	(28)	96.4	89.5	(2)	75.0	47.4	(1)
Tax bills	35.7	41.5	(12)	30.8	22.2	(1)	64.8	33.2	(13)

Source: Compiled by the author.

36

Why was cohesion so much higher in the regular session than in the two special sessions? Interviews and newspaper accounts suggest two reasons for the decline in cohesion. Democrats reported an increasing impatience in the party with appeals for party unity over personal or constituency orientations. On several occasions, veteran Democratic legislators in both caucuses protested what they considered an overemphasis on party solidarity, and, as reported previously, the Democratic caucuses abandoned the practice of voting on policy positions before the end of the regular session. Second, Republican legislators reported an increasing willingness by the party rank-and-file to abandon support of the governor as the threat of a wholesale walkout of school teachers loomed even greater. This willingness was partly due to fear among some Republicans that their party would bear the blame for such a crisis in the eyes of the voters. Republican defections were not so much motivated by a reaction against party as by a different interpretation of the long-run interests of the party. Paradoxically, the Democratic decline in cohesion was largely the result of an impatience with the very conception of party solidarity, while the Republican decline largely stemmed from a concern with party welfare.

Finally, cluster-bloc analyses can reveal factional structures on the three major party-related issues. Cluster-bloc techniques indicate the number of times each legislator voted with every other legislator on a given set of roll calls, and, thus, also reveal blocs of legislators who voted with a high degree of consistency against other such blocs.[27] Here we are concerned with intraparty blocs or factions as revealed in roll-call votes on educational appropriations and motions to override vetoes. These were the issues having the highest Rice indexes of party cohesion, and any consistent minority bloc within a party on these roll calls can be considered as a "hard core" faction.

A "bloc" will be defined as any set of legislators who voted together on 90 percent or more of the aforementioned roll calls. This is an unusually high cut-off point in cluster-bloc analysis; it was selected because a lower cut-off would have included so many legislators in some cases that bloc structures would have virtually disappeared. Therefore, in interpreting the following comments, the reader should recall that intraparty cohesion on these bills was high and that "disagreement scores" of only 10 percentage points were sufficient to differentiate factions within a party. For space considerations, bloc matrixes are not reproduced.

Two blocs appeared in the Senate Democratic party. The larger consisted of ten senior legislators, all but one of whom represented the urban counties of Dade, Duval, and Hillsborough. This bloc included the Senate president and the chairman of the Rules and Calendar

Committee. Another five Democratic senators were on the fringes of this bloc and represented urban districts including Pensacola, Miami, and Orlando. Two other Democratic blocs consisted of five senior senators from rural or mixed urban-rural districts, with a fringe group of three from similar constituencies. Thus, the Senate Democrats continued to reflect the older pork chop versus lamb chop division but only as a pale shadow of the factionalism of yersteryear. Indeed, the fact that a 90 percent cut-off point was needed to demark the two groups testifies to the healing of old wounds and the consolidation of the Senate Democrats on these "party sensitive" issues.

The Senate Republicans also contained two distinct though small blocs. One bloc of four included the minority leader, and the other bloc of equal size clustered around Senator Bafalis, the governor's informal floor leader in the Senate. Each bloc had a fringe of two or three senators. However, there is no noticeable pattern within either bloc with respect to the type of constituencies represented. Apparently, the factors dividing the two blocs were primarily support for and opposition to the governor and, perhaps, to personal ideologies.

In the House of Representatives, there were two Republican blocs with a common fringe group. One bloc of fourteen consisted of all seven Orange County (Orlando) representatives plus six of the eight Broward County (Ft. Lauderdale) representatives, together with minority leader Reed. However, Reed also qualified as a member of the second bloc, consisting of nine members, half from Palm Beach County and the remainder from several mixed urban-rural counties. Eight of the nine Pinellas County Republicans did not have 90 percent or higher agreement scores with any other representatives. However, if the cut-off point is reduced to 80 percent, the Pinellas Republicans form yet a third bloc. As noted before, Republican representation in the House was heavily concentrated in seven districts where the party had captured 100 percent (or nearly so) of the seats; also, separate subcaucuses of district Republican representatives sometimes had met. The cluster-bloc analysis again reflects this district orientation among Republican Representatives. However, there is no convincing evidence that these blocs were based on any substantial socioeconomic differences between the districts. It seems very likely that Republican factionalism, such as it was, consisted of "friends and neighbors" from separate districts having somewhat idiosyncratic political concerns and different reactions to the governor's style of leadership.

The pork chop versus lamb chop factionalism of previous years reappeared in two distinct blocs within the House Democratic membership. The larger of the two clustered around Speaker Turlington and was primarily urban in constituency type. A much smaller bloc consisted of rural Democrats who had been associated with the pork chop group in the past, joined by a few Duval County representatives.

Democratic representatives from mixed urban-rural districts appeared in both groups or their fringes, but most of them were associated with the former bloc.

In summary, factionalism appeared after the 1967 regular session on party sensitive issues. The Republicans in both houses of the legislature experienced a greater decline in cohesion on these issues than the Democrats. But the roots of intraparty factionalism were somewhat different in the two parties. Democratic factionalism apparently derived partly from liberal and conservative ideological differences among legislators and partly from an individualistic view of the legislative role versus a party-oriented view. To some extent, the conservative ideology coincided with the individualistic role perception and the liberal outlook with a greater receptivity to appeals in the name of party. In turn, these lines of division tended to follow urban-rural constituency differences, but far from completely so. On balance, Democratic factionalism seems to have been less a function of fundamental socioeconomic clashes of constituency interests than of the personal political values and role perceptions of legislators.

Republican factionalism was even less clearly associated with differences in constituency characteristics. Rather, factionalism in the minority party apparently was rooted in contrasting attractions to the different styles of party leadership typified by Governor Kirk and Senator Young. Related to these different leadership styles, there were differing perceptions of the kind of legislative record most likely to strengthen the party in the long run, and these perceptions were doubtless colored somewhat by the personal ideologies of Republican legislators. But Republican factionalism was fundamentally different in character from that of the Democrats. In the minority party, there was no hint of any differences of socioeconomic interests between the factions and no evidence of a rejection of the value of party as an organizing principle. Minority factionalism was primarily a disagreement about the process of making party policy and about the policy stance that would best serve the future welfare of the Republicans as a party. Thus, it is easy to speculate that a more conciliatory approach by the governor vis-à-vis his legislative party would have resulted in a continuation of the high Republican cohesion that had existed in the regular session.

CONCLUSION

A wealth of systematic quantitative research has been done on personal attributes of legislators and constituency characteristics as related to party voting in state legislatures.[28] A smaller amount of research has used interviews with legislators to reveal their orientations to party as opposed to other representational roles.[29] As valuable as these studies are in delineating factors tending to promote legislative party cohesion, few of them probe the internal dynamics of legislative parties, no doubt partly because the necessary comparative data would be very hard to obtain. The advantage of a single case study is that it can reveal much of the "infrastructure" of a legislative system. This examination of the Florida legislature has focused primarily on the perceptions and role behaviors of the actors involved, on the group processes that arise largely from the latter, and on the momentum of the legislative party struggle as it responds to issues and events in the course of time. As Sorauf writes,

> The legislature itself presents the final opportunity for the party to enter into the representational process. It is there that the party tests its relationship with its elected candidates and tries to establish their responsibility to a party program.[30]

Insofar as party responsibility comes into existence, it is at least as much a function of the internal dynamics of a legislature as it is to the kinds of personal and constituency characteristics investigated in the past.

That party responsibility did not fully flower in the Florida legislature is evident, yet the system was far removed from that of the one-party era. In the 1967-68 sessions, significant new developments provided a basis for a functioning two-party system: the appearance of legislative leaders with party welfare as a major concern; the rise of party caucuses and the outlines of legislative party organization; attempts to promote party loyalty among the rank-and-file as superior to factional and local interests, and a willingness among many to subordinate older factional differences to party unity; legislative strategies designed to further party interests; a governor who asserted a partisan role as chief legislator and who attempted a reorganization of state government such that party responsibility for public policy might become more of a reality.

To discuss reasons why an even greater degree of party responsibility was not attained is to recite familiar characteristics of American political culture. For example, a degree of antagonism between legislative and executive branches may be present in all governmental systems as it was in Florida. Legislators' perceptions of their roles as constituency delegates or as Burkean individualists sometimes prevails over party orientation. This sort of role conflict appeared in Florida as in other states. Second, beyond such presumed cultural factors, the perceptions and skills of actors involved had an independent effect upon the legislative party system. Legislative leaders in Florida, unaccustomed to a two-party system, at first seem not to have perceived party as a major parameter of the legislative system; at least, their behavior initially was integrative and conciliatory, and they abandoned this role only after the governor laid down a partisan challenge. The evidence of this study points to the role behavior of the governor as critical in activating party conflict in the legislature. The novelty of his legislative proposals on educational appropriations, his insistence on no new taxes in the face of intensive pressures for new spending, his proposal to eliminate the independently elected office of school superintendent—all provided a spark to partisan conflict. It is easy to believe that had the governor adopted a less dramatic and partisan role, legislative party conflict would have been less accentuated. Paradoxically, while the governor initially stimulated party conflict, his perception of his role as hierarchically superior to his legislative party and his intransigence on the issues were a major cause of the eventual collapse of Republican unity and the appearance of bipartisan policymaking.

The strategies and tactics used by parties in the legislative process have received very little attention from political scientists. This study suggests that the kinds of strategies used by legislative parties may reveal a great deal about the character of the party system and, thereby, of the process of policy-formation. Legislative party strategies are worth studying because, in this interpretation, party itself becomes an interest group whose members try to promote the long-run electoral success of the party. Thus, in a two-party system the primary purpose of party strategy will be to divide the opposition party if possible, to place it in untenable parliamentary positions, to force it into actions and pronouncements likely to be unpopular in the eyes of the electorate. This is not quite the same thing as using strategies to promote an ideological viewpoint or to represent the views of interest groups. For a party has at least some range of choice in the specific content of the policies it adopts at any given time in the development of the legislative struggle, and it may even shift its policy grounds to meet counter-strategies of the opposing party. Such a shift was observed in the positions of the Democratic party in Florida on the issue of educational appropriations. The absorption of many leaders in both parties with strategies led officials of the Florida Education Association to characterize the legislative struggle as a "shell game" somewhat detached from substantive policy issues.[31] The officials' greatest animosity was directed at the governor, but at several points they also castigated the Democrats as more interested in defeating the Republicans than in articulating a policy position.

Whatever the inefficiencies of a one-party system in converting public demands into public policy, party itself is not an interest group in the legislative system (although there may be others). As a two-party system develops, conversion is channeled through the presumed interests of parties, as reflected in legislative strategies. If so, then parties do not simply act passively as brokers among competing interests, as one view of two-party systems holds. Further, in carrying out strategies for advantage the parties may not act as the responsible party model demands—the pursuit of well-defined and consistent programs of public policy.

Innovations may be adopted deliberately by a state legislature in order to achieve preconceived goals, as illustrated in several of the case studies in this volume. But also, unintended innovations in a legislative system may be stimulated by changes in the external environment of the system. The elections of 1967 in Florida were such a stimulus, but the election of a considerable number of Republican legislators was not sufficient in itself to produce party responsibility. The initial motives and role behaviors in the new legislature served pluralistic and bipartisan ends. Insofar as a more responsible party system appeared thereafter, it was primarily a result of personal and situational factors within the legislature that could have been altogether different, perhaps perpetuating the initial pattern. Thus arises the theoretical question, under what legislative conditions is the likelihood of a responsible party system enhanced or diminished? This case study provides several hypotheses about such conditions:

1. In an emerging two-party system, party responsibility is unlikely to occur in the absence of the following:

a. The assertion of a clear position on a controversial and highly visible policy issue by one or more leaders of a party;

b. The adoption by the latter of role behaviors designed to increase intraparty cohesion on the issue position;

c. The perception by the opposite party's leaders of a threat from the foregoing to the interests of their party;

d. The assertion of an alternative issue position by the opposite party's leaders;

e. The adoption by the latter of role behaviors designed to increase intraparty cohesion on the alternative issue position.

2. The likelihood of party responsibility increases with the strength of party identification of legislators.

a. Party identification is likely to be greater among legislators in a newly emerging party, and less among legislators in a formerly dominant party.

b. In a legislative party containing incumbents from a previous one-party system, holdovers will tend to have a negative orientation to party as an influence on their legislative behavior.

3. Legislative leaders in a newly emerging two-party system tend to adopt bipartisan, integrative roles in the legislative system instead of accentuating party conflict.

    a. Committee chairmanships (when not determined by seniority) will be awarded to majority party members representing all intraparty factions, rather than to members loyal to the party's policy positions.

    b. Sanctions are unlikely to be levied for party disloyalty.

4. In an emerging two-party system, party caucuses will exist primarily for informational purposes, not for reaching binding party positions.

5. Hierarchical relations between party leaders and rank-and-file legislators tend to decrease the probability of party cohesion.

    a. The likelihood of party cohesion is greater in the presence of intraparty bargaining on policy issues.

    b. Legislative party leaders will tend to value legislative independence from the executive over party loyalty to the governor.

6. Legislative party strategies to defeat the opposite party will take precedence over strategies to enact a consistent policy program.

NOTES

1. The turnover rates for the Florida Senate and House were 62 percent and 65 percent respectively for the 1965-67 period, and these rates were more than double the average for the United States. See Elston E. Roady and Manning J. Dauer, "The Florida Legislature," in William G. Cornelius, ed., Southeastern State Legislatures (Atlanta: Emory University School of Law, 1968), p. 33.

2. Dennis M. Callan, "Intra-Legislative Communications in a Newly Emergent Two-Party System: The Case of Education and the Florida House of Representatives, 1967" (Master's thesis, Florida Atlantic University, 1969).

3. The responsible party model first appeared in Toward a More Responsible Two-Party System, A Report of the Committee on Political Parties, American Political Science Association (New York: Rinehart & Company, 1950). The intellectual roots of the model, as well as a critical commentary, are presented in Austin Ranney, The Doctrine of Responsible Party Government (Urbana: University of Illinois Press, 1962).

4. Toward A More Responsible Two-Party System, p. 43.

5. Ibid., p. 40.

6. E. E. Schattschneider, Party Government (New York: Rinehart & Company, 1942), pp. 57-61.

7. Toward A More Responsible Two-Party System, p. 40.

8. Thomas A. Flinn, "Party Responsibility in the States: Some Causal Factors," American Political Science Review 58 (March 1964), 60-71.

9. Loren P. Beth and William C. Havard, "Committee Stacking and Political Power in Florida," Journal of Politics 23, No. 1 (February 1961), 58-61.

10. Malcolm B. Parsons, "Quasi-Partisan Conflict in a One-Party Legislative System: The Florida Senate, 1947-61," American Political Science Review 56 (September 1962), 605-14.

11. V. O. Key, Jr., Southern Politics in State and Nation (New York: Alfred A. Knopf, 1949), pp. 82-105.

12. William C. Havard and Loren P. Beth, The Politics of Mis-Representation (Baton Rouge: Louisiana State University Press, 1962), chaps. 5 and 7.

13. Callan, "Intra-Legislative Communications," p. 56.

14. Havard and Beth, The Politics of Mis-Representation, pp. 135-144.

15. Ibid., pp. 144-47.

16. Miami Herald, May 13, 1967, p. 12-A.

17. David B. Truman's remarks about the interest group character of local party organizations very probably apply to legislative parties also. See The Governmental Process (New York: Alfred A. Knopf, 1958), pp. 279-81.

18. Christian was a major source of information and consultation for Democratic legislators on educational issues and strategies, according to data from mail questionnaires to House members. See Callan, "Intra-Legislative Communications," pp. 50-52.

19. Miami Herald, June 1, 1967, p. 26-A.

20. St. Petersburg Times, February 3, 1968, p. 1.

21. Tampa Tribune, January 29, 1968, p. 1.

22. Tallahassee Democrat, February 9, 1968, p. 1.

23. Miami Herald, February 11, 1968, p. 2-D.

24. St. Petersburg Times, Feb. 9, 1968, p. 1.

25. Callan, "Intra-Legislative Communications," pp. 46-47.

26. For a more complete explanation of the Rice index of cohesion, see Lee F. Anderson, Meredith W. Watts, Jr., and Allen R. Wilcox, Legislative Roll-Call Analysis (Evanston, Ill.: Northwestern University Press, 1966), pp. 33-35.

27. Cluster-bloc analysis is explained more fully in Anderson et al., Legislative Roll-Call Analysis, chap. 4.

28. See works cited in William J. Keefe and Morris S. Ogul, The American Legislative Process: Congress and the States, 2d ed. (Englewood Cliffs, N.J.: Prentice-Hall, 1968), p. 315.

29. See John C. Wahlke, Heinz Eulau, William Buchanan, and Leroy C. Ferguson, The Legislative System: Explorations in Legislative Behavior (New York: John Wiley, 1962), chap. 15. Also, Frank J. Sorauf, Party and Representation (New York: Atherton Press, 1963), chap. 6.

30. Sorauf, Party and Representation, p. 121.

31. Miami Herald, January 12, 1968, p. 1.

2

LEGISLATIVE REFORM AND POLITICS IN CALIFORNIA: WHAT HAPPENED, WHY, AND SO WHAT?

Alan J. Wyner

Very few states in the nation can match the Golden State in political excitement, and increasingly in the latter half of this century very few can match it for political importance. After the 1970 Census, California gained enough new congressional seats to place it ahead of New York in the size of its Washington delegation. California's importance in presidential nominations and elections is also widely recognized. But perhaps the factor that should be given primacy when assessing its importance is the composition of its population.

If there is a prize for the state that contains the most diverse polyglot of races, ethnic backgrounds, social classes, economic groups, and life styles in this country, California must be considered in the forefront of the race for that blue ribbon. In addition, the population combination is not stable, but ever-changing. As Gladwin Hill phrases it,

> California has never been a state in the ordinary sense of a fixed community of people. Rather, the endless tide of immigration, peculiarities of geography, and the forced-draft growth of California's economy have made it a kaleidoscopic succession of states, changing from year to year, almost from day to day.[1]

Philip A. Rosenberg assisted at both the design and data collection stages of this research. This paper was completed in 1970 and does purport to report more recent events relevant to but not contradictory to the main theses and interpretations.

Hill also reminds us that a certain type of person leaves Oklahoma, Illinois, or Vermont to settle in California. Primarily he is an individualist "with less than ordinary regard for conventions, established norms, and what has gone before."[2] Consequences for politics abound. This American, and typically strange, mixture with its inborn and man-made cleavages generates a political environment supportive of "unusual" ideas and people at the same time it sustains a brand of politics representing a good sample of the "typical" American electorate.

This chapter will not accept the challenge of presenting to the reader a description and analysis of California politics in toto. It will focus on a narrower, institutional and still provocative, topic— the California state legislature. The state legislature possesses qualities that make it representative of the California political environment. It is an exciting institution because emerging from within the Assembly and Senate chambers and committee rooms is the conflict and cooperation, as well as bitterness and friendship, characteristic of the state's political environment. It is in the legislature that one sees and hears all the issues and personalities that divide and unite the state's diverse polity.

There exists no shortage of books and articles devoted to the legislature, so repetition of the organization, functions, and powers of the California legislature will not be necessary.[3] What is lacking, and what this chapter hopes to provide, is attention to a rather unique orientation or characteristic of this institution. That is, its tendency in the post-World War II era, and especially in the decade of the 1960s, to be innovative in its willingness to enact proposals for reforming and (some say) upgrading the quality of the legislative process. The goals of this chapter become twofold: (1) to describe in some detail the changes that have taken place, and (2) to ask a series of questions about the consequences of those changes. Attention will focus on the consequences, if any, for legislative procedures, personnel, and to some extent policy. For reasons that will become apparent later, the lower house (the Assembly) captures the lion's share of our inquiry.

Data for this essay were collected in several ways. Personal observation of the legislature as it conducts its business allows one to garner much of the detail and flavor of legislative life. Contrary to some reports about conducting research in Washington, legislators and staff in Sacramento have not been "plagued" by scores of political scientists demanding large blocks of time for interviews. As a result, it remains fairly easy to interview in the state capitol. Some persistence permitted interviews with several dozen people, including many legislators as well as legislative staff, lobbyists, executive agency personnel, and newspaper reporters. Observation and interviewing were supplemented by extensive use of documentary material. Random techniques were not used to gather data, but care was always taken to assure the data's representative quality.

As is often the case, an understanding of the political framework within which legislative behavior occurs will enhance the clarity and relevance of the material presented here. A short narrative about recent California political highlights, then, becomes the first order of business. The reader should be forewarned that what follows necessarily represents only the top of the iceberg.

A SHORT POLITICAL HISTORY

The Warren Era

Contemporary California political history began with the "Earl Warren Era," named after the man elected California's governor three times, Republican vice-presidential nominee on the Dewey ticket in 1948, and since 1969, retired chief justice of the U.S. Supreme Court. Warren served ten years (1943-53) in the governor's chair. Taking advantage of Hiram Johnson's Progressive heritage, many California politicians have sought shelter under the nonpartisan, "nonpolitical" umbrella. Somehow, this public stance was thought to be held by men possessed of superior virtue, and few were as adept as Earl Warren in cloaking themselves in this mantle. Part of the Progressive tradition was the unusual concept of cross-filing, an electoral system whereby any candidate could file for election as a representative of any or all recognized political parties. In all three of Warren's gubernatorial campaigns he sought both the Republican and Democratic nomination in the primary election. Warren was successful only in 1946 in preventing any ballot competition at the general election. Yet, the fact that one man could seriously seek both major party's nominations in primary contests for the state's highest office speaks handily to both the milieu of California politics in the 1940s and the abilities of one of the system's most able participants.

For the most part, Warren enjoyed success with the Republican-dominated legislatures of that time. Even in the heyday of Artie Samish, the personification of the "lobbyist-as-devil," Warren possessed the skill and popularity to wrangle legislative agreement for most of his liberal social welfare program. At the same time, he lived with some of the special interest shenanigans authored, and reputedly paid for, by Samish's oil, liquor, and race-track employers. Not much can be said about the legislatures of Warren's time,

except that the scandalous revelations about Samish and other lobbyists in the early 1950s helped reduce the public regard for legislators
and the legislative process to its modern low point. Samish, who was
convicted in 1953 in federal court for income tax violations, was
known to boast that he could tell whether legislators wanted "a baked
potato, a girl, or money." Although no legislator was convicted of
accepting a bribe, it was quite clear that somebody received the
Samish money. One outgrowth of the scandal was a conflict-of-
interest law that sought to make it more difficult for the unscrupulous
lobbyist to operate without public disclosure.

The 1951 legislature began a trend that was to bear plentiful
fruit a decade later. In that session the legislature for the first
time made provision in its expenditures and space allocations for
an office and secretary for each member during the session. Modest
as this may seem, it is a step not taken by the majority of states
almost twenty years later.

Earl Warren's appointment to the U.S. Supreme Court by President Eisenhower caused him to resign the governorship on October
3, 1953. The office of the governor was placed in the hands of
Warren's lieutenant governor, Goodwin J. Knight. Not much has
been written about Knight, except his "switch" with William Knowland
in the 1958 election—more about that later. The decade of the 1950s
saw two other men launch themselves into the state political arena:
Edmund G. Brown and Jesse M. Unruh. "Pat" Brown served as state
attorney general for two terms, 1951-58, after laboring as the Ala-
meda County (Oakland) district attorney. Following two unsuccessful
tries, Jesse Unruh was elected to the state Assembly in 1954 from
a district in Los Angeles County. Four years later he became chairman of the powerful Assembly Ways and Means Committee, and at
the age of thirty-nine Unruh was elected Speaker of the Assembly in
1961.

Democrats and the Aftermath of 1958

Republican U.S. Senator William Knowland coveted the California governor's chair in 1958, and he let his wishes be known. He
(and some say Vice-President Richard Nixon) persuaded fellow
Republican Governor Goodwin Knight not to run for reelection so
that Knowland could seek the Republican nomination unopposed.
Knight was then given the Republican senatorial nomination. The
great "switch" between Knight and Knowland infuriated many Republicans because it was obvious that Knight was pressured into the
exchange against his will. Democrats saw a golden opportunity to
elect their second governor in the twentieth century; only Governor

Culbert Olson (1938-42) had saved the Democrats from a total white-wash in the gubernatorial sweepstakes. To challenge Knowland and a divided Republican party, the Democrats selected Attorney General Pat Brown. Aided by Knowland's strong stand in favor of "right-to-work" laws, Brown swept to a landslide victory by a margin of approximately 1 million votes. In addition to the governor's office, the Democrats gained control of both houses of the state legislature. This marked the first time in the century that the Democrats so completely controlled the state government. Yet, too much should not be made of this party feat because California was not (and is not now) one of those states in which a strong party organization dominates the field. The Democratic party is held together (sometimes) only by the energies of its key personalities; to a slightly lesser extent this is also true of the Republican party.[4]

Immediately after victory, the Democrats moved to consolidate their political position. They had long contended that cross-filing served Republican interests by preventing Democrats from taking advantage of the edge in Democratic voter registration. Too many Republicans, went their cry, were able to masquerade as either Democrats or "nonpartisans" on the Democratic primary ballot and "confuse" Democratic voters. It was not at all surprising that the 1959 Democratic legislature and Governor Brown agreed without much debate to abolish entirely this unique method of nominating public officials.

An issue of long-standing contention in California was resolved during Brown's first term: distribution of water within the state. Breaking a stalemate that had existed since World War II, the legislature enacted a plan for a massive transfer of water from the water-rich northern part of the state to the arid south. It was a multi-billion-dollar program that aroused great emotions as well as doubts about technical and economic feasibility. The project was still under construction twelve years later but well along toward completion.

Brown was careful not to become identified as simply a Democratic party politician. Nonpartisanship or bipartisan appeals still were important. This was once again made evident in the 1962 gubernatorial race between Brown and former Vice-President Richard Nixon. While Nixon portrayed himself as a good Republican, Brown stressed nonpartisan issues such as the water distribution plan and school construction. Nixon learned the hard way, as had Knowland, about the phenomenon of "Washington myopia." The California political scene always looks different at the other end of the continent than in the Golden State. A grand entrance into the state political arena from Washington rarely sits well with the voting public. Starting with a great splash and ending with a 300,000 vote deficit, Nixon lost his bid for governor.

All was not well with the Democrats, however. As Jesse Unruh (a Democrat) was emerging as a power in the legislature in the late 1950s and early 1960s, he was also surfacing as an outspoken critic of Governor Brown. These two astute, professional politicians never seemed to hold much personal regard for each other, although they often agreed on policy. The Brown-Unruh disagreements kept the Sacramento gossip mills busy for many years and provided an easy story for many capitol newspaper reporters. The climax, and in many ways the last straw, occurred in 1966 when Unruh managed to stay out of the country for most of Brown's desperate third-term bid against Ronald Reagan.

Throughout the Knight-Knowland and Brown-Unruh conflicts one issue always managed to excite politicians—reapportionment. The way in which legislative district lines are drawn has an overwhelming influence on the distribution of political power within a state. Political parties, geographical regions, and individual politicians themselves have strong vested interests in the decisions made about apportioning the legislature, to say nothing of the citizenry, who will, in the final run, bear the impact of any shifts in political power. California has shared in the reapportionment-generated political agonies that every other state in the union has witnessed during the 1960s.

Feelings ran high when it came time in 1965 to reapportion the state Senate to comply with the U.S. Supreme Court ruling in Reynolds v. Sims. This time boundary lines for senatorial districts had to be drawn according to population. Previously, California had followed a practice that respected county boundary lines and allotted one senator per county except in a few sparsely populated mountain counties. Prior to 1965, one senator from Los Angeles county represented over 6.5 million people compared to a rural, northern district of 15,000 citizens. With a state Supreme Court deadline hanging over its head, the California legislature meeting in special session late in 1965 finally agreed upon a plan to redraw all the Senate districts and a few Assembly ones. The reapportionment combined twenty-three northern senatorial districts into eight and added thirteen more senators for Los Angeles County. Other shifts from rural to urban areas also occurred. The eight southernmost counties now are represented by twenty-two of the forty-man Senate. Depending upon what part of the state one happened to be in, wonderful or unbelievably disastrous consequences were predicted to flow from this new arrangement.

Ronald Reagan: A Whole New Ball Game

As the 1966 election approached, Pat Brown decided to seek something no California governor except Earl Warren had been able to win—a third consecutive term. Brown seemed to be in a reasonably good political position, despite his continued scrapping with Unruh. The Republicans were readying two possible opponents: former San Francisco Mayor George Christopher, and the man who broke into the political limelight as a spokesman for Barry Goldwater in the presidential campaign of 1964, Ronald Reagan. Brown strategists were happy when Reagan trounced Christopher in the primary; Reagan would be an easy touch because of his identification with the "extremists" so badly demolished in 1964. This enthusiasm in the Brown camp quickly dimmed as Reagan moved into the fray. He came across as a moderate Republican (not too partisan) dedicated to shaking up the entrenched money spenders in Sacramento and restoring fiscal integrity to state government, i.e., reduce governmental costs and taxes. The image touched a responsive chord.

This time it was the Democrats who lacked unity. Deep divisions in the party surfaced during the campaign. Some of the differences focused around President Johnson's handling of U.S. foreign policy in Southeast Asia. Added to this were disagreements about how to run the campaign and "deal with" Reagan. It was obvious weeks before the election that Reagan would win, but the size of the victory suprised many. Reagan carried 59 percent of the electorate in beating Brown as badly as Brown had defeated Knowland eight years earlier. Brown and the Democratic upsurge of the 1960s were finished, although the Democrats retained a slim majority in the legislature until 1968.

Claiming that he had walked into a fiscal "mess," Reagan was able successfully to badger the legislature into a series of tax increases providing almost a billion dollars in new revenue. At the same time he ordered a freeze on state employment and a 10 percent across-the-board budget reduction for state agencies. Reagan had promised he would strive to decrease governmental size and activity, and he set about to implement the mandate he felt the voters had provided him. Continued unrest on the university and state college campuses provided, ironically, another boost in his political prestige. Reagan made the issue clear—the use of police and National Guard on campus would be countenanced and ordered much earlier and more often than his critics would advocate. The "hard-line, no nonsense" approach had clear political payoff.

For the politically astute, Reagan's major embarrassment remained his inability to secure the legislature's (by 1968 under Republican control) agreement to any one of a series of comprehensive tax reform plans he and his advisers offered. The governor continued to alter his stance about the appropriate system of state taxes in order to meet his critics objections. Yet a drastic overhaul of the tax system, one of his major 1966 campaign promises, remained an elusive goal.

When the Republicans gained control of the Assembly in the 1968 elections, Jesse Unruh lost his job as speaker. With that the battle lines for 1970 were set. Unruh and Reagan traded "pot-shots" during the 1969 legislative session about issues and personalities that would play a major role in the next gubernatorial race. Jesse Unruh wanted to be governor in 1970, and Ronald Reagan relished another four years in Sacramento. The goals and future plans of these two men dominated California politics as both sides prepared for the showdown in 1970. Although the final margin was smaller than predicted, Reagan had no trouble beating Unruh and returning for a second term.

Against this political backdrop a significant trend developed in California government during the 1950s and especially the 1960s. A continual move toward making the legislature a coequal partner with the executive was apparent. Slowly during the 1950s, and then much more rapidly in the next decade, the legislature provided itself with the capabilities to legislate on a more equal footing with the resources of the governor and the bureaucracy. The impetus and acceptance of this trend occurred primarily in the Assembly. Most of the time the Senate was either a reluctant partner or an absent party. Therefore, the discussion about legislative reform that follows applies largely to the Assembly.

LEGISLATIVE REFORM AND THE
CALIFORNIA LEGISLATURE

At present, a surfeit of literature on the ills of American state legislatures clearly exists. No textbook on state government is deemed complete without at least one section describing and decrying the inadequacies of the state legislative institution. Writing in 1966, William J. Keefe summarized the feelings of most legislative observers when he commented that "the American state legislature is an institution waning in everything except resilience."[5] To offset the quite obvious decline of state legislatures, a number of new organizations have been created and older reform-minded foundations, institutes, and organizations have renewed their efforts. Two such operations derive much of their impetus from Californians. After Jesse Unruh assumed leadership of the National Conference of State Legislative Leaders, that organization began devoting its prime emphasis toward reform proposals. Larry Margolis became the first director of the new reform-oriented Citizens Conference on State Legislatures in 1965. Margolis served for many years as a staff aide in the California Assembly under Unruh.

It is not entirely by accident that these two men have come to play a large part in the national effort to revitalize state legislatures. The Golden State has been a breeding ground for leadership on reform and today serves as an example to many states. Most of the credit for this must be attached to Unruh, although the seeds of reform were always present in the California legislature. As evidence of the national attention the California legislature receives because of its reform efforts, witness the remarks of former North Carolina Governor Terry Sanford: "California House Speaker Jesse Unruh has demonstrated how better pay, modern procedures, and adequate clerical, research, and office facilities can improve legislative effectiveness."[6] Or the comments of Alexander Heard: "[The] California legislature has perhaps done more to improve its capacity to meet the extraordinary problems it faces than has any other."[7] California stands as an exception to the lament usually provoked by state legislatures. After a brief discussion about some salient aspects of legislative reform, the California experience merits close examination.

Legislative Reform

Legislative reform, simply stated, is a change in the legislature's procedures of operation or the means by which legislators are chosen, paid, or serviced by staff. The innovative quality of a reform resides in the perspective one wants to take. A reform is always innovative for the legislature adopting the change. In a broader context, however, a reform may or may not be innovative, depending upon the unique qualities, if any, of the change. An example will illustrate. If a legislature adopts the practice of a consent calendar (whereby business out of the regular order may be acted upon with unanimous consent of the members) it is being innovative vis-à-vis its own procedures and precedents. Yet, the idea of a consent calendar is certainly not new. Consent calendars long have been a practice in many legislative bodies the world over. However, when a legislature adopts, say, a unique manner of organizing its staff, the change may be innovative from both the specific legislature's viewpoint and a global perspective. In this context, California's legislative reforms were rarely unique, but rather implementation of well-known reform proposals.

A legislature always pays a role in the enactment of a reform, but it does not always have the sole prerogative. Only the operating procedures of the legislature are subject to exclusive legislative jurisdiction. Most legislatures write and pass upon a set of operating rules at the beginning of each session. These rules govern the

behavior of members during floor sessions, outline the powers of
the legislative officers, and regulate the flow of legislative business.
Other reforms usually require the concurrence of another authority,
e.g., the governor, or an affirmative vote of the electorate. For
example, changing from biennial to annual legislative sessions in
California required approval on a referendum because it involved a
change in the state constitution. Likewise, an increase in legislative
staff size needs the governor's approval because it necessitates
increased appropriations.

To say that there is a need for legislative reform assumes that
something is awry. Most often this assumption means that the legislature does not exert enough "independence" from the executive,
lobbyists, or press. Yet this proceeds from another assumption,
namely that legislative independence is desirable. Roger Davidson,
David Kovenock, and Michael O'Leary rightly point out the important
relationship between one's perspective on the "proper" function and
role of a legislature and subsequent ideas about the need for legislative reform.[8] These authors suggest the presence of three different
viewpoints on legislative functions, and devotion to any particular
perspective helps determine the kinds of reforms, if any, suggested.

The literary theory adopts a rather strict interpretation of the
separation-of-powers concept embodied in the U.S. Constitution and
all state constitutions. It calls for a legislature possessed with the
capability to be truly a coequal partner in the triumvirate. Both the
executive and judicial branches are seen in recent times as usurpers
of legislative prerogatives. Legislatures, this body of thought pro-
fesses, are supposed to aggregate consensus and make law arising
out of that consensus. They are also to keep a close tab on the administration of the executive branch. In a word, legislatures are
to be initiatory bodies that provide leadership and direction for the
state government. Reform is clearly the order of the day, and, most
emphatically, reform that will return the legislature to its once-
known pedestal of importance.

Those who adhere to the executive-force theory believe in an
almost opposite set of dogma. It is the executive, and primarily the
chief executive, who should exercise most of the initiative and consensus building. Legislatures are to provide a check on any excesses
or mistakes, but a representative body cannot (and should not) provide
policy leadership. A legislature's prime function is to legitimate
executive proposals or, if one prefers to be somewhat cynical, legislatures should serve as a "rubber-stamp" for the chief executive.
Obviously, legislature reform is not a matter of pressing business
for this school. If reform is called for, it is an attempt to make the
legislature more malleable to executive direction.

As an extension of the executive-force theory, some pledge allegiance to a party government theory of legislative behavior. This group is not just concerned about legislatures, but rather the entire political system. Politics in this country ought to be modified so that political parties develop into centralized organizations that establish and act upon clear-cut policy programs. These parties must be able to maintain internal discipline among their members, especially legislative members. Who would serve as the chief spokesman and leader for the legislative parties? Naturally, the chief executive is the logical candidate (without worrying for the moment about the prospect of one party controlling the legislature and another the executive). As with the executive-force theory, the advocates of a strong party government see the need for executive domination of the legislature. If reform is needed here, it is in the direction of increased executive influence over the legislature.

With the advantage of hindsight, the picture of what has happened in California becomes rather clear. Starting in the mid-1950s and increasing dramatically in the 1960s, a group of men who adhered to the equivalent of the literary theory gained prominence in Sacramento. Primarily these were legislators, headed by Jesse Unruh, but another important group came from the press. Both Unruh and his successor as Assembly speaker, Bob Monagan, have made numerous speeches in which they point to the key role played by the press in any move toward legislative change. At a minimum, they suggest, the press must tacitly agree. To effectuate changes envisaged by the literary theory, such as pay increases, the state press can not be in opposition. If they are, the odds favoring approval of reform rapidly diminishes.

As previously mentioned, one's perspective on the appropriate functions of a legislature dictates the kinds of reforms supported. In most states, and California was no exception in the late 1950s, adherents to the executive-force theory were supporters of the status quo. Change in the legislature was not necessary, or at least nothing more than small, incremental change, because the appropriate relationship between the legislature and executive already existed, a relationship dominated by the executive. In a state without a history of effective political party organization and action, those who profess the party government approach are bound to be few and relatively ineffective. The area of contention, then, was quickly reduced to those who supported a literary theory of legislative functioning and those who championed the executive-force notions.

The California legislature is not the first representative body in the world to undergo a period of attention to its own plight and then act accordingly. Two factors make the California experience important. One is the manner in which the legislature conducted itself during the reform period. Unlike the U.S. Congress, which seems to have sporadic bursts of reform sentiment that die almost as quickly as they begin, the California Assembly and Senate managed to sustain an interest and motivation for change during the major part of a decade. Translated into practical terms, legislative leadership encouraged this reform orientation and provided the incentives and punishments necessary to accomplish its purposes. A second unique feature of the reform decade was the self-conscious style in which it was carried out. Jesse Unruh made it fashionable to be in favor of improving the legislating capabilities of the legislature. Through his direction and leadership it became possible to speak openly of improved facilities, higher salaries, more staff, etc. Not that he was without his critics, and surely many legislators had to tread lightly at home on the reform issue, but Unruh and his supporters (in both parties) continued to set legislative reform and improvement near the top of legislative priorities.

Nobody, except perhaps a few academics, publicly calls himself a literary theorist or an executive-force supporter. The issue gets defined on a different plane in the political arena than it does in political science journals. A brief survey of some arguments, pro and con, about legislative reform provides a better insight into the politics surrounding reform efforts.

Those who argue in favor of reform, i.e., those who hold to the literary theory, begin by pointing out the changed nature of the relationship between the executive and legislative branches. They speak of executive dominance and legislative submission. A reform proponent, then, starts by admitting the relatively weak position of the legislature.[9] This mood is best captured by Jefferson B. Fordham when he writes that "the American people, during a period spanning more than a century, have been both witnessing and, in a real sense, participating in the deterioration of the position of the state legislature."[10] Why did this happen? Usually it was not due to an overt power grab by the executive, but rather a steady, continuous growth in size and influence of the bureaucracy and its chief executive. As the role of all government in the United States increased during this century, so too did the activities of state government. This expansion meant an increase in the delegation of responsibilities from the legislature to the bureaucracy and the governor.[11]

Some political participants argue for legislative reform out of a devotion to the concepts embodied in the literary theory, that is, a belief in the vital importance of a representative body in a democracy. At many points during the last decade, Jesse Unruh has been one of these. A very important factor motivating the reformers, however, is the opportunity to enhance one's personal political power or the relative political standing of a particular group. There comes a time when legislators expect to gain advantage from reform (and perhaps ignore the potential disadvantages). Not the least is the opportunity they see for increased pay and other personal perquisities that coincide with legislative reform. Additionally, there are those outside the legislature who visualize increased access or agreement with their viewpoint from a legislature operating different than it is at present. The important point to be made is that the opportunity for increased political power stands out as a very prominent motivating force in any reform movement.

Why would anyone take exception to the literary theory of legislative functions, advocate an executive-force view, and oppose any major changes in legislative operations? Primarily the answer resides in an acceptance and agreement with the status quo. What is wrong, the reply would come somewhat aggressively, with executive domination of the legislature? The legislature should play second fiddle. Any number of reasons may be advanced to support this position. After all, a legislature behaves as a slow, cumbersome body—something no reform can completely change—and this point in history calls for a fast acting, responsive government. Some would argue that legislatures, because of the necessity for continual compromise, are more conservative than governors and their administrators; and for ideological reasons these reformers appreciate a more liberal viewpoint. Also underlying the status quo argument is the fact that many individuals and interest groups are very happy with the current balance between the executive and legislative branches because they feel satisfied with their influence in government. An interest group may enjoy good relations, including the ability virtually to dominate appointments, with a certain administrative agency and therefore fear legislative change because it may lead to increased questioning of its "special" access. Why upset the applecart? Moreover, it is easy to demonstrate the vastly increased cost of operating a legislature that happens to adopt any or all of the usually suggested reforms. Legislative change means increased costs, and that fact can be easily documented. Fighting increased governmental expenditures is a popular smokescreen erected by antireform groups.

Before moving on, one point should be made more directly. The tone of the previous discussion implies that the antagonists in the legislative reform arena operate in a zero-sum game. That is, the "winnings" of the legislative reform advocates exactly equal the "loses" of the executive-force believers. Why not, one might legitimately ask, increase the power and prerogatives of both the executive and legislative branches? The answer remains far from proven fact, but it appears that adoption of a legislative reform program leads to, in practice, a decrease in executive power and discretion. A caveat quickly must be entered. Legislative reform is not a perfect zero-sum game because any one reform may not detract anything from the executive. Yet when taking the whole reform package together, the California experience shows that legislative reform cannot help but subtract noticeably from executive influence. Later discussion should make this even clearer.

No one should form the impression that California's legislature has solved all its problems. There are some topics it has not even addressed, much less solved. Yet it is undoubtedly head and shoulders above all but possibly a few state legislatures in the degree to which it has sought to cope with the decline that seems endemic to representative bodies in the twentieth century.

The California Experience

This section is devoted to a description of the details of California's legislative reform period. What changes have occurred?

Staff

Ask any person in the Capitol building, except someone from the steady torrent of tourists, what has been the most important change in the legislature during the last few decades and the odds are overwhelming that the response will be a single word: staff. Walking around the building, an observer gets many visual confirmations from the plethora of staff offices. Apparently, the title "staff" carries some unwanted connotations because no one on the legislative payroll is referred to by that title. Rather, they are known as Assembly or Senate "attaches," committee "consultants," or "analysts."

One way to classify legislative staff is by placing them into either "line" or "functional" categories; and within each of these two brackets are professional and secretarial-clerical staff. Line staff are those who work directly for individual legislators. The functional staff members are employed by one of the several legislative service organizations, e.g., legislative counsel, or a specific committee. The number of legislators for whom they provide service marks the difference between line and functional staff. While line staff are attached to individual men and perform wide-ranging, diverse services for him, functional staff are available to aid the entire legislature or the entire membership of a committee.

California's legislators are not lacking in staff aid. Because many legislators are sensitive to the charge that they spend too much money operating the legislature, accurate calculation of the exact number on the legislative payroll is not easy. (As an aside, legislators are "touchy" on this subject because of a fear that the press will accuse them publicly of having too many staff aides.) However, a fairly close estimate has been made by the authoritative <u>California Journal</u>, as follows:[12]

	Total Number	Professionals
Assembly	767	217
Senate	450	135
Joint committees		
Legislative analyst	63	49
Auditor general	45	41
All others	46	16
Legislative counsel	125	51
Totals	1,496	509

The relative abundance of staff has not always been the case. In many ways the watershed occurred in 1951. That year saw the additions of the East Wing to the Capitol and for the first time legislators were assigned to their own private offices. Private secretaries were available only during the session. Prior to that time, the legislature functioned, as many legislative bodies still do today, without much privacy for legislators and with very limited staff help. Only the leadership and a few of the busier committees had anything approaching current staffing. Although line staff multiplied some during the 1950s, most increases took place in the secretarial-clerical category and very little professional help was available to the individual member.

Jesse Unruh's election to the Assembly speakership in 1961 brought dramatic changes in the Assembly line staff. Unruh moved immediately to bolster the secretarial and professional staff available to individual legislators. In addition to providing each member with at least one permanent secretary in Sacramento, through Unruh's efforts every legislator could support an office in his home district. Unruh and others who supported this move argued that establishing a district office would permit the performance there of the "case work" and errand running that constituents demand, thus freeing the Sacramento operation from these time-consuming chores. The legislator would then have more time to spend on the "important" part of his job—making laws in the state capitol. The critics cried, "Boondoggle!" Many complained that the new district officers would be used only for campaign purposes, and an assemblyman who must run for re-election every two years is always campaigning. Republicans were afraid that the majority Democrats would become more entrenched. Nevertheless, as the situation stands today, the average "backbench" legislator has at least two secretaries in his Capitol office during sessions and two more persons running his home district office.[13] Those in positions of legislative leadership (committee chairmen, party leaders, etc.) can count on several more people to operate their legislative offices. The usual proclivity to multiply leadership positions means that approximately one-third of the Assembly enjoys a Sacramento office staff above the minimum of two secretaries. For instance, the recent Republican Assembly Speaker, Bob Monagan, has about a dozen people working directly out of his office; seven are professionals. A committee chairman may have two or three secretaries and two administrative assistants on his Capitol staff.

Looking at the Senate, the number of line staff positions is not noticeably different, but it has a little quirk. Starting in 1959 each senator has been authorized to employ one administrative assistant in Sacramento and at least one secretary. Since then, increases in secretarial aid and professional assistance have been allowed by the Senate Rules Committee (the "housekeeping" committee) for any senator in a leadership position. In the Senate usually every one of the forty senators is considered a leader. By establishing twenty-one committees in the 1969 session, for instance, each senator won the opportunity for service as a chairman or vice-chairman of at least one committee, thus making him eligible for additional office help. Most senators now support an average of two secretaries and one or two administrative assistants. No one has a smaller staff, many have larger ones.

Many of the legislative functional staff offices and positions predate 1960. Positions such as the legislative counsel, legislative analyst, and legislative auditor general (all serving both houses) were created earlier. Other functional-type jobs, such as those with committees or the Assembly Office of Research, also have predecessors that trace their birth to earlier days. Although not born in the 1960s, these functional agencies and positions (especially in the Assembly) received a large boost in size and importance during that decade.

As far back as 1913 the California legislature decided it needed legal assistance of its own in the preparation of bills. In that year the office of legislative counsel was founded by statute. Although chosen by concurrent resolution of the entire legislature at the beginning of every session, a tradition of nonpartisanship has served this office well. Most legislative counsels have had long tenure. When a new party or leadership group succeeds to the majority, the old counsel is not turned out as a matter of habit. To help him with his work, the counsel may appoint staff, who are then subject to civil service laws. At the moment, the counsel employs fifty lawyers. This almost doubles the 1955 total of twenty-six attorneys.

A large percentage of all bills introduced (more than 3,700 bills were introduced in 1969) are actually written in the counsel's office. Any member or any state executive agency may request counsel's assistance in translating an idea into the technical language necessary for proposed law. The counsel receives requests for several thousand legal opinions each year. It has been reported that since 1960 the requests for legal services from the counsel's office has increased more than 100 percent.

Another task assumed by the counsel adds immeasurably to the clarity of issues legislators are asked to vote upon. Since 1959 no bill may be introduced in the legislature without an accompanying "Legislative Counsel's Digest." The digest summarizes the pertinent details of each pending bill in a brief statement appearing at the bottom of the first page of each bill. Reading the digest, a legislator quickly learns who sponsored the bill, what section of the current law it would change, the major subject matter and administration of the bill, whether it requires an ordinary or extraordinary majority for passage, and whether money must be appropriated. Because a bill may not be voted upon until it has been printed and distributed, the digest gives every legislator the opportunity to know at least the main provisions of every bill. Simple as this may sound, such is not the case in many states.

One perennial problem facing legislatures is that of coping with the executive-prepared state budget. Anything of major importance requires the expenditure of state monies, so the budget bill usually becomes the battleground for different interests and ideologies in the legislature. A typical budget bill develops into an amazingly complicated piece of legislation, containing (to the uninitiated) a baffling maze of figures and sometimes a detailed description of legislative intent. For the legislative process, the crucial question quickly resolves into whether the legislative appropriation committees, and subsequently the entire legislature, can understand and critically comment upon the budget. At least two authors remain doubtful of such legislative competence. Thomas J. Anton has remarked:

> Lacking the staff personnel required to cope with the intended and unintended complexities of state financial documents, legislatures typically know very little about what is contained in such documents. Constrained by constitution or by custom to dispose of major appropriations within a limited period of time, legislatures have little opportunity to do anything but approve the expenditures recommended by the governor.[14]

And writing about the legislative time schedule for considering the budget, Malcolm E. Jewell described the situation in some states in this manner:

> The governor will deliver his budget to the legislature on Monday. Members of the responsible committee will have a day or two to read and digest several hundred pages of figures. Tuesday the budget director will appear before the committee to answer questions. Wednesday, perhaps after listening to requests from interest groups for more funds, the committee will meet in executive session and approve the budget, often with one or two minor changes.[15]

In order to overcome and prevent some of these handicaps, the California legislature in 1941 created the Joint Legislative Budget Committee. Providing the legislature with an independent and reasonably complete source of information about state budget proposals was the raison d'être of this new joint committee. Seven legislators from each house comprise the committee's membership. They in turn appoint a legislative analyst who oversees a supporting staff now grown to sixty-three. Although every bill requiring an appropriation contains an accompanying recommendation from the analyst's office, the analyst's major effort centers around the annual budget bill. Every specific appropriation proposal in the budget receives a recommendation with critical comments by the analyst in his annual Analysis of the Budget Bill. This document often runs more than 1,000 pages in length in order to appraise a budget bill of some 130-140 pages. Production of such a document demands year-round scrutiny and research on executive agency performance by this legislative office.

Members of the analyst's office are employees of the legislature, and as such are expected to adopt the legislative perspective in commenting upon the executive originated budget. To avoid charges of partisanship or political chicanery in his analysis requires the analyst's walking a very delicate tightrope. The current analyst, A. Alan Post, has been on the job since 1949. Criticisms of the Analysis are heard, though, primarily because some legislators feel that a few senior members of the analyst's office have become too "cozy" with their executive agency counterparts over whose shoulders they continually peer. Stories are told, for instance, of analyst's staff members touring the state to inspect capital expenditure programs with men from the Department of Public Works. Yet, a recent observer and chronicler of the California process of budget-making felt that the analyst enjoyed wide acceptance by legislators. He commented that "(t)he analyst is a valuable ally of the legislative branch in its struggle to avoid being overwhelmed by the political strength of the executive and the expertise and complexity of the bureaucracy."[16] California's legislature relies upon the analyst and it seems fair to conclude that as a consequence of that reliance the legislature can grapple with the executive budget on a more equal footing. Or stated differently, the legislature possesses the information-gathering capability that enables it to ask questions of the executive that may produce some sleepless nights in the bureaucracy. Whether this capability produces a "better" budget or a more "rational" budget-making process is another matter.

The third major functional staff position is also the newest. Through its Joint Legislative Audit Committee, the legislature appointed its first auditor general in 1955. His primary task is an annual postaudit and general perusal of executive agency financial transactions. The enabling legislation establishing the position of auditor general authorizes his access to any records, correspondence, files, bank account, etc., of any state government agency. Prior to 1955, the Department of Finance conducted the only postaudit of agency expenditures. The executive branch retained responsibility for policing itself with little, if any, legislative interference. Through the years, the auditor general, who now has a staff of forty-five, has offered hundreds of recommendations to executive agencies about their accounting procedures; most are adopted eventually. These recommendations usually refer to technical features, and accusations of theft or overt ineptitude are uncommon. However, reports of the auditor general sometimes provide fertile ammunition for the legislator seeking to probe into the operation of a particular agency because these reports list specific instances of questionable agency behavior.

Every legislative committee, of which there are usually forty-five to fifty, has at least one full-time staff consultant. Most standing committees, especially in the Assembly, have more than one consultant. Approximately eighty people served as committee consultants during recent sessions. Consultants work under the direction of their committee chairman, and a chairman can usually replace a consultant. Analysis and evaluation of bills pending before the committee consume most of a consultant's time. To do the job effectively, a consultant must spend considerable time with executive agency personnel and lobbyists (officially known as "legislative advocates") who are affected by the bills in question.

In practical terms, classification of consultants in the functional group may not be entirely accurate. Depending upon the style and political position of the committee chairman, a consultant may work for the committee (and therefore be a functional staffer), or in fact spend most of his time working personally for the chairman. Both situations exist. The chairman's preferences determine a consultant's working behavior.

Compared to the number available a decade earlier, the number of committee consultants in 1970 had more than doubled. Two factors account for this increase. The Assembly made an important decision in 1957 when it decided to participate in an internship program funded by the Ford Foundation and organized by several professors (primarily Joseph P. Harris) from the University of California. September 1957 saw the first group of interns move into assignments with the Assembly, in most cases as committee consultants. For many years after the initial class, the internship program remained a key source of permanent staff as many interns were asked to stay with the Assembly. As the desire and need for committee staff increased in the 1960s, the internship program lost some of its prominence as a supplier of regular staff. Not enough interns were available to meet the growing demand. Applications from "outside" were encouraged and accepted in approximately a 10:1 ratio. That is, out of every ten applicants for consultant positions, financial and political considerations permitted selection of only one.

Attributing the increase in consultants only to the impetus generated by the internships would be inaccurate. The internship program was important, but did not continue the trend toward greater committee staff on its own. Jesse Unruh was clearly the other important factor. Upon assumption of the speaker's office in 1961, Unruh gave the entire staff movement a tremendous shot in the arm. Many observers claim that the pre- and post-Unruh staff arrangements in the Assembly differ dramatically in kind and not just in degree. Unruh labored to ensure Assembly committees the necessary professional assistance he felt they required. Technical expertise, or the ability to acquire it quickly, in substantive areas—e.g., education, mental health, highway construction—became the main consideration when hiring new committee staff. Possibly by coincidence, and then again probably not, most of the committee staff hired during the large increases of the last decade claimed affiliation with the Democratic party.

The Assembly Office of Research is another functional staff agency that bears the imprimatur of Jesse Unruh. Actually, the Office of Research was conceived in 1967, but it bears considerable resemblance to its predecessors—the Chief Consultant's Office and the Assembly Legislative Reference Service. During the early 1960s, Unruh increased the size and research responsibilities of the Legislative Reference Service extensively. With an expanded staff, the office responded to requests from members (and some committees) for in-depth studies of current and future legislative issues. Being out of the daily firing line usually gave the Reference Service more time to investigate complex issues. By 1967 Unruh saw the need for a more centralized direction of Assembly research operations; the switch to annual sessions that year also prompted the reorganization. Because the speaker hand-picked the Office of Research director, Unruh and the director maintained a very close working relationship. In some respects, the Office of Research was the speaker's research agency.

In sum, the legislative staff picture emerges something like this: By the end of the 1960s, both houses operated with relatively large and well-staffed functional agencies, although the Assembly had obviously developed its capabilities significantly more than the Senate. Line staff aid also increased dramatically, once again primarily in the lower house. Staff help abounds, so much so that the writers of a well-known text on California government and politics recommend the need for a "legislative council" to serve as a "super agency" coordinating and supervising staff activities in the legislature.[17] While most states still worry about finding the political will-power and money to bring their staff up to modern requirements, some observers felt that California finds itself in a position where it must think about the potentially stifling effects of too much staff. The man largely responsible for generating this quantum leap in staff and the subsequent legislative dependence upon that staff is Jesse Unruh. His impact on the Assembly stands out in sharper relief by looking at the Senate. Relatively, line staff does not vary much from Senate to Assembly, but the functional staff situation differs. The Senate has not seen the need for a unit comparable to the Assembly Office of Research, and, likewise, it has not augmented its committee staffs to any extent resembling the level of the Assembly.

Procedures

A degree of openness not always found in other legislative bodies characterizes the proceedings of the California legislature. One of the unwritten, but very relevant, rules calls for widespread sharing of information among members. For instance, Unruh always consulted (or at least informed) the minority party leadership on issues such as scheduling of legislative sessions and committee meetings. Monagan operated similarly. Likewise, the author of a bill can rest assured that he will be informed when a committee considers his measure; for a committee to proceed without the author present is considered entirely improper. No bill may be brought up for a vote on the floor before it has been printed, distributed, and announced in the Daily File. The average California legislator probably has a better opportunity to understand the legislative agenda than his counterpart in any other legislature. Of course, he often does not know why an event is occurring. As one assemblyman put it, "You can really get the short end of the stick or stuck in the back around here, but at least you know it's coming."

Repetition of material found in several other sources about legislative procedures, such as the use of electronic voting boards, or the three readings requirement for a bill, serves no purpose in this discussion.[18] Yet, a few important characteristics and changes in legislative procedures could bear some elaboration. The change from biennial to annual general sessions, committee structure and operations, use of a consent calendar, the role of legislative leadership, and the "veto session" are procedural elements deserving attention.

In the November 1966 general election, voters in California approved several changes in legislative operations, one of the most important being a switch from biennial to annual regular sessions. For the twenty years prior to 1966, the legislature met in general session every odd year for a constitutionally stipulated duration of not longer than 120 days. A thirty-day budget session was held in even years. Shortly after the adoption of an even year budget session in 1946, it became each governor's practice to call a special session of the legislature running concurrently with the budget session. Through this means, a limited number of topics other than the budget, but only those specified by the governor, could be discussed. In practice, California had a limited form of annual sessions since the post-World War II period. The constitutional amendment approved in 1966 instituted annual regular sessions of unlimited duration, and in the first three years of annual sessions, the legislature has convened each time for an average of eight and one-half months.

While the California legislature still maintains a large number of committees in each house, the trend is toward reduction through consolidation and elimination of "unnecessary" committees. During the 1969 session, the eighty-man Assembly operated with twenty-one committees, a shrinkage of four from the previous year. The Senate distributed its forty members on twenty committees, also down slightly in number from previous years. No assemblyman served on more than three committees, while senators were usually required to occupy five or six committee seats.

Looked at comparatively, these figures indicate that California has slightly less than the average number of committees in all state legislatures. Yet, twenty committees in a house of forty men taxes human capacities. Surely, the Senate, or for that matter the Assembly, could operate with many fewer committees. Part of the answer to the number of committees is simply tradition. Certain kinds of committees have "always" existed and probably always will.

Politically speaking, a multitude of committees also allows the prestige of serving as a committee chairman to be spread among the membership. Whatever previously passed as the arguments in favor of a large number of committees, the most common reason heard today bears a resemblance to statements made in many parts of contemporary society. The kinds of issues, it is said, that legislatures must face and hopefully resolve today are highly technical and complex ones. Moreover, they are issues that demand specialization by those individuals who must be attentive to them. If the legislative work load were not divided into narrow topics requiring committee proliferation, it would prove impossible for a legislator to gain the expertise necessary for adequate performance. From this standpoint, California, being one of the most difficult and complex states to govern, naturally needs a fine degree of specialization in its legislative operations.

After such decentralized considerations, who puts together all the pieces of specialization and decides whether the total picture is appropriate? The dilemma of reconciling the need for specialization and of overcoming its tendency toward fragmentation, with the desirability of some overall coordination, remains unsolved in California as elsewhere. No easy panaceas may brush away this problem. Some technical and procedural changes are possible, but the cure-all palliative remains to be found.

Legislative leadership, majority and minority, is a force potentially able to provide some coordination of priorities. As California moves into a period of increased legislative partisanship, concentration of (some) authority in the hands of legislative party leaders empowers them with the opportunity for developing programs that create priorities in the state government. Both major parties appear moving toward greater legislative party unity, with the resulting opportunity for leadership coordination. The legislative party organizations hold the potential for performing the priority-setting functions necessary to overcome the dissipating fragmentation by specialization.

A legislative fact of life in the 1960s was the preeminent role played by party leaders in both houses, but especially the Assembly. Unruh became the first speaker in modern times to organize and to solidify his party into an operating entity. Previous speakers had built coalitions of support that cut across party lines, but the increased partisanship of the Assembly (which Unruh helped to create), permitted Unruh's development of stronger party machinery, e.g., a functioning caucus system. The Republicans soon emulated him. Unruh's successor, Speaker Bob Monagan, portrayed the same type of party leadership that Unruh showed when his party held the majority. The Senate also moved toward more partisanship and an increasingly important centralized party leadership. The 1970 Senate session retained much of the partisan flavor exhibited the year before.

Simply saying that relatively strong party leadership developed does not explain it or answer why it is important in legislative functioning. While steering clear of the psychological and moral functions of leadership, the practical aspects can be illustrated. To begin with, leadership selects committee chairmen and assigns members to committee responsibilities. Because committee assignments are important to legislators, leadership (especially the Assembly speaker) uses them as a potent bargaining weapon. As party organizations blossom in the California legislature, the men who lead the parties gain in stature. Increasingly in both houses, the party caucuses make strategic decisions that generate a relatively cohesive party voting position on the floor. If a majority or minority leader can claim the backing of his caucus, his bargaining force on the floor is greatly enhanced. No party leader runs roughshod over all his members, and complete domination by one or two men does not occur, but as party organizations solidify their leaders assume great importance in daily legislative operations.

California's constitution, like that of many other states, requires a roll-call vote before any bill becomes law. As the constitution says, "no bill may be passed unless, by roll call vote entered in the journal, a majority of the membership of each house concurs." Add to this the requirement that each bill be read three times in each house before a vote on final passage may be taken and one sees how an inordinate amount of time must be spent reading and discussing bills, including many of absolutely no controversy. (Approximately 2,000 bills are voted upon in a session.) A device offsetting the constitution's time-consuming requirements on bills of minor importance was adopted in the 1959 session. As part of the joint legislative rules that year, a consent calendar was established for bills not involving appropriations and for those that carried unanimous committee approval. If a bill meets these two requirements, it may be placed on the consent calendar providing no legislator objects. When consent calendar bills are considered (usually a daily occurrence), no debate is allowed and only a few questions about the content may be directed toward the bill's author. The actual time saved by a consent calendar proves difficult to measure, but it is extensive. Even the casual observer of a legislative session notices the speed with which bills on the consent calendar pass. To see more than two or three negative votes on such a bill is a rarity. The consent calendar permits a convenient sidestepping of an onerous requirement, thus saving precious time, without completely depriving the citizens of the protection envisioned by the original authors of the roll-call provision.

Another procedural part of the 1966 constitutional revision creates a "veto session" that convenes thirty days after adjournment of the regular annual session. Meeting for no more than five days, the legislature may consider any vetos imposed by the governor on bills passed less than twelve days before their regular adjournment.

Prior to 1966, the California constitution granted the governor twelve days either to sign or veto a bill presented to him by the legislature. If he did neither, the bill became law without his signature. In a case in which the legislature sent him a bill less than twelve days from its adjournment, the governor than had thirty days to approve the bill. If he did not sign the bill within that period, it was considered vetoed (a "pocket veto"). Inasmuch as a vast majority of the bills were passed during the last few weeks of a legislative session, a large number of bills could be pocket-vetoed. A pocket veto gives the legislature no chance to override the governor, and, contrary to a regular veto, it does not require the governor to explain publicly why he refuses to sign the bill.

By passing the 1966 constitution amendment, Californians destroyed the pocket veto. As the relevant section of the constitution now reads: "If the 12-day period [for bill signing] expires during the recess at the end of a regular sesions, the bill becomes a statute unless the Governor vetoes it within 30 days from the commencement of the recess."[19] In other words, either the governor must veto a bill or it becomes law without his signature, regardless of when it was passed during the legislative session. Those bills vetoed by the governor after the legislature adjourns are open for reconsideration during the veto session, and a two-thirds majority overrides the veto. The obvious intent of the change is to strengthen the legislature vis-à-vis the governor. Whether it has worked remains a matter of some debate, and attempts to scuttle the veto session were planned soon after the amendment was enacted. During the first three veto sessions, not one veto was overridden.

During the 1970 session, Speaker Monagan introduced a constitutional amendment that would have made the legislature a "continuous body" for two-year terms. Rather than adjourn sine die each year, the Monagan proposal would keep the legislative session alive for two years. Proponents of the change argued that it would allow for more efficient planning of the legislative agenda and permit more time for committee consideration of complex bills. After winning Assembly approval, the amendment died a quick death in the Senate Rules Committee. Aside from the usual Senate hesitancy, several lobbyists expressed opposition. They did not like the idea that bills could stay alive and viable during the entire two-year session.

Compensation

Former Assembly Speaker William Moseley Jones, speaking to the 1969 legislature during the proceedings of a "Former Speakers Day" in the Assembly, recalled the days when California legislators were paid hardly anything for their services. The most telling comment he made reflects the enormous changes that have taken place in the last three decades. Jones remembered an occasion during the late 1930s when a destitute but prominent assemblyman from Los Angeles County hitchhiked to and from Sacramento. Salaries at that time were $100 per month with no other expenses allowed and nothing payable until the end of the session's first month. To say the least, matters have changed. The compensation of California state legislators today ranks foremost in comparison with the other forty-nine states.

From 1954 to 1966, legislators were compensated with a salary of $6,000 per year plus small allowances for certain expenses. Voters rejected a proposed raise to $9,000 in 1959. Yet seven years later, as part of a constitutional revision of legislative procedures, the voters of California approved a $10,000 increase in legislative salaries to a new total of $16,000 per year. Expenses allowances were also liberalized. A key feature of the 1966 revision (known in California as Proposition 1A on the ballot) enabled the legislature henceforth to set its own salaries, provided that an increase of not more than 5 percent per year ever be approved and that a two-thirds affirmative vote for the increase be required. Near the conclusion of the 1969 general session, the legislature took advantage of its new salary-setting prerogatives and handed itself a $3,200 per year increase. Beginning in 1970, the new base salary became $19,200. In many states, talk of such a relatively high salary would be greeted by outrage, but the straightforward, matter-of-fact comment of a veteran Republican assemblyman indicates the tone of the California legislature. Assemblyman Frank Lanterman thought the pay raise was "modest" and commented that "we're either worth it or not worth a damn and we ought to be fired."[20]

In addition to the base salary, legislators receive $30 per day living expenses while in session and reimbursement for the cost of leasing an auto. A sizable contribution to the Legislators Retirement Fund, authorized by legislative appropriation, amounts to another fringe benefit. A total of $510,000 was set aside in fiscal year 1967 for pensions. A complete picture of legislative compensation, then, must include not only the salary, but additional payments for items such as living expenses and mileage allowances. For fiscal year 1968, the average cash paid to California legislators (not including retirement) moved to slightly more than $21,000.

Table 2.1 presents the compensation figures for the fiscal years 1950 through 1969. A rising trend is evident, even before the large jump in 1966. The dramatic increases in legislative compensation offer a most striking example of the reform tendencies prevalent in this decade.

Facilities

Every state legislature has a chamber in which it conducts legislative business, but, as anyone who has taken a high school civics course can tell you, much of a legislator's time during a session is spent off the floor of the chamber. Somehow this commonplace notion about the large amount of time spent off the floor has considerable trouble getting translated into physical facilities adequate to cope with the reality of legislative operations. To put it bluntly, most state legislators simply do not enjoy even a reasonable facsimile of an acceptable physical plant within which to work. A recent memorandum from the Citizens Conference on State Legislatures stated that

> most of the 7,800 state legislators in America do not have office space at the capitol. They are expected to work from their desk on the floor of the legislative chamber. Otherwise they are forced to turn to public lounges, stairwells, or their hotel room as alternatives to proper office facilities.[21]

And the same report added that "lack of adequate committee space is more critical than the need for offices for members in a number of states."

These accounts are not exaggerated. They are real and they present immediate and practical problems for the legislator. Professor Duane Lockard, a former Connecticut state senator, recalls from his experience the time that

> a constituent once wrote asking me to help him obtain an automobile license plate with his initials on it; he apologized for bothering me, but he wondered if my office staff could take care of it for him, when I had neither office nor staff. A corner in my hallway at home, piled high with bills, reports, and propaganda, was as near as I could come to an office. . . .[22]

A management consulting firm hired by the state of Pennsylvania to study legislative facilities reported that "except for his

TABLE 2.1

Compensation of California Legislators,
Fiscal Years 1950-69
(in dollars)

Assembly

Fiscal Year	Salaries (Total)	Mileage (Total)	Expenses (Total)	Compensation for 80 Assemblymen	Average Compensation Per Assemblyman
1950-51	285,300	4,964	129,938	420,202	5,252
1952-53	282,178	4,986	130,000	417,164	5,214
1954-55	403,667	4,898	129,472	538,037	6,725
1956-57	477,848	4,486	171,180	653,514	8,168
1958-59	477,435	2,239	225,850	705,524	8,819
1960-61	472,766	2,450	251,539	726,755	9,084
1962-63	464,767	1,317	251,313	717,397	8,967
1964-65	475,739	773	277,431	753,943	9,424
1966-67	880,779	1,489	326,475	1,208,743	15,109
1967-68	1,298,672	3,093	456,325	1,758,036	21,976
1969-70	1,299,342	2,386	399,500	1,701,210	21,265

Senate

Fiscal Year	Salaries (Total)	Mileage (Total)	Expenses (Total)	Compensation for 80 Assemblymen	Average Compensation Per Assemblyman
1950-51	140,885	2,434	64,414	207,733	5,193
1952-53	142,916	2,353	65,618	210,887	5,272
1954-55	202,023	2,366	64,806	269,195	6,729
1956-57	240,000	—	86,148	326,148	8,153
1958-59	234,199	826	86,400	321,425	8,035
1960-61	237,409	1,029	124,355	326,739	9,069
1962-63	234,951	536	125,362	360,849	9,021
1964-65	234,197	291	134,001	368,489	9,212
1966-67	427,563	—	163,050	590,613	14,765
1967-68	639,557	777	226,275	866,609	21,665
1969-70	648,388	90	194,650	843,128	21,078

Source: Annual Controller's Report, State of California. A fiscal year covers July 1 to June 30.

assigned desk position in the appropriate legislative chamber, the average Representative does not have a desk or telephone and the average senator finds himself in a room with three other Senators. Neither Legislator is afforded any privacy." As one consequence of this, the report cited a "Representative [who] allegedly keeps over twenty regular shopping bags in the back of his station wagon to accommodate his needs to maintain files."[23] After examining the facilities available for committees in Pennsylvania, the report found that "the size of many of the committee rooms are insufficient and the present arrangement with other desks in each room cut into the size of the committee room, so that many members are forced to either sit on a chairman's desk or stand while the meeting is in progress."[24]

While the national trend clearly moves toward improvement of legislative facilities, for most legislators it remains a "trend" that has yet to reach them. California legislators are an exception. Since 1951 each legislator has commanded his own private office. Even a newly elected member without seniority is accorded a private office of ample size and very comfortable furnishings; a separate, adjoining office houses his secretaries. Those members who are in leadership positions, e.g., committee chairmen, find themselves in the midst of a suite of offices. Legislative committees also enjoy a reasonable allocation of space. Thirteen rooms in the Capitol are reserved for the exclusive use of legislative committee hearings, eight for the Assembly and the remainder for the Senate. Adequate space in committee rooms is provided for members and committee staff at the front of the rooms, with seating for the public filling the remaining space. Some of the rooms accommodate as many as 300 people, so public seating is usually more than adequate.

When considering the California legislature's physical facilities and its use thereof, one could be persuaded very quickly of the validity of Parkinson's Law: "Legislative business expands to fit the space available in which to perform it, and then overflows." Individual legislators, too, have been struck by Mr. Parkinson. Their offices, spacious by comparison to most states, are usually packed with staff, equipment, and the ever-present memoranda and reports. During a session the Capitol bulges with people. Staff growth has been the greatest contributor to overcrowding.

What probably must be regarded as the inevitable occurred late in 1969. Rumors circulating the Capitol about plans for a new Capitol building were confirmed by a persistent newspaperman. Acting in secrecy, an ad hoc legislative committee, working with the state architect, designed a new twenty-four-story twin-tower Capitol that would more than double the space now occupied by the legislature. Preliminary plans for the proposed $65 million structure allow each legislator a complex of rooms, including his own private office, conference room, space for two administrative assistants, and room for three secretaries. Committee chairmen and other leaders would have more than one and a half times the space of the average legislator.

What is the justification for additional legislative space? Assemblyman Joe A. Gonsalves, who helped develop the new plans, claims that large and increasing staffs are necessary if the legislature means to wrestle with the problems encountered in governing the largest state. Housing this staff requires space, and that space, he claims, is a commodity not readily available in the current facility.[25]

Conflict of Interest

Generating support for all political institutions from the body politic continues to present its perennial difficulties, and state legislatures probably suffer more than most. For instance, it seems fair to assume that most adults would be unable to name their state legislative representatives or provide much basic, factual information about their legislature such as the frequency of legislative sessions. Similarly, if public esteem for that occupational group known as "politicians" remains relatively low, state legislatures most likely contribute heavily to that depressed rating. Much of the low esteem may be attributable to a belief that politicians, and especially state legislators, are "on the take," and enjoying a standard of living considerably greater than their ostensible public salary permits. Partly out of a desire to improve their public image and also motivated by a genuine wish to rid politics of some flagrant abuses of overt and excessive influence by certain groups and individuals, legislatures from time to time enact laws designed to separate public officials from associations leading to dubious relationships. In a word, "conflict of interest" legislation periodically moves to the forefront of legislative activities.

Such legislation is either designed to prevent certain kinds of behavior by public officials or to make public the relations between them and other private parties. Laws preventing or discouraging lawyer-legislators from representing clients before state regulatory agencies demonstrates an instance of the first type, while the latter appears in laws requiring lobbyists to register and make known their employers and salaries received. Another pertinent example of conflict of interest laws demanding public disclosure of relationships are those laws requiring public acknowledgement of campaign donations.

Conflict of interest legislation in California captured the spotlight at two different points in recent history, once in the post-Artie

Samish era and the other during the 1969 session. The alleged escapades of Samish produced laws affecting lobbying; and Jesse Unruh secured agreement from the legislature and governor in 1969 on a new policy of regulating campaign financing and other potential conflicts of interest.

Following revelations of Samish's influence with legislators and the amount of money reputed to be involved (some said in the millions), the legislature approved a bill that forced registration of all lobbyists with the legislative analyst. The registration procedure is simple. At the beginning of a session each lobbyist records his name, address, and employers. In addition, every month he must submit a statement of his salary and expense account. How he spends money from his expense account need not be disclosed. A man said to be one of the most influential lobbyists in Sacramento, James D. Garibaldi, reported a salary of $7,000 and "expenses" of $5,500 during one month of the 1969 session. Most lobbyists, of course, do not have that kind of money to spend. Not many people actually look at the registration files, but newspaper reporters sometimes check them. As a result, about once every session a brief flurry of stories appear about such factual information as the number of lobbyists, their salaries and expenses, and (often implicitly) their supposed influence. Beyond that, any restraints imposed on lobbying because of registration can only be surmised.

A recent conflict-of-interest action deals with campaign finances and an even more sensitive topic—public disclosure of the financial status of public officials. As the new law says in its preamble, "the legislature hereby intends to sustain, to the extent necessary, public confidence in government at all levels, by assuring the people of the impartiality and honesty of their officials in all governmental transactions and decisions." Two provisions contain the heart of the bill. First, every public official in the state, including all elected ones and most high level appointed ones, must file annually a "statement describing the nature and extent of his investments." Second, both before and after an election, every candidate for public office must file a statement detailing the amount and sources of all campaign contributions over $500.

Shortly after legislative and gubernatorial approval of Unruh's conflict of interest legislation, the California Supreme Court found the act unconstitutional because it represented "an over-broad intrusion into the right of privacy and thereby invalidly restricts the right to seek or hold public office or employment." This incident illustrates again legislative inability to enact reform measures without the concurrence of outside persons or agencies.

"Good Government Literature" and the
California Experience

Political reform movements come and go in U.S. history. The 1960s witnessed much talk and some activity by those individuals and groups interested in bringing changes to state government, especially their legislatures. Much has been written as a result of these endeavors, and taken together they comprise the latest "good government"* literature on state legislative reform.[26] Even the most casual reader of this literature should notice the similarity between its suggested reforms and the account of California's experience with legislative reform presented above.

When reformers advise state legislatures to raise their salaries and provide themselves with office space and staff assistance, Californians today are wont to frown a bit and wonder what all the fuss is about. The changes in California's legislature were sharply contested at one time, but as with so many other things, once implemented the changes gathered a momentum of their own and became difficult to reverse. California's legislature and citizenry conformed to the spirit of the good government movement and adopted almost all the standard reforms suggested. Because most of the good government literature on state legislatures follows the literary theory in its preachings, one must assume that advocates of the literary theory predominated in California's recent past.

Two questions naturally follow. First, why reform at this point in history? Second, what consequences flow from these changes? The first question is answered briefly in the next section, but the latter question requires lengthier consideration and is the subject of the last section of this chapter.

WHY REFORM AT THIS TIME?

The 1960s saw changes encompassing many aspects of the legislative process. Additionally, the 1950s were also a time of some change and in several cases, like the internship program, the birthtime of the next decade's reforms. Was there something peculiar about the last two decades that generated the movement for legislative change? Or, alternatively, were these decades merely further examples of change in a state in which reform movements are commonplace? And, to throw in one more question, regardless of whether

---

*In all of the following discussion the term "good government" is used in a neutral, nonprejudicial way.

California has or has not always been in a condition of change, what role did political leadership play in all this?

Land of Change

More than most political units, since its Americanization in the mid-1800s, California has been immersed in the constant turmoil of societal change. This has had consequences for state politics and government. Consider population growth alone. Since 1850 the state has grown in population by a factor of approximately two or more every twenty years. In numerical terms, the growth rate looks like this:

1850	92,000
1870	560,000
1890	1,213,000
1910	2,377,000
1930	5,677,000
1950	10,586,000
1970	19,953,000

California's state boundaries enclose an enormous area, more than 150,000 square miles. Combine this territorial size with its climatic and economic attractions and one might expect such a large continually expanding population. Yet, the figures above should be interpreted with care because they alone cannot tell the whole story. Although approximately equal in growth rate, the population growth in the period 1890-1910 did not have the same impact as the population doubling that took place from 1950 to 1970. Those settlers coming to California at the turn of this century were journeying into a rather sparsely populated state, while those who now arrive in the Golden State aboard a four-engine jet move into a heavily populated, and in some cases overpopulated, state. Growth rates are important, as are the absolute numerical population increases, but they must be coupled with a changing perception of government's role for a more complete picture.

A half-century ago governments (at all levels) simply did less and intervened less than today. Especially since World War II, all U.S. governments, naturally including California, have moved in a sometimes unprecedented and often extensive manner into fields such as public health and welfare, education, highway development, and regulation of economic transactions. California's government size, whether measured in dollar terms, number of employees, or economic intervention, has more than doubled in the last twenty years while trying to keep apace the population. Another point to keep in mind is that population growth from 1950 to 1970 means, for the most part, more than a doubling of the urban population. The different order of problems generated by a populous, urban society clearly accounts for much of the increase in governmental activity.

It would be wrong to conclude that California's government has been subjected to pressures for internal change only in the last two decades. On the contrary, change and agitation for reform have always been a part of California, albeit a small part at times. The continual influx of newcomers provided one intermittent, yet common, force for change. The last twenty years, with a population increase of about 10 million, has been a time of greater than usual reform sentiment.

In sum, population has grown and so has government. The changes in the legislature must be viewed against this background. A certain amount of change, a desire to engage in a little experimentation, has usually been the norm of California politics. The same holds for the legislature. Some would say that change in California political institutions like the legislature are inevitable, almost foreordained. That may be the case, for without question reform builds momentum of its own to keep it moving. Perhaps this momentum was prevalent in the 1950s, but such reasoning does not begin explaining what occurred in the 1960s.

Jesse Unruh's Reform Leadership

What happened in the legislature during the last ten years cannot be explained solely by reference to California's tendencies for change. It was a period of heightened activity and attention by the legislature to the legislative process and reforms thereof. In addition to some usual reform sentiment, another very important part of the reason for change in the 1960s resides in the person of Jesse Unruh. Upon assuming the speakership, Unruh picked up the slowly rolling ball of legislative reform and gave it a new momentum.

Despite what some "public mythmakers" tell us, Jesse Unruh did not originate the drive for legislative improvement and reform. As previous discussion indicates, reform sentiments were floating in the legislative chambers before his rise to leadership. But the undeniable fact remains—Unruh turned that sentiment into the hard reality of legislative reform. He worked at two levels: (1) out of public view among his colleagues in the legislature, and (2) at the same time publicly, in what almost amounted to a public crusade, arguing the case for strong state representative bodies and the reforms needed to make them so.

Unruh's Assembly colleagues, especially those in the Republican party, needed some persuading in the early 1960s when he began
implementation of his reform ideas. One of his first moves was to
increase staffing. In addition to complaints about the "excess" cost
of more staff, many expressed a real fear that a sudden increase in
staff would evenuate in a staff highly partisan and/or one owing personal loyalty to Unruh. To some extent the critics were right. As
time passed, however, and most legislators realized the advantages
for themselves in such reforms as staffing, opposition diminished.
By the mid-1960s, partisan differences on reform had almost totally
dissipated and both parties worked together in supporting the big
changes of 1966. Either through the kinds of political pressures a
speaker has at his command or from a realization of the potential
personal benefits, a large majority of legislators soon came to agree
with (if not appreciate) Unruh's efforts.

The turnabout in legislative attitudes must not be minimized.
It was a dramatic example of strong political leadership at work.
Unruh's task assumes even larger proportions when extralegislative
pressures are kept in mind. Alteration in existing relationships
between the legislature and others such as the governor, lobbyists,
and the press will certainly meet opposition. Even a perceived threat
to the status quo produces reaction. What Unruh proposed, especially
by way of staff and pay increases, is just the type of change that
generates a reaction by many "outsiders." For example, if a governor and those under him in the bureaucracy enjoy some dominance
over the legislature (based in part on their accumulation of expert
information), an attempt to create legislature staff for research
purposes will provoke negative reactions. Those who see themselves
in favored positions vis-à-vis the legislature will work against changes
that could challenge them. And because governors, bureaucrats,
lobbyists, and mass media personnel often luxuriate in such favored
positions, they usually can be counted upon to oppose most major
legislative reforms. Unruh made himself a lightning rod for legislative reform opponents and successfully withstood their animosity
while he dominated the legislative arena.

While the continuing fight over reform unfolded in Sacramento,
Unruh took his case to the public, both in and out of California. A
significant portion of Unruh's speeches in the early and mid-1960s
dealt with legislative reform and the need to "upgrade" the legislature.

The most glaring theme that strikes a reader of Unruh's speeches
is the oft-repeated idea that current societal problems require a
stronger legislative branch if there is to be an appropriate governmental response to these problems. He starts from the admission
that state legislatures have fallen to low graces in the governmental

trilogy. Strong executives and interest-group representatives dominate the legislative process, he asserts. Why is the legislature at
such a disadvantage? The primary reason lies in the absence of
adequate legislative staff.

Another theme is easily identified in Unruh's speeches. He
makes no false pretensions about the current image of state legislatures. Their public esteem rests at a low level. Permanent and
meaningful change requires changes in the public's image of the legislature. One way to accomplish this, Unrugh suggests, is passage
of and adherence to a stronger legislative code of ethics.

Fully in keeping with the two previous themes, Unruh often
declares the inappropriateness of Jacksonian beliefs about the virtues
of high turnover among public officials. A corollary argument that
politics does not demand full-time politicians receives equal criticism.
If the legislature assumes the role Unruh envisions, it follows that
legislators will be on the job full time. Naturally, legislators' financial compensation ought to reflect their full-time commitment.

Unruh's public utterances all point in one direction. Representative bodies should exert their theoretical primacy in law-making
because they are uniquely suited to collect, to aggregate, the legitimate demands of the citizenry. Legislatures should be fully competent
and a truly equal part of the governmental structure if the excesses
of either executive or interest group domination are to be prevented.
His speeches evidence his commitment to the literary theory.

Why Jesse Unruh made legislative reform such an important
issue was a favorite topic for politicos throughout his tenure as
speaker. Did he push for reform because of a genuine belief in the
importance of the potential offered by the legislative process or did
he simply see this as a way to glorify and enhance his own personal
political power? Reasonable inferences in response to the question
can be made from interviews with the principals involved in the reform efforts, including Unruh, and a reworking of the decade's political history.

A fair assessment of Unruh's motivations must include both
his striving for political power and his strong belief in legislative
improvement. To do otherwise would be naive or overly cynical,
depending upon which option one selected. Without question, Jesse
Unruh was moving fast in political circles and by 1961 he probably
had visions of the bright political future awaiting him. To think that
a man of his intelligence, political experience, and commitment to
politics would not use the speakership to enhance his own political
power would be a very naive thought. Unruh argued far and wide for
legislative reform and improvement knowing full well that any increase in the relative position of the legislature would also mean a
concurrent increase in his own power. If the legislature, for instance,

hired more staff, Unruh would clearly dominate the hiring through his role as speaker. Any move by Unruh toward reform included some calculation of its meaning for him.

However, to assume that personal political power was the only reason for Unruh's reform activity is unwarranted and requires a very cynical view of politics and politicians. Anyone who has talked to Unruh, read his speeches, followed his career and recent California political history must conclude that he harbors a deep commitment to the potentials the legislative process can offer to a democratic system. Lacking this commitment, he would not have been so active nationally in the legislative reform movement. For that matter, it is doubtful that in the absence of a strong commitment he could have sustained the drive for reform as long as he did in California.

If one accepts the proposition that both power motivations and a true commitment to legislative reform were present, some still might want to ask which came first. Did Unruh latch onto the reform campaign after starting simply with a few ideas to increase his own power or, conversely, did he only see the potential for his own career after engaging in reform efforts? Given the public record about Jesse Unruh, it would seem likely that he first moved into the reform arena for personal political reasons. No moral repudiation is intended; far from it. As a professional politician Unruh deserves respect precisely because he took the step into reform in what turned out to be such an astute way. The intermingling of personal ambitions and idealistic motivitations is the reality of any meaningful reform effort.

Would the legislative changes have occurred without Jesse Unruh? Not most of them, unless someone else, an equally committed and acknowledged leader, chose to follow a path similar to Unruh's. The point is simple: reform demands strong political leadership, someone with organizational and personal skills that make him capable of withstanding the inevitable criticisms that accompany any change in the status quo.

SO WHAT?—SOME CONSEQUENCES FOR THE LEGISLATIVE PROCESS

Reform always implies change. The actual changes may be of some import or of minor significance, they may be functional or dysfunctional, or they may be intended or unanticipated. Certain consequences stemming from California's experience fall into each of these categories.

Forgetting for the moment the usual difficulty of acquiring good data on consequences, another problem looms large. How can one be assured that an observed outcome has been produced in fact by a specific change or series of changes? To be entirely accurate, one must assert a cause and effect relationship between a reform and its alleged impact. Profound methodological and intellectual difficulties are encountered along a road establishing cause and effect relationships. At the very least, an awareness of the multicausal world of political phenomena is required. Rarely can a political event be attributed to one antecedent act or policy choice. The discussion quickly becomes metaphysical; what is knowledge and how do we really know that A caused B? These concerns are not trifling, for they have important bearing on the understanding and explanation of political reality. For the nonmetaphysician, one of two possibilities exists, assuming a commitment to explaining consequences. First, statistical techniques make it possible, given certain assumptions, to ascertain causal relationships. Obviously, this requires data amenable to appropriate statistical manipulations. Such is not the case in this essay. Second, one can adopt a less precise but more practical "test of reasonableness." The test calls for the researcher to exercise his "reasonable" judgment, in the context of his knowledge about the subject and the available data, about the likelihood of cause and effect relationships.

Impact on Procedures

Cost of Operations

Documenting the monetary cost required for legislative operations is an easy task, and the results of the reforms discussed earlier should be obvious—today's California legislature costs considerably more than its predecessors. The cost of legislative operations rose from $3.4 million in fiscal year 1951 to $7.0 million in 1961 to $24.5 million in 1970. Increases in the raw total cost figures give a somewhat misleading impression because total state budget expenditures also increased dramatically during the two decades. A more accurate description of legislative costs is achieved by asking what percentage legislative costs contributed to total state government expenditures. Table 2.2 indicates that although legislative costs as a percentage of total state expenditures have increased since 1950, the gains are not as striking as the raw legislative cost figures. Very little change takes place until 1968. Annual sessions of unlimited duration (coupled with the large salary hikes of 1966) exact a heavier burden on state expenditures.

TABLE 2.2

California Legislative Cost of Operations as a
Percentage of Total State Expenditures, 1951-70

Fiscal Year Ending June 30	Legislative Cost*	Legislative Cost/ State Expenditures
1951	$ 3,388,000	.0033
1952	2,418,000	.0023
1953	3,274,000	.0028
1954	3,070,000	.0023
1955	3,816,000	.0027
1956	3,894,000	.0025
1957	4,836,000	.0027
1958	5,495,000	.0029
1959	6,587,000	.0033
1960	6,074,000	.0029
1961	7,069,000	.0028
1962	6,635,000	.0028
1963	8,311,000	.0031
1964	8,408,000	.0028
1965	11,300,000	.0033
1966	11,877,000	.0033
1967	13,831,000	.0034
1968	19,253,000	.0043
1969	21,004,000	.0041
1970	24,502,000	.0041

*Figures are rounded to nearest thousand.

Source: Annual reports of the controller of the State of California, 1951-1970.

Work Load

Critics of the literary theory argue that implementation of the oft-suggested reforms results in more legislation. That is, the "beefed-up" legislature will perceive a need for more activity (i.e., introduce more bills) in order to make its influence felt. More bills will be introduced, so the argument runs, and more law will be legislated. Examination of Table 2.3 gives some indication of the California legislature's work load and its propensity to pass legislation.

Until the annual session's advent, the number of bills thrown into the legislative hopper hovered around the 5,000 mark. The sharp increase in percentage of bills enacted into law starting in 1959 coincides with the Democratic domination of state government. Deterioration in the relations between Governor Brown and Speaker Unruh accompanies the declining ratio of bills passed to bills introduced in the mid-1960s.

Note the figures for 1967-68 and 1969-70; the critics are right. Bill introductions for any two of those years are considerably higher than in any previous biennium. Likewise, the number of bills passed represents a large increase. Part of the explanation lies in the longer (annual) sessions starting in 1967. More calendar days are available for bill introduction and, apparently, legislators take advantage of it. The availability of staff, when coupled with annual sessions, also contributes to more legislation.

Another aspect of legislative work load refers to committee efforts. The pattern of bill assignments to Assembly committees since 1950 reveals interesting characteristics. (All bills must be

TABLE 2.3

Number of Bills Introduced and Passed in the
California Legislature, 1951-70

Calendar Year	Number of Bills Introduced	Number of Bills Passed By Both Houses	Bills Passed/ Bills Introduced
1951	5,303	1,896	.36
1953	5,522	2,088	.37
1955	5,841	2,103	.36
1957	6,863	2,669	.39
1959	4,401	2,363	.54
1961	4,703	2,401	.51
1963	4,761	2,373	.50
1965	5,021	2,243	.45
1967	4,135	1,808	.43
1968	3,374	1,533	.45
1969	3,792	1,698	.45
1970	3,960	1,628	.41

Source: Annual Final Calendar of Legislative Business, California Legislature.

assigned to a committee and the speaker makes such assignments.)
Looking only at the original committees to which bills were assigned,
a major shift in policy occurred in 1961. Speaker Unruh began assigning more bills to the "substantive" committees and less to the
Assembly Ways and Means Committee. Part of Unruh's efforts called
for a strengthening of the committee system, ergo, more committee
staff. Entirely in keeping with this plan, he also distributed the committee work load more evenly by allowing the substantive committees
the first opportunity to examine bills in their specialty before sending
them to Ways and Means (if they involved expenditures). As a net
result, the substantive committee research, debate, and decisions
have taken on new importance.

Annual Sessions

A switch to annual sessions is usually thought to have two major
consequences: (1) preventing the traditional end-of-session logjam
of legislation, and (2) creating a full-time, professional legislature.
Discussion of the latter supposed consequence will be delayed because
it fits neatly into a broader discussion about the effects of reform
on legislative personnel.

No matter how long or frequent a legislature meets, approaching
adjournment sine die means that confusion on the floor increases.
Wilder Crane and Meredith Watts characterize the situation as one
of "utter confusion." They claim that "roll call quickly follows roll
call, to the point that members may have little notion of what they
are deciding."[27] The problem is acute in states in which the legislature meets every other year and/or for short duration (e.g., sixty
days). A giant logjam develops as the session nears its constitutionally mandated deadline. When the jam breaks, confusion often reigns.
Perceptive reformers have realized that a change to unlimited annual
sessions will not totally prevent this problem. They have long argued,
however, that unlimited annual sessions, by giving the legislature as
much time as it wants for deliberation and allowing it to meet every
year, go a long way toward alleviating the confusion. As Blair and
Flournoy say, "Annual sessions would . . . relieve the pressure for
final enactment at the end of a session, and work to reduce the logjam."[28]

Examining the chronology of bill passage in the California legislature for selected years reveals a strong confirmation of the reformers predictions. The percentage of bills passed during the last
four weeks of the session drops remarkably after the inauguration
of annual sessions. A logjam does not develop with annual sessions
because bills are passed at more even intervals throughout the session. Conversations with legislators and staff personnel indicate

that the switch to annual sessions allows the legislature to dispense with more of the noncontroversial, trivial, and local bills by mid-session. This leaves more time for matters of considerable importance.

Annual sessions have had an unanticipated effect on the legislature's ability to produce "interim studies." When the legislature met in regular session every other year, many committees (often twenty-five to thirty) were created to conduct investigations and carry on research in the interim between biennial sessions. Unpressured by the day-to-day grind of the legislative process, and able to meet at selected points across the state, interim committees became a prime vehicle for the development of necessarily complicated legislation. As committee staff size increased in the early 1960s, the capabilities of the interim committees increased apace.

The time now available for interim committees is exceedingly brief. The annual sessions held since the late 1960s have met for at least eight and one-half months each. Weary legislators usually take a respite from legislative responsibilities immediately after the session. Therefore, not much time is left before an election campaign is under way (even years) or plans are being laid for the next session. At first blush it appears that the added length of the regular session provides appropriate time for the same kinds of investigation and research completed previously during the interim. However, no matter how long a session lasts, during it attention is directed at the immediately pressing bills and not much time is allocated for non-immediate items. To the extent that one feels legislatures ought to concern themselves with long-range research, this effect of annual sessions is dysfunctional.

Staff

Several predicted consequences of staff increases have been advanced.[29] More staff allegedly means: (1) more information for legislators; (2) more independence from the governor, bureaucracy, and lobbyists; and (3) more help with many time-consuming "service" chores.

Little doubt now exists that more "bits" of information are inserted into the California legislative process as a result of staff increases. This is true whether one speaks only about the number of formal, written statements and research reports now generated or about the more casual verbal interjections from staff. Exact quantification of the amount of information and information usage is impossible, but some rough indicators can suffice. Every functional legislative staff agency (i.e., legislative analyst, auditor general, etc.) reports large increases in requests from legislators for information during the last decade. Likewise, an obvious repercussion of larger committee staffs is more information put into the legislative communication network, e.g., analysis of bills, memoranda, etc.

A prime justification for large legislative staffs reflects the concern over excessive legislative dependence upon bureaucrats, lobbyists, and governors. Without their own staff, where do legislators turn for information about pending issues but to lobbyists and executive branch personnel? Information is power, as the saying goes, and a legislature that must accept at face value the comments of bureaucrats and lobbyists is in an inferior position. Therefore, the mere presence of a staff owing its allegiance to and adopting the perspective of the legislature almost guarantees a less dependent legislature.

Two facts support the proposition that today's California legislature has more independence than in prior times. First, the role of most lobbyists and almost all bureaucrats today requires different kinds of interactions than in the past. The people with whom lobbyists and bureaucrats now must communicate most of the time are staff personnel, not legislators. Much of the negotiating that takes place either before bill introduction or at the committee hearing stage involves the staff. Most observers agree that the California legislative staff, especially in the Assembly, does a good job of forcing lobbyists and bureaucrats to present a more detailed and widespread justification for their proposals. As an Assembly leader remarked, "The lobbyist used to be able to dictate, now he must persuade." Oftentimes, staff can accomplish this better than legislators. This is not true because legislators lack determination or knowledge, but because the staff man has the time and prime responsibility to seek out information. Legislators' role expectations demand great attention to aspects of their position other than research.

The second point follows from the above and also demonstrates the increased independence of the legislature. Without staff, legislators are often placed in the position of simply saying "yes" or "no" to even the most complicated piece of legislation. In a 1964 speech, Assemblyman Unruh summarized the problem:

> With the exception of occasional uses of the tactic of bill amendment, legislatures are generally limited to these few, crude, all-or-none responses to questions formulated elsewhere in the structure of government. The capacity of legislatures to deal with alternatives, with gradations of support, or with problems of inter-program coordination, are limited by the form in which questions are put to legislative bodies, and even more crucially by limited independent capacity to design program alternatives

and, generally, to take a creative role in the formulation of policy questions to be debated.[30]

Having access to a nonexecutive and noninterest group source of data grants legislators the ability to ask some necessary and embarrassing questions. No matter how diligent or well-staffed they are, California legislators still find themselves overwhelmed at times or unable to probe sufficiently in committee hearings. Yet, interviews with long-time lobbyists and senior bureaucrats reveal their belief that their own position has become more difficult because of the increased ability of legislators to "put them on the spot" in committee hearings. A perusal of some committee hearing transcripts from the early 1950s and more recent times also confirms the more intensive and penetrating line of questioning that now takes place.*

California's legislators are called upon to perform a wide variety of services for their constituents. Help in finding a job, arranging for a "special" automobile license plate, providing copies of the state constitution, and taking some constituent's plea to an anonymous bureaucrat are some examples of these time-consuming requests. No particular rationale demands that the legislator himself perform these politically necessary errands. Speaking with the authority of the legislator, staff can effectively handle constituents' requests and free the legislator to "make laws." So runs the reform argument. In practice, however, California's experience suggests that the presence of legislative staff only ameliorates the situation. It does not permit the legislator to escape constituents' errand-type demands.

Some constituents or some kinds of requests simply cannot stand delegation to staff. For instance, every district has its relatively small band of politically important constituents who want the personal attention of the legislator, no matter how trivial their particular problem or question. Ignoring their request for personal attention would be imprudent. Sometimes a legitimate grievance by a constituent bears no hope of resolution without the direct, personal intervention of the legislator. In California the most commonplace instances of this are the situations in which some persuasion and political arm-twisting are needed to move a reluctant (and civil-service-safe) bureaucrat toward favorable action for a constituent. Reformers were right when they said that staff could relieve the nonlegislative

---

*This discussion should not give the impression that California's legislature has been able to examine completely and effectively the totality of state governmental actions and policies. The ability to examine and comprehend the whole picture still eludes this legislature as well as all others.

burdens of the legislator. They were wrong, at least in California, when they implied that the legislator would be completely free from his "case work."

Legislative-Gubernatorial Relations

Given the apparent dominance of the literary theory in the California legislature during the last decade, an increase in the conflictual nature of legislative-gubernatorial relations might be predicted. To be sure, some conflict between the two institutions is guaranteed almost by definition, but an upsurge in legislative reform sentiment may provoke a heightening of the conflict level. This prediction contains the seeds of an important consequence. If the "cost" of legislative reform is more legislative-gubernatorial conflict, the question of whether this conflict is dysfunctional to the operation of an already hard-pressed state government must be raised.

The end product of California legislative-gubernatorial conflict appears most frequently in two places: gubernatorial reductions in the appropriation bill passed by the legislature and vetoes of legislation. Table 2.4 presents data on legislative-gubernatorial conflict using these two indicators as evidence. Both indicators point in the same direction, namely, slight increases in conflict as reform progressed. The trend in the percentage of the legislative appropriation bill reduced by the governor seems clear enough, but tendencies of the second indicator remains somewhat cloudy. Between 1951 and 1965, the total bills vetoed as a percentage of the total bills passed by the legislature fluctuates up and down with a mean percentage of 7.5. At first glance the figures from 1967 to 1969 seem to tip the scales toward an affirmation of a decrease in conflict, but this is misleading. In the 1967-70 sessions, the governor could no longer exercise a pocket veto, so all vetoed bills were returned to the legislature with a statement of reasons for the veto. A regular veto represents a more direct confrontation with the legislature than the pocket veto. Therefore, the large increase in the governor's use of the direct veto suggests an increase in head-on conflicts. The elimination of the pocket veto foreordained this repercussion.

Although the two indicators of legislative-gubernatorial conflict used here show some increase in the prevalence of conflict, no evidence exists to suggest that the conflict threatens the viability of California's state government. Such a threat always exists, but the conflict that legislative reform has generated so far creates no such problem.

TABLE 2.4

Two Indicators of Legislative-Gubernatorial Conflict in California, 1951-71

Fiscal Year Ending June 30	Governor's Reductions in Legislative Appropriations[a]/Total Legislative Appropriations for State Government (percent)	Bills Vetoed			Total Bills Vetoed/ Total Bills Passed (percent)
		Pocket	Direct (during session)	Total	
1951	.0000	89	42	131	.069
1952	.0041	158	35	193	.092
1953	.0000	129	8	137	.065
1954	.0000				
1955	.0000	222	23	245	.091
1956	.0000				
1957	.0000	139	29	168	.071
1958	.0000				
1959	.0003	153	16	169	.073
1960	.0019				
1961	.0000	145	15	160	.068
1962	.0000				
1963	.0029	165	8	173	.077
1964	.0006				
1965	.0040	b	83	83	.048
1966	.0001				
1967	.0084	b	59	59	.038
1968	.0028				
1969	.0196	b	79	79	.046
1970	.0000				
1971	.0690	b	77	77	.047

aCalifornia's governor has the constitutional authority to reduce or delete appropriation items in the budget bill; he may not increase an item.

bThe governor no longer can use a pocket veto.

Sources: Final Calendar of Legislative Business, 1951-68; D. Jay Doubleday, Legislative Review of the Budget in California (Berkeley: Institute of Governmental Studies, 1967); and the Los Angeles Times and Sacramento Bee, 1951-71.

Impact on Personnel

Legislators' Backgrounds

Will the different character of the legislature result in any
changes in the kinds of men who serve? An easy way to look at the
question is to survey the background characteristics of legislators
from 1950 to 1969. Such data have been collected only for assemblymen, so comments must be limited to them.

Only a few changes appear in legislators' backgrounds during
the last two decades. The overwhelming majority of assemblymen
continue to be white, married males. Few women and equally few
nonwhites are elected to the lower house. Other social characteristics show some change, however. More of the current assemblymen have earned a college diploma and an advanced degree than a
decade ago. California is a state of newcomers, and the reflection
of this demographic fact is seen in the large proportion of assemblymen during the last twenty years who were not born in the Golden
State. In recent years, a slight shift toward more native sons is
apparent, but as late as 1967 one-half the representatives were born
in another state. The only major shift in background features of
assemblymen occurred in their occupational profile. In the last two
sessions, only one-half as many representatives as in the early 1950s
listed their occupations as "businessmen." The occupational category
that absorbed most of the decline in businessmen is the law. Thirty-
one of the eighty assemblymen in the 1969 session classified themselves as lawyers.

Turnover

A high rate of turnover among legislators remains a characteristic of state legislatures. It is not exactly commonplace, but neither
is it unusual, for a state legislature to begin a session with half its
membership being sworn in for the first time. In recent times, reformers have lamented this fluidity because of its supposed derogatory
effect on legislative expertise and quality.

For the last two decades the number of freshmen assemblymen
has varied, but the trend points toward a decrease in freshmen and,
therefore, longer average tenure. The last (1971) California session
had a fewer number of freshmen assemblymen than any other session this century. The figures for the last eleven sessions show
this:

	Freshmen Assemblymen
1951	15
1953	19
1955	19
1957	15
1959	16
1961	11
1963	34
1965	10
1967	33
1969	7
1971	6

The 1963 and 1967 sessions should be regarded as exceptions. Both were held immediately after extensive reapportionments; such turnover was expected. The sessions of 1961, 1965, 1969 and 1971 all show a smaller number of freshmen than any of the preceding sessions in the 1950s. This is far from conclusive evidence that legislative reforms have produced a decrease in personnel turnover, but it does suggest that some move in that direction is occurring. The trend is probably owing to the increased attractiveness of the legislative job, which is a consequence of the reforms.

For the politically ambitious, a seat in the California legislature holds more attraction today than during the 1950s and earlier. To state the case differently, more men today view the legislative role as one worth achieving. If being a state legislator is perceived as a more important and/or rewarding job, increased competition for party nominations should be expected. Data show that competition in primaries was more prevalent in the 1960s (especially in the latter half of the decade) than ten years before. That is, in the 1960s an increasing number of primaries for Assembly seats were fought out by two or more candidates. For example, in 1968 Assembly primary elections, 66 of the eventual 160 candidates (two per district) gained their nomination by defeating an opponent in a primary campaign. In 1958, only 28 candidates suffered primary competition.

One more strand of evidence suggesting the increased attractiveness of the legislature ought to be mentioned. As seen above, the number of freshmen elected in the last decade shows a decline (except for the intervention of reapportionment). An obvious corollary is that more incumbents find the job attractive and worth keeping.

Two reasons account for the increased attractiveness of the legislature, and they are a direct result of the reform efforts. First, and most obvious, is the dramatic upsurge in monetary renumeration.

A high salary rate and increased fringe benefits have at least two consequences. In a few instances the pay itself will be motivation enough to push a politically active individual into a race. Yet, most observers and many participants agree that the primary result of the pay increases has been the retention of already elected legislators. The pay raises made it economically feasible for many legislators, especially those with children in school, to remain in the legislature. They did not have to use the state legislature as a quick stepping stone to something more lucrative.

A second reason for the legislature's increased attractiveness is the slowly but steadily increasing prestige of the body. The national attention accorded the California legislature in both the good government reform literature and many popular news sources raises its prestige in the eyes of those who are potential legislators.*

The California legislature receives its share of publicity. California state government is big; only five other governmental units in the world have larger budgets. As the legislature in the 1960s came to play a very prominent public role in this active and large governmental complex, it increased its institutional prestige.

One indication of legislative prestige is voter turnout. Legislative races rarely attract as much public notoriety as gubernatorial ones, even when governors and legislators run at the same time. A smaller percentage of the electorate votes for state representative than for governor. Extreme fall-off, or voter fatigue, is common for campaigns lower on the ballot than the governorship. One device for testing the public prestige of the legislature, then, is to measure the amount of electorate voting fatigue. Simply taking the ratio of total votes cast for legislators over the total votes cast for the governorship provides such a measure. Using only the California Assembly for illustration, the slow increase in legislative prestige becomes apparent.

Number of Citizens Voting for Assembly/
Number of Citizens Voting for Governorship

1950	.79
1954	.91
1958	.93
1962	.95
1966	.95
1970	.96

---

*In February 1971, the Citizens Conference on State Legislatures released its study of the quality of the fifty state legislatures.

Campaign Costs

To stand for election in a California legislative district requires large monetary expenditures. The increasing use of (and perceived necessity of) professional campaign public relations firms,
coupled with the augmented attractiveness of the legislature, produces very expensive legislative campaigns. The most extravagant
Senate campaign in 1970 saw officially reported combined expenditures of approximately $244,000, a sum hardly reminiscent of the
typical "shoestring" legislative campaign. Combining both candidate's
expenditures, the more typical and average Assembly campaign now
costs about $70-80,000.

Only a rare candidate has the personal financial capability to
wage a legislative campaign. As in early times, the lobbyist continues
to supply a certain proportion of campaign funds. Without debating
the merits of this means of financing, it is important to point out that
dependence upon lobbyists for campaign funds reduces one of the
alleged advantages of higher legislative salaries. Higher salaries
have led to less dependence upon lobbyists for such essentials as
hotel bills, transportation, and entertainment, but this reform outcome is quickly dissipated when the source of campaign contributions
is taken into account. In many ways, candidates for today's legislature, are almost as dependent upon lobbyists as their predecessors.
The difference is that now a legislator needs the third house every
two or four years at election time, but he is not as dependent upon it
during sessions as were earlier lawmakers. This distinction is real,
but not crucial. High salaries notwithstanding, lobbyists still retain
their influence.

Full-Time Legislator

Most states still cling to notions of the citizen-legislator, the
man who gives a small percentage of his time every year or two and
travels to the capitol to make the laws that will govern the state.
A citizen-legislator remains a part-time legislator. In rather explicit fashion, the California electorate in 1966 abolished the part-
time legislator. Meeting in session every year for approximately
eight months, returning for a veto session, and then holding a few
interim committee hearings is hardly a part-time demand on a legislators resources. Being a California legislator quite clearly has

---

By combining categories of functionality, accountability, information-
handling, independence, and representativeness, the conference
ranked the legislatures from one to fifty. California ranked first.

become a full-time preoccupation. Most legislators still have other occupations—a law office, insurance agency, etc.—but legislating pre-empts the overwhelming majority of their time. The myth of citizen-legislator still lingers; most legislators persist in identifying them-selves as teachers, attorneys, and businessmen. However, in the 1969 session, eleven representative broke with tradition and classified themselves as full-time legislators. More will follow suit in future sessions. Given the assumptions of the literary theory, which are widely shared among legislators, the change to full time is not only necessary but very desirable.

Impact on Policy

Policy content, the specific declarations and actions taken by the legislature, has been affected in some instances by the reform efforts. Although not usually noticed by the public, a change for the better in the "technical" characteristics of policy is evident. For instance, fewer mistakes (unintended or unclear sections) that re-quire correction in the next session creep into current legislation. More attention, especially by staff, is paid to the details of a bill so that such mistakes do not occur. As part of the whole trend toward reform, a greater degree of openness prevails. More participants in the process know what in fact is happening and this encourages technically better legislation. The openness mitigates against a tactic that at one time was much more prevalent—hiding special legislation for a particular group, section, or individual deep in the content of unrelated bills. Not that the California legislature no longer serves special interests, but it is done with more candor and op-portunity for legislative and public criticism.

Legislative reform has also had some impact on policy content through the legislature's resumption of an initiatory stand in several policy areas. Some bills of major importance would have either not been written at all or written in significantly different form except for the legislature's new-found ebullience. Three policy areas that immediately come to mind are mental health, air pollution, and educa-tion.[31] In each of these, the legislature has demonstrated decreasing reliance upon administrative agencies. For example, in 1969 the state Senate originated and passed a bill that would have banned all internal combustion engines in the state by 1975; the bill was sub-sequently defeated in the Assembly but will be revived again.

Despite these policy-related implications of legislative reform, looking back at the last two decades does not permit the observation that as a result of the reforms any one particular group, section, or interest has been significantly better served by the policy content of legislation.* A claim that the pressing issues of our times—race, poverty, and ecological protection—have been addressed because of legislative reform cannot be legitimately advanced. Today's legislature is generating different policy than its predecessor of twenty years, but to attribute the major responsibility for these differences to reform efforts is, in the eyes of most participants and observers, an inappropriate assessment. Reform is not meaningless vis-à-vis policy, but other variables, e.g., social and economic pressures, probably account for more of the variance than reform.

Dismay or condemnation are not apt emotions, however. To expect such consequences from structural and procedural tinkering is inappropriate. Wholesale change in policy content rarely occurs, and it will not occur as a consequence of reform efforts alone. What the reforms have accomplished, and all they should reasonably be expected to accomplish, is to grant the legislature an improved capability to cope with our ever present societal and political problems. For the most part, California's legislature possesses that capability after two decades of reform. It has the potential to play a full role in state government, and it regularly exercises that opportunity.

CONCLUSION

The California legislature has accomplished much in the last two decades. Combining California's penchant for change with strong leadership, the legislature adopted most of the standard reform suggestions. In doing so it has demonstrated its adherence to a literary theory about the proper role of representative bodies. Not only has it served itself well, but in many ways it has provided an example for other states.

Both line and functional staff show dramatic increases in size during recent years. With these increases has come on augmented role and importance for these nonelected members of the legislative institution. Without question, California's legislators now depend heavily upon their staff. Most legislators seem to enjoy this dependence because it also gives them some freedoms and opportunities they would not have otherwise. Staffing has resulted in more independence

---

*A possible major exception, and a topic that has not received much attention in this study, is the court-ordered and legislative-implemented reapportionment of 1965. The enormous shift toward greater Senate representation for the Los Angeles metropolitan area may eventually cause significant differences in policy. At this writing, changes in policy as a result of reapportionment are not at all apparent.

for the legislative branch in its relations with the executive and the third house (lobbyists).

California legislators are the highest-paid state representatives in the nation; they meet in long annual sessions; and the sessions are characterized by several changed procedures that enhance their operating efficiency. Consent calendars and more equitable distribution of committee work loads are examples. A more centralized and partisan leadership is obvious in the Assembly and the Senate is moving in the same direction. Although they complain about their facilities, or lack thereof, California legislators work in luxurious quarters when compared to their colleagues in most other states.

Changing to annual sessions has apparently fulfilled most of the predicted consequences of such a switch. The chaotic nature of the session's last few weeks has lessened, more bills are passed, and the legislature has become de facto a full-time occupation. As a result of the reforms, the legislature holds a great appeal for both incumbent and prospective legislators. More lawyers and more men with college degrees are winning seats today than previously.

Of course, the legislature is not without its critics. Some very stinging rebukes to the reforms are voiced in the state bureaucracy and among some lobbyists. Constructive criticisms are also made by legislators. Procedurally oriented reforms are always an appropriate topic, but the major reforms of the 1970s probably will be geared more directly to specific policy areas.

NOTES

1. Gladwin Hill, Dancing Bear: An Inside Look at California Politics (Cleveland: World Publishing, 1968), p. 10.

2. Ibid., p. 20.

3. For example, George S. Blair and Houston I. Flournoy, Legislative Bodies in California (Belmont: Dickerson Publishing, 1967); Henry A. Turner and John A. Vieg, The Government and Politics of California (New York: McGraw-Hill, 1967); Bernard L. Hyink et al., Politics and Government in California (New York: Thomas Y. Crowell, 1969); and Joseph A. Beek, The California Legislature (Sacramento: California Office of State Printing, 1965).

4. Hill has written, "A party organization in California hence really consists of a letterhead, offices in San Francisco and Los Angeles with skeletal staffs, and a dispersion of unpaid, spare-time officers who have no way of mobilizing efforts on behalf of the party except through unpredictable tides of sentiment. In the virtual absence of patronage, they can offer no rewards; nor can they impose penalties, for noncompliance with their exhortations." Dancing Bear,

p. 111. For a fuller discussion of political parties in California see Turner and Vieg, Government and Politics of California.

5. William J. Keefe, "The Functions and Powers of the State Legislature" in Alexander Heard, ed., State Legislatures in American Politics (Englewood Cliffs, N.J.: Prentice-Hall, 1966), p. 37.

6. Terry Sanford, Storm Over the States (New York: McGraw-Hill, 1967), p. 183.

7. Heard, State Legislatures in American Politics, p. 158.

8. Most of what follows owes its inspiration to the discussion of reform in Roger H. Davidson, David M. Kovenock, and Michael K. O'Leary, Congress in Crisis (Belmont: Wadsworth Publishing, 1966). See the many sources cited in this book for extended discussion of the points made in this chapter. The categories these authors create (which are used in this discussion) are rather "pure" types and over-lap and exceptions surely exist.

9. For a discussion of this point from the perspective of the governor's office, see Alan J. Wyner, "Gubernatorial Relations with Legislators and Administrators," State Government, 41 (1968), pp. 199-203.

10. Jefferson B. Fordham, The State Legislative Institution (Philadelphia: University of Pennsylvania Press, 1959), p. 16.

11. On this point, see William W. Boyer, Bureaucracy on Trial (Indianapolis: Bobbs-Merrill, 1964). Boyer applied this reasoning to executive-legislative relations at the federal level, but it seems very appropriate in the states as well.

12. California Journal, April 1971, p. 96. This compares to much higher estimates of the congressional payroll. A figure of 2,000 for the U.S. Senate alone is cited in Randall B. Ripley, Power in the Senate (New York: St. Martin's Press, 1969), p. 187. One source estimates over 10,000 congressional employees: Louis Cassele's UPI story in the Santa Barbara News-Press, July 9, 1969, p. A-10.

13. A columnist for the Santa Barbara News-Press, Tom Kleveland, relates the difficulty he encountered when trying to learn the cost of maintaining district offices for the Santa Barbara area's representatives. Based on figures in a recently published column, the district's assemblyman spends about $17,000 (per year) to operate his two district offices. See Kleveland's column in the Santa Barbara News-Press, September 20, 1969, p. B-1.

14. Thomas J. Anton, "Roles and Symbols in the Determination of State Expenditures," Midwest Journal of Political Science 11 (February 1967), pp. 34-35.

15. Malcolm E. Jewell, The State Legislature, 2d ed. (New York: Random House, 1969), p. 60.

16. D. Jay Doubleday, Legislative Review of the Budget in California (Berkeley: Institute of Governmental Studies, 1967), p. 99.

17. Turner and Veig, Government and Politics of California, p. 130.

18. See the works cited in note 3, supra.

19. California State Constitution, Article IV, Section 10a.

20. See his comments in the Los Angeles Times, July 31, 1969, p. 3.

21. Citizens Conference on State Legislatures, Research Memorandum No. 11, August 1969.

22. Duane Lockard, "The State Legislator," in Heard, State Legislatures in American Politics, p. 114.

23. A report on legislative facilities prepared by E.B.S. Management Consultants, Inc., appearing in "Toward Tommorrow's Legislature," by the Pennsylvania General Assembly's Commission for Legislative Modernization, January 1969, p. 95.

24. Ibid., p. 99.

25. As reported in the Santa Barbara News-Press, June 11, 1969, p. B-8. Whether the new edifice will actually be constructed remains in some doubt. The price tag attracts many opponents.

26. For purposes of this study I have chosen to rely on the following examples of the reform literature. The list is far from all inclusive. Committee for Economic Development, Modernizing State Government (New York: The Committee, 1967); Donald G. Herzberg, "An Intelligent Citizen's Checklist for State Legislative Improvement," prepared for The Public Affairs Training Program, International Telephone and Telegraph Corporation, 1968; Heard, State Legislatures in American Politics, chap. 6; Sanford, Storm Over the States, especially chap. 16.

27. Wilder Crane and Meredith Watts, State Legislative Systems (Englewood Cliffs, N. J.: Prentice-Hall, 1968), p. 77.

28. Blair and Flournoy, Legislative Bodies in California, p. 55.

29. For a good collection of reform proposals about staff, albeit on Congress, see A. de Grazia, ed., Congress: The First Branch (Garden City, N.Y.: Doubleday Anchor, 1967).

30. Speech by Jesse M. Unruh to the Western Political Science Association, Salt Lake City, March 20, 1964, entitled "Scientific Inputs to Legislative Decision Making."

31. See a recent article by Arthur Bolton, former head of the Assembly Office of Research, entitled "Legislative Initiative in the Mental Health Field," State Government, 41 (Summer 1968) pp. 187-93.

3

POLICY IMPLICATIONS OF
LEGISLATIVE REORGANIZATION
IN ILLINOIS
Samuel K. Gove

   In recent years state legislative reorganization has been a
popular cause. With the impetus of foundation grants, many studies
of reorganization have been made, innovative programs such as legislative intern programs have been popular, and new reform organizations devoted to the problems of state legislatures (e.g., the Citizens
Conference on State Legislatures) have been established. Academic
units, such as Rutgers' Eagleton Institute, have devoted much of their
time and talents to studying and promoting legislative reorganization.
An American Assembly, with subsequent regional conferences, was
convened on the topic of the problems of state legislatures. Older
organizations, such as the National Municipal League, received special grants for state legislative programs and have developed publications like The State Legislative Reporter. The American Political
Science Association has a foundation-sponsored state legislative service project, with academicians designated as fellows in several
states.
   Older organizations of legislators and legislative staff, such as
the National Legislative Conference, which is affiliated with the
Council of State Governments, have been more active, devoting a good
part of their conference programs to reform, and have established
several special study committees. In addition, new organizations of
state legislators have been established including the National Conference of State Legislative Leaders and the National Society of State
Legislators. In addition to these new developments, there has been

   The author wishes to thank Mrs. Ashley Nugent for her most
helpful editorial assistance. This chapter was completed in September
1970; notwithstanding several developments in Illinois since then, the
author would not change his conclusions.

a simultaneously expanding body of academic literature on state legislatures and legislative reform. The number of doctoral dissertations
on the topic has increased sharply.

The overriding reason for such considerable legislative reform
activity undertaken by legislators and other participants rests on the
premise that the state legislative institution needs to be strengthened—
the term "strengthened" being undefined. The state legislatures as
a group are widely regarded as out of date, subject to the status of
horse and buggy branches of state government. These bodies are
usually said to be unresponsive to the problems of the state and to
be in need of renewed viability and innovation. Statements like these,
which could have significant policy implications, are not heard as
frequently as statements that argue change is needed for the sake of
efficiency and economy—desirable goals in themselves. When the
"innovative" cliches are heard, however, the discussion is extremely
vague, with few suggestions what the innovations might be.

Typical of the comments on the efficiency and economy theme
are those from an Illinois reorganization report:

> State legislatures throughout the nation have not de-
> veloped adequate procedures to cope with the increasing
> problems and responsibilities they now face. There is
> not present in government the pressure of business compe-
> petition that compels efficient operation within the private
> sector of the economy. As a result, modern techniques
> that are commonplace in industry have seldom been ap-
> plied to the day-by-day operation of state legislatures.
> It is paradoxical that our state legislatures should lack
> the qualities of streamlined efficiency which are the
> very qualities the world associates with the concept of
> the American society.

Further in this same report's introduction, the other general theme,
strengthening the legislature, appears:

> It is our expectation that by furnishing the State legis-
> lature with adequate procedures, staff, and facilities, we
> can revive the faltering partner in the federal system
> and help stay the tendency toward overcentralization of
> power. It is our hope that the states may be encouraged
> to resume their historic role as experimenters and
> innovators in the American system of government.[1]

In this chapter we will examine the attempts at legislative reorganization in one state that has devoted much time and effort to

this undertaking and has met with considerable success. Throughout a ten-year period, the Illinois legislature, which had most of the common shortcomings cited above, adopted many of the reforms long advocated in Illinois and elsewhere. Although the reorganization efforts were not related to specific policy goals—at least none were openly espoused by the reform proponents—we will inquire whether indeed there were state government policy changes and trends that can be attributed to Illinois legislative reorganization developments.

THE ILLINOIS GENERAL ASSEMBLY

The Illinois General Assembly has had a long and colorful history. As might be expected with any legislative body, its character has changed frequently. Some of the most marked changes have come, however, in the 1960s.

Although until recently the legislature has not received close scrutiny from scholars and writers, a few studies indicate the flavor of the legislature in earlier days. Paul Simon, then lieutenant governor, for example, told of an early experience with one of Illinois' illustrious citizens who served in the general assembly. What Abraham Lincoln is most remembered for in the special session of 1840 was an episode he wanted people to forget in later years—a jump out the window to prevent a quorum. The Illinois State Register described the scene:

> Mr. Lincoln, of Sangamon, who was present during the whole scene, and who appeared to enjoy the embarrassment of the House, suddenly looked very grave after the Speaker announced that a quorum was present. The conspiracy having failed, Mr. Lincoln, came under great excitement, and having attempted and failed to get out at the door, very unceremoniously raised the window and jumped out, followed by one or two other members. This gymnastic performance of Mr. Lincoln and his flying brethren did not occur until after they had voted and consequently the House did not interfere with their extraordinary feat. We have not learned whether these flying members got hurt in their adventure, and we think it probable that at least one of them came off without damage, as it was noticed that his legs reached nearly from the window to the ground! By his extraordinary performance on this occasion, Mr. Lincoln will doubtless become . . . famous. We learn that a resolution will probably be introduced into the House this week to inquire

into the expedience of raising the State House one story
higher, in order to set in the third story so as to prevent
members from jumping out of windows! If such a resolution passes, Mr. Lincoln in [the] future will have to climb
down the spout.2

Over the years the general assembly was involved in incidents
that did not tend to improve the body's image. For example, in the
late 1930s, a senator writing anonymously in the American Mercury
charged widespread bribery in the legislature. More recently, in
1953 the Illinois General Assembly was the subject of a lengthy article
entitled, "What Those Politicians Do to You," by John Bartlow Martin
published in the Saturday Evening Post. For the image of the legislature and for the legislators involved, the timing of the article was
unfortunate. At the same time Martin was gathering his material late
in the 1953 session, a Chicago legislator was kidnapped and has never
been seen since. The article highlighted this incident although the
author had attempted

to tell the uninformed—and misguided—galleryite what
goes on in the Legislature, not only on the floor but in
the lobbies and hotel rooms. What does the Legislature do? How does it do it? And what kind of people
are the members? Let us study the 1953 session of
the Illinois Legislature as an example of an American
legislature at work.3

The author answered these questions well, but the reader could hardly
dismiss the fact that a legislator had been kidnapped. The 1953 session produced some positive accomplishments, nonetheless, and that
year Illinois was one of the first states to move by constitutional
amendment toward legislative reapportionment, a change that was to
have an impact on the legislative process and the legislative image.
Change in the legislative image was not all one way. In 1964,
state Senator Paul Simon, drawing on his background as a journalist,
wrote an article for Harper's, "The Illinois Legislature: A Study in
Corruption." Covering some ten years of the legislature's history,
Simon related many charges of alleged payoffs and political deals.
He concluded by quoting an American Political Science Association
report that "modernization of American state legislatures is considered by many to be the most important piece of unfinished business
in the area of government reorganization." He added, "From my
experience in Illinois and my knowledge of other legislatures, I would
consider that an understatement."4 Needless to say, the reaction to
Simon's article from his fellow legislators was something less than

warm, although it apparently did not hurt Simon four years later (it may have helped) when he was the first person from the opposite political party of the governor to be elected lieutenant governor of Illinois, a position he now holds.

After the Harper's article, a series of publications appeared in various periodicals all with the common theme of how bad legislatures were across the country. Illinois was one of the main targets in another article in the Saturday Evening Post, and again the Illinois legislature was the victim of bad timing. While preparing his 1966 article, "The Octopus in the State House," Trevor Armbrister visited the 1965 legislative session. The opening sentence of his section on Illinois indicates his approach: "In no state do so many of the body sores afflicting state government fester quite so appallingly as they do in Illinois."[5] Armbrister seemed bent, in the best muckraking journalistic approach, on painting the worst possible picture of the Illinois legislature. Unfortunately, it was made easy for him when late in the session an unknown person planted a tape recording machine in the Springfield hotel room of lobbyists for currency exchanges. On the fifteen rolls of tape were devastating statements that legislators had been offered various sums of money for their votes. The tapes containing the names of sixty-one legislators—not all cast in derogatory roles—were published in a Chicago newspaper.

By 1965, the Illinois General Assembly was ready for reform, to paraphrase a Chicago alderman. Most of the efforts discussed were procedural reforms, but certainly reform proponents and legislative leaders were hopeful that the legislative image might be improved. Policy implications were not mentioned except that the reforms might counteract the favored position of special interests.

REAPPORTIONMENT

Before proceeding it might be well to discuss the changes that were occurring in the legislature, mostly as an outgrowth of reapportionment, prior to 1965. It should be pointed out that in Illinois reapportionment and legislative reorganization are closely related and the latter seems to be an outgrowth of the former.

The Illinois Constitution of 1870, still the state's basic document, originally provided for the redistricting of fifty-one congruent House and Senate districts every ten years. However, there was no reapportionment of the legislature from 1901 until 1954 when the voters approved a constitutional amendment changing the method of apportionment. The new article divided the state into three geographical regions: Chicago, Cook County outside of Chicago, and the remaining 101 downstate counties. House districts were to be based on population, while area was to be "the prime consideration" in fashioning Senate districts. In 1955, the general assembly enacted legislation based on the new constitutional provisions for apportionment, which provided for fifty-nine House districts and fifty-eight Senate districts. Reapportionment of the House was called for in 1963 and every ten years thereafter. Senate districts appeared at the time to be permanent.

In our analysis of the reapportioned Illinois General Assembly of 1957, we could find little new. We said that

the expectations of the reapportionment supporters in the 1954 campaign were both general and specific. In general, it was surely anticipated that greater equity in representation would improve the functioning of the democratic system. Equity for its own sake was a real and legitimate objective, and it was stressed. In addition, however, it was assumed that, because the interests of a substantial number of people of the state had been inadequately represented under the old districting system, the new system would result in proposals, attitudes, and opinions that either had not been expressed in the legislature at all or had been previously understated or overstated.[6]

Our findings, summarized, were that

reapportionment of the Illinois legislature, judged by the product of the first session of the "new" General Assembly, created no profound changes. Party organization and committee activity were no less informal after reapportionment than before. The dominant role of the Governor was not affected, nor was the eagerness of most members to be at peace with the press. The old blocs persisted, and a few new ones developed. The test of a legislator's capability as far as his colleagues were concerned continued to be whether or not he could "pass a bill," and this, in turn, depended on whether he did not involve himself in every issue that came to the floor, delivered his vote after having promised it, and did not deliberately misinform his colleagues.

If reapportionment did not shift the power balance, however, and did not change the ways in which the legislature organized itelf, it is obvious that it did produce two kinds of extremist blocs, one with a reform orientation and a second with an intense local orientation.

Half of the small reform group were Cook County suburban Democrats; all of the localists were suburban
Republicans. Aside from these two groups, the new members fused into the formal and informal pattern of the
legislature without disturbing those patterns at all. Indeed, in the Senate, where neither group had active adherents, the addition of seven members made the only
significant difference from the situation as it was before
1957.[7]

The newcomers in 1957 did later seem to have an impact on the
legislature. The reformers among them were able to get their views
and positions across in the press, at least. They probably had an
impact on new laws, but this impact is hardly quantifiable. The product of the legislature, taken as a whole, did not seem to change
greatly—and if it did, it was a result of gubernatorial action, not of
reapportionment.

In 1963, the legislature passed a House reapportionment plan
that was subsequently vetoed by the governor. The state constitution,
in the event of such a deadlock, provides that a special bipartisan
commission made up of ten members chosen by the governor from
lists supplied by the state chairmen of both parties draw a suitable
map. The commission was unable to agree on a map before its four-
month constitutional deadline passed, and in 1964 all House members
were elected at large. Reliance on this device was unexpected as the
specter of an at-large election had been originally envisioned as an
effective catalyst for agreement by either the legislature or the reapportionment commission. Early in 1964 the governor called a
special session of the general assembly to pass the necessary tempo-
rary legislation for an election that was without precedent in Illinois,
or in any other state.*

---

*For the at-large election, state nominating conventions re-
placed the regular party primaries. Each party was limited to 118
nominees, two-thirds of the 177 to be elected, in order to insure a
third of the House seats for the minority if the entire majority slate
were elected. Each party nominated 68 incumbents and 50 new candidates. The orange ballot listing the 118 candidates of each party was
nearly three feet long. All but a small percentage of the orange-
ballot voters marked one party circle or the other, rather than
splitting their tickets and voting for individual candidates. The size
of the Democratic vote that year was large enough to elect all 118
Democratic nominees. The remaining 59 seats went to Republicans
receiving the most votes.

The House produced by the 1964 at-large election differed from its predecessors in three major respects. It had a higher proportion of new members than any House in the previous forty-five years. Since at least 1920, except for one session, new members never comprised more than a third of the House. The exception was the 1957 session, elected after the only reapportionment since 1901, in which 38 percent of members were new. In the three following sessions, 12 to 18 percent were new. In 1965, 42 percent of members served their first terms; twenty-eight of the fifty-nine Republicans were newcomers.

Election at large produced a second difference: an unusually high proportion of seats held by one party—67 percent. In the eight sessions before 1965, the majority held no more than 56 percent of the House seats. In the three sessions prior to the 1964 at-large election, the majority party's advantage was five, one, and three members. In 1965, the advantage was fifty-nine.

Normally, the House majority approximates the proportion of the popular vote received by that party's candidate for governor or, in nongubernatorial election years, for state treasurer. In 1965, although Governor Otto Kerner and the Democratic House slate received about equal shares of the popular vote, the proportion of Democrats in the House far exceeded his popular majority.

In spite of the heavy Democratic majority, members of the House elected at large almost perfectly represented the divisions of population between metropolitan and nonmetropolitan areas, between northern and southern areas of the state outside major cities, and between Cook County and downstate. A shift of only six representatives, four of them from the southern to the northern half of the state, would have given perfect apportionment among these divisions in accordance with their populations. This was the third difference in the 1965 House: the lowest number of malapportioned seats since the early years of the century.

Among the new legislators brought in by the at-large election were a number of so-called blue ribbon members. They were interested in innovation and reform of all branches of government. They profoundly affected the legislature—they shook up the legislative institution. Few major changes of policy resulted, however, primarily because of the majority party division between the two houses—the Senate remained strongly Republican. But that chamber had a new leader, Senator W. Russell Arrington, who also was receptive to reform. One reform he supported was legislative reorganization, and bills providing for legislative self-study committees did not have much difficulty being adopted.

The reapportionment picture was further clouded when the U.S. Supreme Court, in Reynolds v. Sims, ruled that both houses of a state legislature must be apportioned on the basis of population. Applying the "one man, one vote" principle to Illinois, the Court later invalidated the Senate apportionment in Germano v. Kerner and placed the burden of reapportionment of both houses on the shoulders of the 1965 general assembly.

In 1965 the legislature was unable to enact reapportionment legislation for either house. The responsibility for drawing the Senate map shifted to the Illinois Supreme Court. The special bipartisan commission again tried to reapportion the House. This time the commission was successful and agreed upon districts from which House members were to be elected until 1970 census figures became available. The Supreme Court succeeded in drawing a constitutionally valid map from which all fifty-eight senators would be elected in 1966 and 1970. The court made no provision for staggered Senate terms required by the constitution, feeling that such a provision "would unnecessarily encroach upon the legislative domain." Senate elections are usually staggered so that members from odd-numbered districts are elected at one election and those in even-numbered districts are chosen in the succeeding election.

REAPPORTIONMENT OF 1965

With the 1965 prereapportionment legislature and the 1967 post-reapportionment legislature, one had an opportunity to take a first-hand look at the public policy implications of reapportionment. Both periods indicated that one policy change would affect urban legislation. Reformers, after all, had been highly critical of slow-moving, conservative legislatures dominated by rural interests. Thus, if the urban areas were given fair representation, it was expected that they would be more favorably inclined to legislation that would provide solutions to urban problems. To test this proposition, we took a hard look at the urban legislation in 1965 and 1967.[8]

The 1965 prereapportionment legislature was, as mentioned, made up of a House of Representatives elected on an at-large basis and a Senate elected from districts established in 1955 when area was "the prime consideration." The Republicans had control of the Senate but by a much smaller majority than the two-to-one majority by which the Democrats controlled the House.

The 1965 legislature passed many bills that would qualify as urban under almost any definition. A state Office of Economic Opportunity was established, as was a state Department of Business and Economic Development. An expanded Police Training Program was adopted, and an Interstate Air Pollution Compact was approved. The Chicago Transit Authority was granted $7.3 million in payment of school children's transportation, and a compensatory education program for culturally disadvantaged children was approved. A consolidated medical assistance program for the needy was adopted as was a new Consumer Credit Corporation Act to help reduce the number of personal bankruptcies. Also approved were recommendations implementing the master plan of higher education. All of these bills, and there were others, had significant impact on urban areas and also throughout the rest of the state.

No broad-based taxes for urban governments were adopted, although several individual taxes were established or rates raised. The legislature created the usual number of study commissions, and a few of these were instructed to study urban problems. For example, one commission was to study high-speed rail problems, another full-value tax assessment issues, another planning problems of Springfield as the state capital, and another low-cost housing.

The 1965 legislature, like its predecessors, defeated many bills, several of which would meet most of the criteria of urban legislation. The reasons for their defeats are many, and an analysis of the reasons is beyond the scope of this chapter. It should be realized, however, that in few, if any, cases was the reason a clearly antiurban one. Given the divided partisan composition of the legislature, the defeat can usually be traced to a partisan position.

The 1965 legislature devoted much time to civil rights. Most of its legislation, including open occupancy bills, was defeated. Also defeated were some bills that could be considered as attacks on the recently created Fair Employment Practices Commission. A study commission on civil rights legislation was defeated. Little attention was given to a constitutional home rule proposal. Other proposed commission bills would have provided studies of the feasibility of departments of metropolitan affairs, metropolitan area problems, mass transportation, and northeastern Illinois mass transportation. Several proposals for broad tax increases for cities were defeated. Defeated labor legislation included minimum wage proposals. Two urban bills were passed, but both were vetoed by the governor. The first would have exempted smudge pots from air pollution regulations, and the other would have created halfway houses for newly released penitentiary prisoners. In the first case, the veto rather than the passage of the bill can be classified as a pro-urban move.

The 1967 postreapportionment legislature, controlled in both houses by Republicans, was the first elected on a "one man, one vote" basis. The session passed many bills of interest ot urban governments, probably the most notable being the increase in the city tax. This bill, however, was part of the compromise to increase the state sales tax and was not a completely separate measure. Another controversial bill approved provided for gun registration. The general assembly also authorized that $40 million worth of bonds be issued for rebuilding the burned-out McCormick Place in Chicago.

On a statewide level there was a $1 million issue for air and water pollution control—a major proposal subject to approval of the voters. The bond issue had far-reaching implications for urban areas, particularly in regard to air pollution.

Among other bills passed were measures creating the office of municipal budget officer, the office of coordinator of federal and state aid in municipal governments, and a division of local governmental affairs and property taxation, all in the state Department of Revenue. Other measures were approved strengthening the administration of the property tax—a major source of revenue for local governments. An act making municipalities liable for damage occasioned by mob violence was repealed. A general prohibition on residential picketing was adopted. A tax was authorized on hotel rentals in Chicago to promote tourism and conventions. Authorization for two new higher education institutions, one in the Chicago area, the other in Springfield, was given. A special grant of highway money for Cook County government was approved, as was another grant to the Chicago Transit Authority for reimbursement for transportation to school children. And two commissions concerned with urban problems were created— one would study police relations, the other local government generally.

Other new laws set minimum salaries for police and firemen. These bills were usually opposed by city officials as violating the home-rule principle. Henceforth no conscientious objector to military service could be appointed to local police departments. An assault on a fireman executing official duties was made a specific crime. Another law outlawed B-girls from taverns. The state superintendent of public instruction was made the recipient of money for a new urban program. An appropriation of $500,000 was made for a program for disadvantaged children. Also the legislative School Problems Commission received a $10,000 appropriation (reduced from the original request of $50,000) to establish a subcommittee to study specific needs of urban schools.

As in 1965, probably the most important 1967 urban proposal that did not pass was an open occupancy law. Some twenty different measures were introduced, and at the adjourned session reconvening in September, open occupancy was an almost daily controvery. Several tax proposals were offered in addition to the one-quarter-cent sales tax increase finally adopted. Minimum pay bills for workers were again introduced and again defeated. An educational opportunities act directed at high school dropouts was defeated as was a commission to study this subject. Several other study commissions were defeated. These included an urban areas problems commission and a northeastern Illinois mass transit commission. Another commission would have studied the need to rewrite laws that classify on the basis of population.

These, then, are some of the measures considered by the 1965 and 1967 general assemblies. One can look at either session and point to one or more noteworthy new pieces of urban legislation. One is hard put, however, to find a significant difference in the legislative recognition of and approach to urban problems. An impressionistic observation shows no marked difference, and it is doubtful there would be a significant difference if a meaningful quantification of legislation could be developed.

In our pre- and postreapportionment analysis we noted that reapportionment has had little effect on the urban legislative product. This is not to say that the 1967 legislature did not pass some significant measures pertaining to urban Illinois. It did. The general assembly raised the city sales tax, passed a $1 billion air and water pollution bond proposal, and enacted some significant housing legislation. The passage of these measures, however, certainly cannot be traced directly to a legislature composed of members selected on a "one man, one vote" basis. It is a much too simple argument to say that reapportionment was the main factor. Undoubtedly it was a factor, as were many other factors.

Although the measures mentioned were passed in 1967, one could examine measures adopted at other legislative sessions and find significant urban legislation. This was done for 1965 and the results as reported do not vary greatly. In no year, before or after reapportionment, did the legislature enact a sweeping urban program.

This is not surprising because the state's role in solving urban problems has not been settled. Part of the dilemma is caused by the contradictory arguments for more home rule and for more state involvement. The cities cannot consistently argue that they prefer to be left alone to handle their own affairs, and then, on the other hand, argue that they want the state to adopt a far-reaching program to handle housing, education, transportation, or other major urban problems.

The lack of state involvement in urban affairs has come about because no one—state officials, local officials, political parties, or pressure groups—has formulated a program for the legislature to consider. The legislature is only one unit in a larger governmental system, a system that has much rigidity. Several factors militate against the legislature's devising and implementing its own program. Its large size is one factor. Further, the general assembly is equipped and accustomed to reacting to proposals presented to it rather than taking the initiative. The legislative machinery is designed to consider bits and pieces rather than broad-ranging programs. Finally, the general assembly has an active two-party system, and partisanship

has been, and will be, an important consideration in attempts to present solutions to urban problems.
We concluded our analysis:

> Will the General Assembly itself in the future come forward with state solutions to urban problems? If the system proceeds in the future as it has in the past, the answer is probably "no." But if some outside force—city officials, civic organizations, or others—comes up with a well thought through plan, the answer may be "yes." This will be so if they offer their requests through the accepted legislative channels. The state solutions, it must be reiterated, will result from the efforts of the outside forces, not from legislative reapportionment.[9]

REORGANIZATION—THE COOGA COMMISSION

These are our conclusions on the impact of reapportionment in Illinois. It is possible that the situation might be different in another state, but the Illinois experience is probably typical. If reapportionment per se can be said to have had no great impact, can the same be said for its related phenomenon, legislative reorganization? Illinois again affords an instructive case study. One piece of legislation that the 1965 general assembly approved created a commission to study legislative organization and procedures. The commission was a product of the session distinguished by a House elected at large, and undoubtedly its creation was a reaction to the critical articles cited earlier that had given the Illinois General Assembly a bad image.

Surrounded as they were by criticism from both inside and outside the legislature, the members of the 1965 general assembly could not help but be aware of certain deficiencies of their institution. Owing to the constant increase in the number of bills introduced and passed in the general assembly, the end-of-the-session logjam became an ever more serious and universally deplored problem. Even the less progressive members were acutely aware that inadequate consideration was given to bills because of lack of time, and many of them were openly critical of the functioning of the committees.

Several superficial efforts to improve certain aspects of the legislature's operation had been made early in the post-World War II period. The most notable of these was the Jenkins Commission, which was established by the general assembly in 1946. However, this commission, which was composed entirely of legislators, recommended only technical changes in the rules of the House. As late as 1965, it was true that of the three branches of the Illinois state government, only the legislature had not been systematically reorganized. (The executive branch, which had been dominant in Illinois, had been subject to frequent reorganizations.)

One member of the 1965 general assembly who was very much aware of this fact was Harold Katz, a Democratic freshman representative from Glencoe. A lawyer who had served as an aide to Governor Kerner, Katz was well aware of the legislature's shortcomings. During his campaign for election in 1964, Katz had made a strong appeal for legislative reorganization to the voters of Chicago's North Shore area, and had promised to sponsor a bill for a study commission for that purpose.

Katz was one of the "blue ribbon" candidates who served their first terms in the general assembly following the at-large election of 1964. These members were devoted in the cause of good government. Katz found substantial support among his new colleagues for his study commission bill, House Bill 163, which he introduced with the cosponsorship of a very large group of representatives, including a number of other blue ribbon members from the Chicago area.

House Bill 163 called for the establishment of a commission to "study and evaluate the operation and organization of the general assembly, . . . to recommend more efficient uses of manpower and facilities, . . . to study the operation of the legislative service agencies."

Simultaneous with the introduction of House Bill 163, a similar bill was introduced in the Senate by Senator Harris Fawell, a young legislator who had been voted "Outstanding Freshman Senator" in 1963.*

Little opposition to House Bill 163 developed. Bills creating commissions to study various subjects are quite common in the general assembly and are usually adopted. Furthermore, to oppose a measure aimed at improving the legislature was, in the words of the bill's sponsor, "like opposing motherhood." The Katz bill passed both the House and Senate by wide margins, and was signed into law on May 29, 1965, by Governor Kerner, who later vetoed the Fawell bill. The passage of House Bill 163 attracted no great attention, and most Springfield observers expected no more of this new commission than they had previously experienced with numerous other commissions created by the general assembly.

The Katz Commission, as it was quickly labeled, differed from most legislative commissions in that the public members were

---

*Representative Katz won a "Best Legislator Award" from the Independent Voters of Illinois in 1965 and again in 1967.

appointed by the legislative leaders rather than the governor. The Senate members and five of the public members were appointed by the Republican president pro tem of the Senate, W. Russell Arrington, with the appointment of the remaining public members and the five House members left to the Democratic speaker of the House, John Touhy. Both of these legislative officers served as ex officio members of the commission, In keeping with the bipartisan nature of House Bill 163, both Arrington and Touhy were limited to appointing no more than three legislators of their own political party, thus presumably establishing a commission composed of three Republican and two Democratic senators appointed by Arrington, three Democratic and two Republican representatives appointed by Touhy, and the same number of public members chosen by each. Following the Illinois practice, the two house leaders acted on the advice of minority leaders in their minority appointments.

In contrast to other commissions, the caliber of the appointees to the Katz Commission was above average. About half of the legislators appointed were relatively new members of the legislature, having served one or two terms, and most of them had been classified as blue ribbon legislators during their freshman session.

The other legislators on the commission were, for the most part, men who had served at least five terms in the legislature and who held positions of influence in their houses. More by virtue of their long experience in and attachment to the bodies they served than by basic attitudes, these men were professional legislators.

The predominance of legislative leaders in the professional group indicates the importance that Arrington and Touhy accorded the commission. However, as a corollary to high political position, these legislators tended to be more firmly attached to the status quo of the legislative institution, at least in regard to any change that might affect their positions with the institution. Unlike previous legislative commissions, these two ex officio members were active and fully participating members of the commission. Senator Arrington, in particular, was in regular attendance at the commission's meetings and exercised a great deal of influence over the decisions of the commission. The importance of the participation of these two men in the Katz Commission cannot be overemphasized; their concerted support or rejection of the commission's recommendations was enough to determine the action taken by the general assembly.

The public members also tended to fall into two groups. The first group consisted of the academicians, men whose profession was the study of government and who were attached to the political science faculties of universities. All three men in this group had a wide range of experience in studying and dealing with the problems associated with the general assembly and, in a sense, were profesionals in the business of the legislature and state government. The other seven public members appointed to the Katz Commission had a variety of experience, much in the public sector.

The four categories of membership set out above refer only to similarities of experience or contact with the legislature. Although in some cases the behavior of the members reflected these categories, as, for example, in the relative influence of the groups at different stages of the decisionmaking process, in many cases no such pattern was discernible.

In considering the pattern of action taken by the members throughout the commission's work, however, one underlying attitude was evident in almost all of them: This was a genuine desire to improve the operation of the general assembly. Although this attitude was not always the dominant interest of the commission's members, its appearance during the commission's work was frequent enough to render it one of the stronger factors.

The adjournment of the Seventy-fourth Illinois General Assembly in June 1965 and the appointment of the commission's twenty regular members paved the way for the organization of its activities in summer 1965, an unusually early start for a legislative commission. The initial meetings, held in August and October, were devoted to a selection of the problems to be studied and to organizing subcommittees to deal with these areas.

The election of the commission's officers at the first meeting, on August 10, previewed several factors that would be present throughout the commission's work. Katz, having introduced House Bill 163, was a candidate for chairman of the commission. However, Senator Arrington threw his support behind Senator Fawell, who had been to some extent a protégé of Arrington's. Arrington, the ranking Republican on the commission, had shown a personal interest in Fawell's election, and this led to the support by most of the Republican members for Fawell. The Democrats, similarly, formed a bloc supporting Katz. The defection of one of the Republicans put the balance in Katz's favor, and he was elected chairman, while Fawell was named vice-chairman. The interplay of personal and partisan interests, and the formation of blocs behind the party leaders, was repeated often in later commission meetings.

At the first meeting, it was decided to call the body officially the Commission on the Organization of the General Assembly, usually rendered as the COOGA Commission. During its work it was usually referred to as the Katz Commission, both in the press and by many of the people associated with it, although Republicans tended to call it the COOGA Commission.

After he was elected chairman, Katz acted as the commission's principal organizer. By means of a constant flow of letters and memoranda he functioned as the main liaison between the various subcommittees and members when the commission was not meeting and continually pushed the subcommittee chairmen for the completion of their final reports. Katz also arranged for a variety of informational resources to be available to the subcommittees, including reports and memoranda from various agencies and organizations connected with the legisalture. Katz, as a cohesive and motivating force, was largely responsible for the success of the commission. That the commission was something more than the usual mediocre legislative commission was attributed, by several members, to the fact that "Harold Katz worked like hell."

Although Katz tended to dominate the commission's organization outside the meetings, this was not true in the meetings themselves. The first organizational meetings were characterized by a loose consensus on action to be taken, with most members' suggestions for preliminary work accepted with little opposition.

From the very first it was evident that most of the members had strong opinions concerning the problems of the legislature that should be studied. Among the most commonly mentioned problems were the lack of facilities and staff assistance, the functioning of the committee system, the appropriations process, the end of session logjam, and annual sessions for the legislature. So far as concerned commission procedure, it was proposed by Katz at the first meeting that the commission hold public hearings to obtain ideas from legislators and other interested persons, and that it prepare a questionnaire to be circulated to all members of the general assembly.

At the September 24 meeting of the officers and academicians who comprised the Research Committee, seven topics for study were decided upon. The inquiry of the commission had already begun to crystallize around certain subjects, such as committee effectiveness, staff assistance, facilities, and the budgetary process.

At the second meeting of the full commission, held on October 13, the topics outlined by the Research Committee were unanimously approved and arrangements were made for the organization of subcommittees to study them. In the following months the subcommittees were established, and Katz outlined a tentative schedule for their operation. The work of the commission was to cover two stages. In the first stage the subcommittees would study the subjects assigned to them and prepare a tentative list of recommendations. This was to be accomplished in the first three months of 1966, so the recommendations might be used as trial balloons in a discussion for the University of Illinois Institute of Government and Public Affairs' annual assembly on March 31, which was to be devoted to legislative reorganization. After the university conference, the subcommittees were to prepare their final list of recommendations, which were to

117

be presented as their final reports in the late spring and summer of 1966. In the second stage, the subcommittee reports were to be considered by the full commission and, upon being given approval, would be combined in the commission's final report, which was to be prepared in the fall of 1966.

With the leading students of the legislature serving as chairmen of or consultants to subcommittees, commission members had available all data that could possibly be of any use. However, the types of reports the subcommittees produced were determined, not so much by the quantity of information available to them, as by the attitudes that members had toward their task. When the subcommittees were first formed, the attitudes of the commission members could be loosely correlated to the previously cited four groupings—blue ribbon legislator, professional legislator, academician, and public member. In general, the blue ribbon group of legislators showed special concern for revitalizing the legislature and tended to think of the commission's report as a target document of recommendations that would constitute a comprehensive program to be implemented by the general assembly. One member of this group talked of the commission's report as a statement of "what ought to be."

The professionals, on the other hand, tended to conceive of the commission's task as that of determining solutions to individual problems. Hence, from the outset, Representative Elward and Senator McGloon, both Chicago Democrats, began discussions on specific problems of committee functioning. Another attitude found among the professionals, from Senator Arrington in particular, was a desire to limit the report's recommendations to immediately realizable goals. Having had a greater amount of contact with legislative politics, the professionals tended to take a more individual and immediate stance toward the individual problems they had encountered in the legislature. Similarly, the academicians seemed to have a more individual orientation toward the problems of the general assembly, partially because their experience with it had been concentrated in narrow fields. The predominant concept held by the academicians on the commission was epitomized by a remark, "This is really a commission on the efficiency of the general assembly, not on its organization."

The remaining public members, having had less experience with the legislative process and with the legislature's problems, did not share the attitude of the progessional legislators or the academicians. They tended to be neutral and subject to opinions of the other groups.

The commission's approach to its task was necessarily tied to the members' conception of the goal, or overall purposes, of the commission. At no time, however, was a definite statement of the commission's goals forthcoming, nor was such a statement ever discussed. The commission members took it for granted that they knew

118

what the commission was working for. Hence, the goal of the commission's report was the sum total of the goals and interests of its most influential members.

One of the most important determinants of the nature of the commission's report was the members' conception of the political framework within which the commission was functioning and to which its efforts were directed. Each member of the commission was aware of certain limits on political change in the legislative institution, which were enforced by the personal or partisan interests of the legislators; beyond these limits, change in the legislature would be thwarted. All of the commission members, with perhaps one exception, were aware that these limits existed and felt it was useless to recommend solutions to the legislature's problems that lay beyond these limits. Therefore, one of the concerns throughout the decision-making process was to present a report that would be acceptable to the general assembly. An attitude stated often was, "We don't want to produce an ideal blueprint for a utopian legislature that will be thrown in a filing cabinet to gather dust." Because this was a common attitude, the factor determining the nature of the recommendations was how narrowly (or widely) the members conceived the practical political limits to be drawn, and how far within these limits they were willing to act.

A final attitude that was common early in the organization period was expressed by one member at the first meeting: "We already know what the problems are; we want to find the solutions." Considering the experience that most of the commission members had had in the general assembly, it would be impossible to conceive of the Katz Commission as a group of objective researchers eagerly searching for the defects of the legislature. By and large, the commission members knew what the problems were. Indeed, they should have, because the underlying principle on which the Katz Commission functioned was the assumption that there was a "better way of doing things" in the legislature. In fact, many of the commission members, particularly the academicians and the legislators, knew what some of the solutions were and were quite willing to advocate them.

In certain areas of the commission's investigation, then, the process was one of deciding which of the various solutions offered was best suited to the problem, and in what specific form.

The subcommittees proceeded with their work. The commission participated in a University of Illinois conference on state legislature reorganization and then worked as a full commission to develop its report and recommendations.[10] The report—and the commission itself—was well received by the press. To differentiate the report from those of other commissions, Chairman Katz arranged to have it published by the University of Illinois Press.

Improving the State Legislature, the report of the commission, was divided into six chapters: the constitution and the legislature, legislative procedures and techniques, modernizing legislative publications, realizing the potential of committees and commissions, improved tools for an improved legislature, and the appropriation process. Essentially the chapter topics followed the subcommittee structure. There were eighty-seven specific recommendations; some required constitutional change, some statutory change, some rules changes, and others leadership action.

It is difficult to summarize the recommendations. They ranged from important constitutional changes for annual sessions to providing the legislators with access to state telephone service providing toll-free calls to or from the Capitol building.

The commission did not enter some subjects that the members felt were outside its jurisdiction and could better be left to other study commissions. These included conflicts of interest and lobby regulation, and such controversial constitutional questions as reapportionment, unicameralism, the size of the legislature, and Illinois's unique cumulative voting method of selecting House members. One public member sharply dissented from omitting these constitutional questions because he considered them essential if the legislative institution in Illinois was to be reformed. According to the chairman, however, his dissent was filed too late and was not included in the report. The report was essentially unanimous, and there were only three specific dissents included in the final published version.

The commission report contained one fundamental philosophical position: that the concept of the citizen-legislator should be continued. The preface to the report said:

> The predominant view among the members of the Commission strongly favors the retention of the concept of the citizen-legislator in Illinois rather than that of the full-time professional legislator. Unless the part-time concept is retained, many of the very ablest legislators will find themselves unable or unwilling to serve. . . .
> Through our recommendations, we have tried to make service in the legislature more attractive—by making the legislative process a more rational one, by providing legislators with reasonable facilities such as offices, secretarial services, and professional assistance, and by proposing reimbursement for the unreimbursed expenses of legislators. Even though there are greater demands on the time of the members of the legislature than ever before, we are persuaded that men of quality can be attracted to serve in the

legislature and that such a legislative body in Illinois can, on a part-time basis, meet the constitutional demands upon the legislature. But this goal can only be attained if serious consideration is given to the task of reorganization and modernization of the General Assembly.[11]

We next turn to the legislative reaction to the Katz Commission's recommendations.

THE LEGISLATIVE REACTION

The commission's report was distributed to the legislature at the beginning of the 1967 session. The Republicans had regained control of the House, and the new speaker had not been involved with the commission. He was not, however, antagonistic.

No organized program of implementing the report was established; rather, coordination of efforts by the legislators was achieved through informal meetings with Katz and through one full commission meeting held on February 7, 1967. Nor was any attempt made to have the commission report as a whole considered by the general assembly. Instead, action was taken on individual recommendations according to the priorities established by members of the Katz Commission and determined by the political situation in the legislature during the session. Some changes, such as the recommendation that each legislator be given a private office, were postponed simply because practical circumstances (in this case the lack of available office space in the Capitol) would not permit their implementation.

The process of implementing the recommendations was accomplished either by the introduction of bills and constitutional amendments, or by having recommendations incorporated in the rules that the houses adopted for the session.

Bills incorporating various recommendations were introduced by commission members and other legislators at various times throughout the session. At the beginning, recommendations for annual sessions, committee staffing, and rules changes were presented to the legislature. Later, Katz and Fawell introduced a series of bills on electronic voting in the Senate, modification of bill size, and other, mostly noncontroversial, measures. Katz and Elward introduced bills changing the function of the Budgetary Commission in line with the concept of an executive budget.

A number of major issues faced the 1967 session of the general assembly, and this factor affected implementation of the Katz Commission recommendations. Action on the Katz report was definitely subordinate to the legislators' concern for Chicago revenue, open housing, gun control, and a host of other questions. Thus, there were limits to the amount of legislative improvement that could be accomplished in the session. Despite this, however, a considerable amount of attention was paid the report, and occasionally legislators quoted from it (Republicans referring to it as the COOGA Commission, Democrats as the Katz Commission) while making some unrelated point.

The fate of the recommendations that were considered initially by the legislature brought to light factors that would act upon all the recommendations introduced in the general assembly that session. This first group included reduction in the number of committees, annual sessions, and committee staffing—three measures that most of the commission members considered the "heart of the report."

As a result of a series of compromises, the commission report recommended committee reduction and consolidation leading to ten legislative committees in the House and twelve in the Senate. It was assumed that the majority leadership in each house would support this provision. However, the elections of 1966 changed the situation significantly, and there is some justification for saying that the fate of committee reduction in the House was decided on November 6. In the contest for speaker of the House, the winner had promised a rather large number of committee chairmanships to his supporters. Therefore, after his election it was impossible for him to acquiesce to large-scale committee reduction. Another factor that prevented the implementation of committee reduction in the House was the lack of political power held by those commission members in the majority party. Thus, what had begun as an ambitious program of committee reduction in the Katz Commission ended without change in the number of House committees from the previous session.

Committee reduction fared no better in the Senate. The Senate caucus agreed to a consolidation resulting in a total of fourteen legislative committees, a nominal reduction of four committees from the previous session. However, the reduction was more apparent than real. When the full commission had originally debated the commission reduction plans, Senator Arrington remarked that large-scale committee reduction would never win legislative approval unless subcommittees were created and their chairmen were assured the status of congressional subcommittee chairmen. Arrington's prophecy was fulfilled, and it seems likely that his acceptance of the twelve-committee plan for the Senate was based on an understanding that subcommittees would be established. What happened was this: the fourteen legislative committees that were adopted by the Senate caucus included three committees with subcommittees (called "divisions") attached to them. There were seven of these divisions altogether.

Soon after the session was under way, it became apparent that these divisions were actually functioning as full legislative committees, and that the division chairmen did, indeed, enjoy the status of congressional subcommittee chairmen. Moreover, the divisions did not report through their parent committees, as did their congressional counterparts. Thus, from eighteen legislative committees in the 1965 session, the Senate had progressed in 1967 to what were, in practice, twenty-one legislative committees.

Senator Arrington's reference to the subcommittees in Congress was extremely apt, as the proliferation of subcommittees in the general assembly was exactly analogous to the establishment of subcommittees in Congress following the committee reduction of the legislative reorganization of 1946. The proliferation of subcommittees came as no surprise to one legislator, who stated that it was "in the nature of the beast."

As with committee reduction, the fate of annual sessions was influenced by factors outside the legislature proper. In this case, the factor was the coalescing of support for a constitutional convention (con-con) that followed the elections of 1966, partially as a result of the defeat of the revenue article. Much of the rationale for con-con was based on the supposition that piecemeal amending of the document would not work. Thus, after Governor Kerner threw his support behind a resolution for a convention, the annual sessions amendment took a subordinate position to con-con. Many of the legislators felt that the amendment would be unnecessary if the convention were called, since annual sessions could be implemented by recessing rather than adjourning the legislature, as was actually done in 1969.

Of the three recommendations, committee staffing was the newest idea to the general assembly. The original plan had been to provide each legislative committee with staff; however, with the failure of committee reduction this became impractical. The staffing bill introduced by Arrington on January 24, 1967, Senate Bill 181, called for the employment of ten staff members for each house with the important provision for equal majority and minority appointments. Owing to vigorous support by Arrington, the bill passed the Senate in eight days and was sent to the House on February 1. After reaching the House, however, Senate Bill 181 was delayed, owing largely to the opposition of the Republican floor leader.

On April 6, Senate Bill 181 passed the House and was sent to the governor who approved it. Considerable difficulty was encountered in retaining competent staff, however, and although at the beginning of the year a committee chairman expressed the hope that staffing might be an accomplished fact by March 1, the attitude expressed by Senator Arrington in April was, "well, these things take time. . . ."

Along with staffing, provision was made for reimbursing legislators for limited secretarial and research assistance in their district
offices—an important development. Most of the bills pertaining to
legislative printing were readily approved as noncontroversial. The
more controversial bills for Senate electronic voting and changes in
the powers of the Budgetary Commission were defeated.

Aside from these bills and bills on annual sessions, committee
staffing, and committee reduction, most of the successes or failures
of the Katz Commission involved suggested changes in legislative
rules. In both houses, commission members succeeded in having
adopted a legislative deadline schedule whereby no bills could be
introduced after May 1. There was widespread support for this measure, probably because of a desire to avoid the universally deplored
end-of-session logjam. It has effected some change, although decisions on important matters are still postponed until the last minute.
One study has shown that in the 1969 session the new schedule has
merely advanced the logjam to May 1. A number of recommendations
supported by Katz and other commission members were incorporated
in the House rules. Several altered the process for constitutional
amendments. Six procedural recommendations became House rules,
including elimination of proxy voting, automatic tabling of bills not
heard in sixty days, and seven days' notice for committee hearings.
No such support materialized in the Senate, however, and none of
these recommendations was adopted.

In addition to rules and statutory changes, several technical
changes recommended were quickly implemented.*

Not all reaction to COOGA recommendations was favorable.
One example is the recommendation that the Legislative Reference
Bureau be directed by statute to undertake planning for the adoption
of an official code of laws and for its continuous revision as to form.
The legislature responded by adopting a resolution directing the
bureau to study the session. The bureau staff, which was neither
close to nor enthusiastic about the commission's work, undertook a

---

*A bill continuing the life of the commission for two more years
to follow up on the COOGA recommendations was approved by the 1967
general assembly. Katz was reelected, but it was understood that
the commission was to function as a watchdog. The funding of the
commission was to come from outside grants that the commission
was specifically authorized to accept. In 1969, another bill to extend
the commission was vetoed by the new governor. He thought the
constitutional convention could handle the commission's assignments.
In 1970, however, he approved a similar bill. Katz was again elected
chairman.

study concluding that the development of a code was not feasible because of lack of interest on the part of the bar association. (The bureau staff is composed of lawyers and works closely with the organized bar.) In its report, directed by a 1967 resolution, the bureau concluded:

> The only expression of a need for the adoption of an official revision or codification of the Illinois statutes that has been noted is that of the Commission on the Organization of the General Assembly. The widespread use and acceptance of the Illinois Revised Statutes had been indicated, and the problems of adoption of an official compilation, including a proposal using the Illinois Revised Statutes as the base, have been discussed in this report. Finally, it should be observed that there has been no formal or substantial expression from the bar associations, attorneys, judges or legislators that the present system of setting out the Illinois statutes should be revamped. It is strongly recommended that no change to an official compilation of Illinois statutes should be undertaken unless in response to the demands of a substantial representation of the bench and bar.[12]

This rather clearly indicates that the legislative establishment was not wholeheartedly behind the COOGA report, although on most matters the leadership supported the recommendations. Some agencies looked for direction to their clientele outside the legislature, rather than to a report written without their participation.

Like the legislators who were members of the commission, the leadership of the general assembly shared an underlying concern for the improvement of the legislature. All too often, however, the legislators' interests—like those of the commission members—kept them from approving recommendations that would have been ultimately beneficial to the general assembly. Usually the leaders accepted only changes that did not conflict with any party or group interest; even this, however, could not be said about much of the rank and file of the general assembly.

Were the 1967 and 1969 legislatures noticeably different because of the adoption of the COOGA recommendations? Not markedly. The legislature still has to fight last-minute logjams although some improvement has been made. The legislature continued to expand its staff, and this may very well produce a more pronounced impact in the future. It could well mean that the legislature will play a more positive role in budgetary review and in overview of state agencies and programs. In recent sessions the legislature has experimented with devices such as consent calendars, which may mean less attention need be spent on legislation deemed noncontroversial.

Although the Commission on the Organization of the General Assembly supported the concept of the citizen-legislator, Illinois is surely moving toward full-time professional legislators. The time demands on legislators for legislative business has increased markedly over previous sessions. In recess periods, members spent much time on commission business, as in the past, and now standing committees are beginning to function in recess periods, a new development. The practice of recessing from time to time, rather than adjourning on June 30 of the odd-numbered year, has been met with mixed feelings. After a two-week session in July 1968, a veteran lobbyist, Joseph Meek, was quoted in an Illinois Legislative Council study as saying: "After nearly 40 years of observing the Legislature, I can say with malice toward none, that it is at its lowest performance in history. Visiting the Legislature used to be fun. Now it's startling, a bit scary." It was frightening to Mr. Meek because of the "hasty action on hundreds of bills." While others were less critical of the recessed sessions, according to the Legislative Council, the typical feeling among members was displeasure at being drawn from their normal livelihoods.

The Illinois State Chamber of Commerce was also critical of the recessed session.[13] In a publication of that organization, the attorney general, then a candidate for U.S. senator, is quoted as saying that the general assembly "passed bills at this last session with such great speed that the printers couldn't even get the House and Senate Journals (the official proceedings) printed." Asked to give an opinion on the constitutionality of some newly passed legislation, the attorney general stated:

> The bill is constitutional, subject, however to the following conditions. We have not had access to any Legislative Digest, Journals or synopsis, and, therefore, cannot say whether or not the bill was read three different days in each house nor whether there were amendments made to the bill which were germane and, if the bill was amended, we are not aware as to whether or not it was read three different days in each house.
>
> We are not aware that another bill may or may not have been passed at this session of the General Assembly amending the same statute, and if so, whether such amendments are constitutional, harmonious, inconsistent or repugnant. Neither are we aware of the fact, if it is a fact, that the bill received the necessary two-thirds vote in the Senate and in the House.[14]

One action of the recessed session was a unanimous vote of the House requesting the Commission on the Organization of the General Assembly to study the problems and procedures of extended sessions. Because of some problems, primarily political, this was never done.

The reason for focusing on the 1968 special session is to suggest that there have been problems in legislative reorganization in Illinois, despite the adoption of many COOGA recommendations. This brings up the question of whether the Illinois General Assembly can be accurately described as a reorganized legislative body. Most would agree that the legislature is a changing body, but arguments can be heard on whether it has been truly reorganized.

OTHER FACTORS EFFECTING CHANGE

As has been suggested several times earlier, the Illinois General Assembly is a changing body. In recent years changes have been many. One of the most significant has been legislative reapportionment. Other changes have altered procedures and attitudes, and still others have affected the personnel serving in the legislature. Implementation of the recommendations of the Commission on the Organization of the General Assembly contributed to only one part of the changes, those affecting procedure. In fact, it can well be argued that the establishment of the Commission was a result, not a cause, of the changing legislature.

One significant factor in the changing legislature was the ascendancy of Senator Arrington to a leadership role. Possessed of a strong and aggressive personality, he was devoted to strengthening the legislative branch and the role of political parties within the legislature. Before becoming Senate president pro tem, he had been one of the two moving forces in establishing the legislative staff intern program, a program originally funded jointly by the Ford Foundation and the legislature, and now supported entirely by state appropriations. Many persons have felt that because it showed the value of legislative professional staff where staff had previously been nonexistent, this program really started the legislative reorganization movement. When he became a leader, Arrington pushed to develop a permanent legislative staff, which was in accord with COOGA recommendations.

Another way in which Arrington helped change the legislative pattern was his insistence on longer legislative sessions. He was willing to spend as much time as needed on legislative pursuits, and he expected other legislators to be willing to do the same. At the conclusion of the 1967 regular session, he broke precedent by having the legislature recess from time to time in order to be available initially to review vetoes, and then to attend to other necessary matters. Ironically, the only veto overridden was on January 8, 1969; it permitted the legislators a salary increase.* This action was taken in the morning, before the new legislature convened at noon.

The 1969 legislature did not adjourn <u>sine die</u> on June 30, as had been the custom prior to 1967, but recessed from time to time. The recess until March 31, 1970 (the House until April 1) was to establish annual budget sessions, a move in accord with a COOGA recommendation. Despite the recess to a specific date, it was necessary for the governor to call a special session to permit the legislature to reconsider aid to local transportation districts, a matter unresolved at the time of recess. The new timetable had not, obviously, made it possible for the legislature to solve all the state's problems.

This change in the timing of sessions is only one of many changes brought about primarily by Senator Arrington, although he obviously had to have the cooperation, albeit reluctant, of other legislative forces.

Senator Arrington also became very active in the various national legislative organizations, something no previous leader had taken seriously.† He made the Illinois legislature more visible on the national legislative scene.

In probably his most important accomplishment, Arrington undertook to strengthen the role of the Republican party in the legislature. He, with the consent of the Republican speakers, developed Republican legislative programs. He helped his fellow Republican senators in their campaigns with funds and technical assistance. The natural Democratic reaction to these developments was to strengthen their own operations to counteract the Republican moves.

At the conclusion of the 1969 regular session, his fellow senators said of Arrington:

> Few legislators in the history of Illinois have done as
> much as this man to restore energy and purpose to
> state government. . . . His reputation as an innovator,
> and his devotion to improving the legislative process
> have brought honor to each member of this body. . . .
> The boldness of his leadership has always been charac-
> terized by a deep concern for the welfare of every part
> of Illinois. . . .[15]

---

*This was only the fourth veto overridden since the adoption of the present constitution in 1870.

†Arrington's predecessor, President pro tem Arthur Bidwill, had been a founder of the National Conference of State Legislative Leaders, but he had been neither as aggressive nor active as Arrington and had not participated in other legislative organizations.

On the whole, the impact of Senator Arrington as a legislative leader can not be underestimated, and a case can be made that his ascendency to a leadership position was more important in changing the legislature than the report and recommendations of any study commission. Had Senator Arrington not sympathized with the purposes of the COOGA Commission, he could have stopped the commission's efforts at any point.

Another very recent outside development that contributed to changing the legislature was the election of an aggressive governor in 1969. Richard Ogilvie had a wide-ranging program for state reform. He was a strong executive and this, of course, had ramifications for the legislative branch. He believed in a truly executive budget and actually withheld budget information prior to the release of his budget, thus cutting into the functioning of the legislature's budgetary Commission—a commission that had historically included the power structure of the legislature. By law the commission was to receive agency requests before the governor presented his budget and, in fact, by law was to make recommendations to him. This they could not do in 1970 because the usual fiscal information was withheld.

There were other ways the forceful new governor disrupted the accepted legislative-executive relations. These included the effective use of his veto power, such as the one making the pensions laws commission solely a legislative body. He was willing to veto "strong legislature" bills such as the one continuing the COOGA for another year. He did not, however, veto bills providing more staff for the legislature. By introducing a one-year budget when he took office in 1969, he effectively forced annual legislative sessions.

The point in mentioning the governor in a discussion of legislative reorganization is that he can indeed become a force for the legislature to contend with. If he is aggressive, as was Governor Ogilvie, he can be important and not necessarily in a "negative" way. Thus, we still have to remember that the legislature is only one part of a bigger picture, albeit an important part.

In addition to new legislative leadership, a more aggressive executive, and changes in the role of parties, there are other factors not originating with the COOGA report which contributed to legislative change. For example, as an outgrowth of the 1965 session, the session that established the COOGA Commission, the Sixth Illinois Constitutional Convention was convened in 1969. The 1965 reform-minded session created a Constitution Study Commission, which in turn recommended that a convention be called, a recommendation approved by the general assembly and then by the state's electorate. The convention thoroughly reviewed the legislative provisions of the constitution and placed before the voters a greatly revised legislative article, and related articles, that will provide for many procedural changes (many in accord with COOGA recommendations) and will broaden the substantive powers of the legislature. Even if the proposed constitution is defeated, many of its suggestions may well be adopted later by the legislature in constitutional amendments.

While the COOGA and the Constitutional Study commissions were sitting in 1965 and 1967, other related commissions were busy at work. For example, one commission devoted itself to conflict-of-interest legislation, legislation that was eventually adopted. Another commission examined the space needs of the legislature, a problem that must be rectified if the Illinois legislature is to have facilities resembling those of Congress or such states as California. After five years of study, the problems have not been resolved. The long-awaited separate legislative building has not been started, and for the time being the legislature must be content with additional space allotted in the state capitol building. A Joint Committee on Legislative Information Systems was created by resolution in 1969. Already it has an experimental computer project under way and hopefully will have the record-keeping procedures computerized for the 1971 legislative session.

These developments demonstrate the existence of a climate of change in the Illinois General Assembly. Change is not automatically rejected, as it would have been in the past. Furthermore, change and suggestions for change are not the province of any one individual or any one commission; there are many participants.

What impact do these numerous changes appear to have had on the legislature? To the long-time observer, the level of floor debate seems to have improved. It is quite obvious that the members are working harder and longer and taking their jobs more seriously. One hears fewer remarks on the floor and in the committees to the effect that "we should find out how the governor stands on this." There is more concern for the legislative image and the legislature as an institution. Many agencies of state government have become more aware of legislative scrutiny, which means the strategy in the old legislative game for the executive agencies has been changed. Lobbyists also have found that the rules are different. One lobbyist nicely put it: "There are some legislative questions upon which facts are important, there are others upon which all the facts in the world wouldn't make the slightest difference—but the area in which facts are important is getting bigger all the time." A more negative opinion came from a legislative staff person who said real decisions are still made outside the legislature, and there is not much legislators can do until they really become involved in the decisionmaking process.

POLICY IMPLICATIONS

We now turn to the main question: What are the policy implications of legislative reorganization? To write meaningfully about
policy implications and policy outputs of a legislative body is difficult,
especially in a state as complex as Illinois. Illinois is sharply divided
both geographically and politically, and this division obviously affects
the legislature.

It would be helpful if there were some method of quantifying
the results so that greater precision in measuring the legislative
product could be achieved. It is possible, however, to make a qualita-
tive evaluation of the legislative product, and this will be done. In
our earlier attempt at a quantitative analysis of the legislative product
before and after reapportionment, we faced the problem of identifying
urban bills. Even if the bills could be so identified, a count of bills
in the Illinois legislature is rather meaningless. If one could say that
in 1965 so many urban bills passed, and in 1967 so many more passed,
this would not necessarily be a very significant statement. For one
thing, important bills are combined with relatively unimportant ones.
And because of the peculiarities of the legislative process in Illinois,
the number of bills is articifially inflated. Often in Illinois one bill
can establish a new program, while another new program might require
twenty bills. Frequently, the bills that were prepared but were not
introduced because of an unfavorable climate may be more significant
than those introduced and defeated. Finally, looking at an amended
bill as finally adopted may actually confuse the question of whether
a bill was passed or defeated. Often the public policy decisions made
at the amendment stage are more significant than final action on the
bill.

Despite these difficulties, we decided to compare the products
of the 1967 and 1969 legislative sessions in the same way that we had
earlier compared the 1965 and 1967 sessions. We felt that if there
had been significant policy changes from the reorganization efforts
of the 1967 session they should begin to become visible by 1969. We
picked the same type of legislation—urban—because cities are the
most pressing problem facing state governments and state legislatures today.

The 1969 session was a productive one, but any difference in
the urban output owed more to the new governor than to a reorganized
legislature, if indeed the adjective can be applied with any accuracy
to the 1969 general assembly. The 1969 legislature, for example,
created a new Department of Local Government Affairs. Although
this agency may well have an effect on urban affairs, its origin was
not in the legislature but in a campaign promise of the governor.
Another innovation was the block grants to local governments from

the state's new income tax. Again, this was the recommendation of the governor.

There were some other significant pieces of legislation adopted in the 1969 session. These included a new, free school lunch program and the establishment of a Commission on Urban Education. The state's housing agency was significantly reorganized, and air-pollution legislation for both state and local governments was strengthened. Significant new local housing and public assistance legislation was adopted. Failing were a rental assistance program, unlimited business regulation powers for municipalities, and statutory municipal home rule. And once again fair housing legislation failed. The other usual urban "housekeeping" bills were introduced, such as bills on tax rates and municipal civil service, and these met with the usual response, some becoming law, others failing.

The results of our comparison of subsequent sessions of the general assembly with earlier ones are not startling. There was in fact no significant change in the urban product of the 1969 legislature that would greatly differentiate it from the 1967 session or any of its earlier predecessors. And certainly what significant new legislation was adopted can not be credited to the work of the Commission on the Organization of the General Assembly.

CONCLUSION

Legislative reorganization is not a fixed, orderly process set in motion by a body established for that purpose. In fact, as we have seen, reform is brought about in a haphazard, piecemeal fashion, and many forces at work in and out of the legislature—an aggressive governor or legislative leader—may bring about change. The fate of recommendations by COOGA, which was set up specifically to reform the Illinois General Assembly, was affected by these forces. Various COOGA recommendations that were introduced passed or failed according to the mood of the legislature, the presence or absence of leadership support, and a multitude of other factors.

To date, legislative reorganization (or more properly, legislative change) has not had an identifiable impact on policy in Illinois. Whether this situation will hold true in the future is unclear, but in any event it will be difficult to establish a clear cause and effect relationship. Those changes recommended by the Commission on the Organization of the General Assembly that may have the best chance of influencing policy are the move to annual sessions and the development of adequate professional staff. The latter has the greater potential, as is substantiated by the literature on legislative staffing.

The creation of COOGA and the commission's report were never intended to change public policy, although this may have been implied because the commission members were generally liberals and reformers. The discussion in the commission and discussion about the report in the legislature revolved around the subject of efficiency and economy. It was argued that there were justifiable ends in themselves, an assertion that is hard to challenge.

There are many reasons why the road to legislative reform is long and difficult. Some have been mentioned earlier—the large size of the general assembly, its resistance to change, the existence of partisanship. Another part of the legislative system is the pressure groups. Despite reorganization, these groups will remain present, and they can learn to deal with new procedures and organizations. They will make their views and positions known, as is certainly proper in a representative system. Where the committee system is significantly restructured, the lobbyists will still strive to place their friends on "their committee." In time, it may be that some groups, now powerless, will become influential, and vice versa. These things may happen and may be encouraged by reorganization, but, in the future as in the past, it will be difficult to identify clearly the cause.

If legislative reorganization and legislative reapportionment have not caused significant policy change, then it might be asked what will. The answer seems to be people. Thus, if an imaginative staff is recruited and encouraged to participate and develop new programs, this could work important changes. More influential still are the people who will sit in the legislature in the future. If the legislature is made more attractive through legislative reorganization and improved facilities, as recommended by the Commission on the Organization of the General Assembly, then new legislators committed to change might be drawn into service.

We will very likely witness a gradual shift from the citizen-legislator advocated by the COOGA Commission to a professional, full-time legislator. This seems an inevitable result of the increased demands on government at the state level. What effect it will have on the legislature's receptiveness to change and innovation can only be conjectured at this point.

Lastly, in regard to people, the type of leadership that arises in the legislature is crucial to change in public policy. Strong commitment to change on the part of the legislative leadership is essential for the possibility of public policy change.

NOTES

1. Illinois Commission on the Organization of the General Assembly, Improving the State Legislature (Urbana: University of Illinois Press, 1967), p. viii.

2. Illinois State Register, December 12, 1840, quoted in Paul Simon, Lincoln's Preparation for Greatness: The Illinois Legislative Years (Norman: University of Oklahoma Press, 1965), p. 229.

3. John Bartlow Martin, "What Those Politicians Do to You!" Saturday Evening Post, December 12, 1953, p. 20.

4. Paul Simon, "The Illinois Legislature: A Study in Corruption," Harper's Magazine, September 1964, p. 78.

5. Trevor Armbrister, "The Octopus in the State House," Saturday Evening Post, February 12, 1966, p. 76.

6. Gilbert Y. Steiner and Samuel K. Gove, Legislative Politics in Illinois (Urbana: University of Illinois Press, 1960), p. 118.

7. Ibid., pp. 132-33.

8. There are serious difficulties in trying to determine what is urban legislation.

> For [some] urban legislation [means] broad, sweeping measures that would solve the social, economic, and physical problems of the cities. For others, there are other definitions. City officials, if asked about urban legislation, probably would talk about money and the declining tax base because of economic decline. Planners would talk about the less newsworthy legislation affecting zoning, planning, and annexation. Newspapers are apt to get as exercised about gun control legislation "to make our streets safe," as any other matter. They might also direct much attention to newsworthy measures to control air and water pollution. . . . From the perspective of the governmental official in the urban areas, money is the overriding consideration. The local official is looking to the state for money in the form of grants, or at least revenue sources.

Samuel K. Gove, Reapportionment and the Cities: The Impact of Reapportionment on Urban Legislation in Illinois (Chicago: Center for Research in Urban Government, Loyola University, 1968), p. 13.

9. Ibid., p. 34.

10. The procedures used by the commission are well analyzed in Stephen Moeller's "The Katz Commission: A Study of Legislative Reorganization," (honor's thesis, University of Illinois Department of Political Science, 1967). The present author has relied much on

this work to refresh his memory, as a commission member, on the commission's procedures.

11. Improving the State Legislature, pp. x-xi.

12. Illinois, Legislative Reference Bureau, "The Revision, Codification and Official Publication of Illinois Statutes" (Springfield, n.d.), p. 22.

13. On the status of legislative reform, however, the state Chamber of Commerce concluded in September 1968 that "the need for streamlining Illinois' legislative process is vitally important to cope with the present and future needs of the state." Illinois State Chamber of Commerce, Springfield Scene, No. 31, September 18, 1968, p. 2.

14. Ibid., p. 1.

15. Senate Resolution No. 145, adopted June 30, 1969.

4

THE IMPACT OF REAPPORTIONMENT ON THE WASHINGTON HOUSE OF REPRESENTATIVES

James J. Best

Legislative apportionment became an increasingly salient concern for political scientists during the past fifteen years. Much of the research and writing in the period prior to Baker v. Carr focused on the causes of legislative malapportionment and its impact on state legislative policymaking.[1] Malapportionment was regarded as a deliberate attempt by rural interests to underrepresent urban residents by legal or constitutional means, using the rationale that "a balancing of interests was required for good government: a balance of rural against urban, of virtue against unprincipled power, of the minority against the majority."[2] Faced with the threat of economic dominance by rapidly growing urban centers, the small towns and cities of the United States looked to the state legislature for protection from political dominance as well. Many state constitutions provided protection for rural interests by basing representation in at least one house of the legislature on something other than population, preferably geography. Finding that some state constitutions required that representation in both houses be based on population, legislatures moved to change the base of representation in one house or neglected to reapportion after dicennial censuses, thus permanently and effectively locking representation patterns into a rural base. As farm populations decreased, they nevertheless retained their representation in the state legislature.

Malapportionment did more than give political protection to rural areas. Because legislative districts in many states serve as the basis for party organization, malapportionment conferred advantages on rural leaders within each party; rural leaders, because they

The author would like to express his appreciation to Susan Campbell, Fred Maerkle, Peter Dott, and Muhammed Saleh for their assistance in collecting much of the data for this study.

had the votes within county and state committees, could exercise disproportionate power with the party and, equally important, control who advanced where, at what speed, within the party. Party platform gave corresponding emphasis to rural problems; urban problems were discussed but rural proposals received first priority. Legislatively, malapportionment gave added political power to the party that drew its heaviest support from rural constituencies, virtually insuring that party control of at least one house of the legislature. Legislatures thus constituted were often unwilling to confront pressing urban problems within the state, forcing the cities to turn increasingly to the federal government for financial aid.[3]

The Supreme Court's decisions in Baker v. Carr and Reynolds v. Simms resulted in a shift in emphasis in the research and writing on apportionment. No longer interested in detailing the extent of malapportionment or its causes, research has focused on the legal, philosophical, and constitutional problems of apportionment.[4] The Court's argument that legislators should represent people rather than trees or cows brought rejoinders that equal representations would do more harm than good to minorities and others seeking a voice in government.

Given that one of the foci of research prior to the reapportionment cases dealt with the political consequences of malapportionment, it is surprising that there has been comparatively little research on the political consequences of reapportionment. Malcolm Jewell, writing prior to 1962, noted that since the state party structure is tied to legislative districts, "a reapportionment based on population would literally revolutionize state politics."[5] Just how reapportionment would "revolutionize" state politics is not clear. If reapportionment could correct some of the egregious consequences of malapportionment, its political impact would be noticeable. There would be a shift of power in many states within and between political parties as legislative district boundaries are redrawn to make districts more equal in population; one expects a shift in power to urban and suburban leaders within the parties and the opening of the party structures to urban and suburban hopefuls. Parties within the state that draw their strength from urban and suburban areas presumably would profit from reapportionment and see their strength grow in the legislature. At the same time, rural legislators, acting by themselves, would be expected to find it more difficult to protect their interests or veto legislation vital to the state's urban areas.

While the rural areas may lose seats owing to reapportionment, the central cities may not be the greatest benefactors; between 1950 and 1960, nine of the ten most populous cities in the United States lost population, ranging from a 3 percent loss in New York City to a 15 percent decline in Boston. At the same time, the suburban areas surrounding the central cities grew at record rates. While the central cities may pick up some seats in the legislature, the suburbs will claim even more and in the future the central cities will lose more and more legislative seats to the suburbs that surround them. "The suburbs own the future. Big city politicians, rather than dominating the legislatures, are going to find they have more numerous and articulate opponents in their suburban rivals than ever before."[6] The increase in suburban representation may well result in state legislatures more familiar with urban problems (they can see them across the river or the city line), but not necessarily more amenable to finding solutions that must be financed with suburban tax dollars. Urban legislators, once faced by a rural majority, may now and in the future find themselves faced by a suburban-rural coalition majority.

Has reapportionment accomplished what its proponents hoped and its opponents feared? There are serious problems in answering the question. For example, many states reapportioned during their 1963 session and first elected representatives under new districting plans in the 1964 election. The Goldwater candidacy and reapportionment cost the Republican party more than 500 legislative seats at the state level; what percentage of that loss can be attributed to reapportionment is impossible to ascertain, particularly inasmuch as Republicans recaptured many of those seats and others in the 1966 legislative elections.

One way to assess the impact of reapportionment would be to examine the kinds of bills passed in the mal- and reapportioned legislatures to see whether urban-oriented legislation had any greater success in the reapportioned legislature and to see whether there was any difference in patterns of expenditures. One would assume that if reapportionment was to accomplish what its advocates hoped, then a reapportioned legislature would pass more urban-oriented bills and be willing to spend more money for urban-oriented projects. There may be very little change, however. Research by Thomas Dye indicates that the degree of legislative malapportionment has had little bearing on the way a state spends its money; the crucial variable in determining spending patterns is the economic climate of the state, a climate that provides resources and sets limits that a legislature, malapportioned or not, cannot ignore.[7]

In studying state budgetary patterns, Ira Sharkansky and Thomas Anton concur that it is extremely difficult to alter drastically existing expenditure patterns.[8] The politics of the budgetary process at the state, as well as the national, level leave little margin for innovation, and, subsequently, changes in expenditure patterns typically occur over a substantial period of time.

In addition to legislation and expenditures, reapportionment might be expected to have a noticeable effect on the personnel in the state legislature. There should be new faces. The change in personnel may have two major consequences. Politically it will mean the dissolution of old alliances and the need to create new ones. The legislative "rules of the game" may have to be redrafted in some state legislatures. This fact, in and of itself, may enable the legislature to change its style and mode of operation and result in different legislative output. Second, the new participants may well bring with them new and different orientations toward the legislature, their role in the legislature, and legislative service. New people, with different perceptions and orientations to the legislature, may be more willing to consider and pass different kinds of legislation.

REAPPORTIONMENT

In order to assess the impact of reapportionment on state legislatures, one should undertake comprehensive surveys of both houses in all fifty states. Cost makes that research strategy prohibitive. This case study is confined to one house of the legislature in the state of Washington. Washington was chosen, apart from considerations of opportunity and access, because it is a rapidly growing and urbanizing state that had not been equitably apportioned since 1930. The state has also undergone several initiative campaigns regarding reapportionment so that it is a salient and controversial issue in state politics.

The House of Representatives was chosen for study for several reasons. The House was the focal point of the legislative dimension of the battle over reapportionment and the greater realignment of districts took place in the House. The fact that House members are elected every two years makes it easier to analyze than the Senate, in which half the body is elected every two years (senators serve four year terms). Studying the House enables us to delineate clearly the end of the influence of the malapportioned House and the beginning of the reapportioned one. And lastly, the larger size of the House (99 members in contrast to 49 in the Senate) made it easier to analyze the data and insure a large enough number of members who had served in the legislature but who had not returned.

Analyzing the impact of reapportionment in Washington State will tell us precious little of the impact of reapportionment nationwide. It will provide us with some clues as to what conditions are necessary for reapportionment to have significant impact.

Unlike many state constitutions, the Washington State Constitution stipulates that both houses of the legislature be apportioned on

139

the basis of population. Despite this constitutional injunction, the state legislature has never voluntarily redistricted since 1901. Instead, the initiative has traditionally been used as a device to reapportion the legislature or to prod the legislature into reapportioning itself. The first successful reapportionment initiative measure was passed in 1930; in addition to redistricting the state, it increased membership in the House from 97 to 99 and in the Senate from 42 to 46.* At the same time, it established coterminous House and Senate districts. The 1930 districting plan remained in effect until 1956 when, after a long struggle, a League of Women Voters-sponsored initiative redistricting the state was accepted by a plurality of more than 41,000 votes.[9] An amendment to the Washington State Constitution, passed four years earlier, empowered the state legislature to amend any initiative proposal adopted by the voters. Because the League's reapportionment had not taken sufficient political factors into consideration, the state legislature proceeded to do so in their amendment of it.

In amending the initiative the legislature operated on the familiar apportionment principle of saving as many incumbents as possible. The final redistricting plan, as amended by the legislature, created only three new districts and was generally agreed to have done the least possible harm. The legislature's action withstood a court test, instituted by the League of Women Voters, by a narrow 5-4 vote.[10]

There matters stood until the Supreme Court's decision in Baker v. Carr. In June 1962, James Thigpen, a South King County justice of the peace, brought suit in federal court against Secretary of State Victor Meyers, charging that Washington's legislative and congressional districts were grossly malapportioned.[11] The state argued for dismissal of the suit on two grounds: the case questioned congressional districting, which the Supreme Court had not ruled on in Baker v. Carr, and the plaintiff had not exhausted all avenues of redress available. The initiative process in Washington presented a route not tried by the plaintiff. Interestingly, the League of Women Voters filed a brief in support of the state's second point. Following the failure of the legislature to reapportion after the 1960 census, the League had mounted yet another initiative drive and suggested that the court stay a decision until after a vote on the reapportionment initiative. The court postponed action until after the November 1962 election.

The 1962 initiative battle pitted the League of Women Voters against the Washington State Grange. As William McDermott notes,

---

*The Washington State Constitution stipulated that the maximum size of the House be 99 and that the Senate be no larger than one-half the size of the House.

"Where the League of Women Voters saw redistricting resulting in
'fairness' the Grange saw only undue influence for the metropolitan
area."[12] Rather than opposing reapportionment directly, the Grange
favored a constitutional amendment increasing membership in both
the House and Senate and guaranteeing each county at least one member in the House. Such a plan would ensure that the rural counties
east of the Cascade Mountains would receive continued representation
in Olympia. On November 6, 1962, the reapportionment initiative
failed to receive a majority of the votes, and the reapportionment
battle moved to the federal courts.*

Oral arguments were heard before district Judge William T.
Beeks on November 30. The plaintiffs alleged that a minority of the
state's population, approximately 38 percent, could elect majorities
in both houses of the legislature. The state rebutted by arguing that
it should not intervene in the case, particularly since a majority of
voters had recently refused the opportunity to reapportion by initiative.

In returning his verdict two weeks later, Judge Beeks ruled that
the Court dismiss the complaint regarding congressional districts by
noting that charges of discrepancies were unfounded. His review of
legislative districting found "invidious discrimination" that could be
remedied by judicial action. In reference to the reapportionment
initiative, which had been defeated, Judge Beeks ruled:

> We have no way of knowing whether the measure was de-
> feated because a majority did not desire reapportionment
> or whether they didn't understand it (there were numerous
> other complicated matters on the ballot) or whether the
> opponents were better organized than the proponents. It
> makes no difference. The inalienable constitutional right
> of equal protection cannot be made to depend on the will
> of the majority. . . .

Having ruled the legislature malapportioned, the Court was
faced with proposing an acceptable remedy. Judge Beeks alertly noted
that the legislature was to meet within a month and stayed judicial
action until then, in hopes that the legislature would reapportion itself.

The scene shifted to the legislature, in which the Democrats
controlled the Senate 33 to 16 and the House by a 51 to 48 margin,

---

*After the failure of the initiative, the League of Women Voters
received permission from the court to switch sides and act in conjunction with the plaintiff.

and to the Democratic governor. On the surface it appeared that the Democrats could reapportion the state to suit their interests, drawing district boundaries to meet their own needs, so long as the districts were roughly equal in population, and have the subsequent reapportionment bill signed into law by a Democratic governor, Albert Rosellini. Seven Democrats in the House defected, however, and by forming a coalition with the Republicans gave the Republicans organizational control of the House and gave one of the dissident Democrats the speakership.[13] Throughout the session, Democratic Senator Robert Greive and Republican Representative Slade Gorton worked to forge a reapportionment package acceptable to both parties and capable of passage in both houses. The formal session ended without agreement and discussions continued on into the following special session. In the special session, the House and Senate passed separate and widely different reapportionment bills and the conference committee could not settle the differences before adjournment of the special session.

Throughout the reapportionment battle in the legislature, the governor stood strangely aloof. The aloofness is less strange when one realizes that the governor was planning to run for a third term and viewed reapportionment as an albatross that could wreck his political chances in rural eastern Washington.

The failure of the legislature returned the case to the federal courts for disposition. Judge Beeks had warned before the session,

> We take notice of the fact that a new legislature will convene on January 14, 1963. Believing as we do, that redistricting should be accomplished by the body constitutionally responsible thereof and that the sins of the fathers should not be visited upon the sons, we are deferring final action to afford it the opportunity of discharging its constitutional mandate. If it fails, we, ever conscious of our oath to uphold the Constitution of the United States, will unhesitatingly take appropriate action to correct the inequity. [Emphasis added]

The remedies open to the judge were numerous. The court could reapportion the legislature, it could appoint a master to reapportion the legislature in its behalf, it could declare the existing districts null and void and call for at-large legislative elections, or it could force the legislature to act using weighted votes, to name just a few of the alternatives. McDermott feels that the threat of at-large elections was the most salient for the parties concerned.[14] Lawyers for Thigpen and the League of Women Voters pressed for at-large elections while the state replied that the expense and chaos of at-large elections would be more than the state and the voters should bear.

On May 3, 1963, Judge Beeks expressed deep regret that the legislature had not acted to reapportion itself, but then disclaimed any intent to have the court do the job. He declared the 1957 districting laws (under which the 1962 legislature had been elected) null and void and prohibited the secretary of state from holding elections with those districts. At the same time he neither prohibited nor recommended at-large elections for the 1965 legislature. Instead, he postponed action for one year, until May 1964. This left two options available: the governor could call a special session of the legislature to reapportion or the legislature could face at-large elections. Governor Rosellini, however, refused to call another special session of the legislature. There is some evidence that he feared the reemergence of the dissident Democrat-Republican coalition in the House blocking action on a reapportionment plan and the recognition that a special session of the legislature could concern itself with matters other than reapportionment, matters that might be potentially dangerous in an election year.

The state appealed the district court's ruling to the U.S. Supreme Court and on February 18, 1964, the Court took the case under advisement. In mid-June 1964, the Court delivered its second landmark reapportionment case, Reynolds v. Sims, ruling that both houses of the state legislature must be apportioned according to population and a week later reaffirmed Judge Beeks' decision in the Thigpen case. In reaffirming the district court decision, the Supreme Court ordered a twenty-five-day delay before the order might take effect. The state contended to the district court that the twenty-five-day delay would make judicial remedy difficult because state law required that filing for the 1964 election begin too far in advance of the November election for the court effectively to intervene. The attorney general asked Judge Beeks to allow one more election under the 1957 districting laws since there was too little time to do otherwise.

On July 22, 1964, Judge Beeks once again spoke to the issues in Thigpen v. Meyers, a case that had been before him for almost two years. After reviewing the alternatives available, the court recommended that the governor call a special session of the legislature to reapportion and threatened weighted voting in the 1965 legislature if redistricting was not completed by the end of August 1964.

The months of July and August were spent discussing the governor's refusal to call another special session and the mechanics of weighted voting in the legislature. Calling a special session stood to gain the governor very little and cost him a great deal. A Democratic legislature, unable to reach agreement on reapportionment and able to conduct other business, posed more political costs than the governor was willing to pay. If he had been unwilling to call a special session in May, he was far less willing to call one in August.

Given the governor's reluctance, party leaders began to discuss the mechanics of weighted voting. Would weighted votes count on all votes or merely final votes on bills? "The Attorney General concluded, after much study, that weighted voting would be very complicated and highly questionable."[15]

The August 31 deadline passed without judicial notice, and it was not until October 5 that the court acted. By that time it was clear that the governor had no intention of calling a special session and that it was too late to postpone legislative elections scheduled for the following month. It appeared that the court was faced with ordering the to-be-elected legislature to conduct its business in 1965 with weighted votes. Instead, Judge Beeks ordered the 1965 session of the legislature to consider reapportionment as its first order of business; in fact, the legislature could not pass other legislation until a reapportionment statute had been passed.

In the course of two years, from 1962 to 1964, the reapportionment issue had bounced yo-yo-like from one political arena to another, searching for a solution. Neither the legislature nor the courts seemed willing to resolve the conflict and the governor refused to intervene. The court's refusal to intervene forcefully in the conflict may be traced to three basic reasons: the court's premises that it should play a minimal role in the act of reapportionment, that it should not issue orders with a high probability of being ignored, and that it should attempt to time its decisions so as to leave the legislature and the governor the widest possible latitude for acting. Judge Beeks was faced with the problem of attaining the courts' end without doing serious injury to the political process in the state. At the same time, the dignity and power of the court could not be threatened.[16] As Richard Neustadt points out in his discussion of presidential power, the power to persuade others to do one's bidding is the essence of political power.[17]

The political situation in the state after the 1964 election was substantially different than before. Governor Rosellini had lost his bid for a third term to Republican Dan Evans, the 1963 minority floor leader in the House of Representatives and active participant in the reapportionment struggle. The Republicans had not fared as well in the legislature; Democrats controlled the House and Senate by 60-39 and 32-17 majorities, respectively. To reconstruct the dissident Democrat-Republican coalition, eleven Democrats in the House would have to defect, a substantially more difficult task now that the Democrats controlled both houses of the legislature.

With control of state government divided again in 1965 as in 1963, the chances for reapportionment looked none too bright.

Democratic control of the legislature would enable them to redistrict the state to suit their taste but the probabilities were correspondingly high that Governor Evans would veto a reapportionment plan that seriously weakened his party. Two factors made 1965 different, however. Governor Evans viewed himself as an active and interested participant in the reapportionment struggle, willing and able to deal with the Democratic leaders in the legislature, most of whom he knew from 1963. In addition, the court's ruling that reapportionment was to be the first order of business for the legislature made it imperative that the legislature deal with the issue if it wished to enact other legislation during the session, or face the possibility of a long and costly special session.

The Democratically controlled legislature attempted to blunt Evans' role by passing a reapportionment plan during the first two days of the session, while Rosellini was still in office and could sign the bill into law. A reapportionment plan drafted by majority leader Senator Robert Greive passed the Senate on a party vote, but the House Democratic caucus could not insure a stable majority and the bill did not reach the floor for a vote. The recognition of some Democrats that they would have to lose their seats under the reapportionment plan and the unanimity of the Republicans forged a majority coalition against the Senate-sponsored bill.

Shortly after Evans' inauguration, the House passed the Senate-sponsored reapportionment bill 55-43 (only four Democrats defected) and the Senate repassed the slightly amended bill 30-16. Governor Evans, as expected, vetoed the bill. Eight days after the first bill was vetoed, a second bill passed the Senate by a 27-20 margin. House Democrats were critical of the Senate plan and passed one of their own by a 57-40 vote. The two chambers finally ironed out their differences and on February 12, 1965, the second reapportionment plan passed both houses. Once again Governor Evans vetoed the plan. On February 19, the federal court ordered a hearing for February 26 on what additional action would be necessary to insure compliance with the court order. Obviously, the pressure was building for the legislature and the governor to reach agreement before the court co-opted the arena.

Governor Evans' repeated vetoes of Democratic reapportionment plans and the court's movement into the arena prompted Democratic leaders, particularly Senator Greive, and Governor Evans to reach agreement on reapportionment, an agreement that allowed Greive to redistrict the Senate as he saw fit with the Republicans doing the same in the House. The House, however, was unwilling to accept the fruits of the compromise. It passed a reapportionment plan that the Senate rejected, while the House subsequently rejected a Senate substitution. On February 26, 1965, thirty months after the filing of Thigpen v.

Meyers, a coalition of thirty-nine Republicans and seventeen Democrats passed the Senate redistricting bill and Governor Evans signed it into law. Forty-seven days of the legislative session had passed, during which the only business upon which the legislature could act was reapportionment.

The reluctance of House Democrats to support the reapportionment bill was based on the realization that Republicans stood to gain the most in the House while the Democratic losses in the Senate would be minimal. It was acknowledged that the Democrats would be able to retain control of the Senate with a 3-7 vote margin. In the House the Republicans were assumed to gain at least five seats, with some estimates ranging as high as twelve seats. The House Democrats had good reason to be dismayed, for a substantial number would not be returning for the 1967 session. Urban and suburban areas profited handsomely from the redistricting. Metropolitan areas west of the Cascades received three additional representatives from rural areas east of the Cascades. The populous Yakima area in central Washington received additional representatives from its rural neighbors, "so that more than 90 percent of the voters were in changed voting precincts. All but 153 precincts out of 1,103 were given new numbers."[18]

The redistricting did alleviate some of the more invidious discriminations of the 1957 apportionment plan. The new districts deviated by only 15 percent from the norm for equal population districts, and only two districts deviated by that large an amount. The new districts also required 47 percent of the electorate to elect a majority of both houses of the legislature.

The legislative redistricting plan of 1965, while reapportioning the state, brilliantly conformed to William J. D. Boyd's satiric insight:

> With but few exceptions, one can characterize the underlying philosophy of every new adopted redistricting plan as preservation, to the maximum degree, of the "stability" of the past. It is as if the slogan SAVE OUR SEATS appeared miraculously upon the walls of every legislative chamber in the nation. Imagination has been shown in fulfilling that self-administered admonition.[19]

Given the need to achieve a workable plan, party leaders in both houses acted on the assumption that as many incumbents as possible had to be protected. In the House, if the choice was between protecting a Democratic and Republican incumbent, the Republican incumbent won. Subsequently, a number of Democrats found themselves running against other Democrats in new districts. In addition to the principle of protecting the incumbents, the reapportionment plan also managed

146

to strengthen party control, Democratic or Republican, in a number of districts. Bone reports that legislators and newsmen saw a net gain of five seats for the Republicans from the redistricting with both parties making their own districts more secure.[20]

The 1966 election results exceeded even Republican expectations. The Democrats held onto old or newly gained central city seats but did badly in suburban districts, particularly in the rapidly urbanizing areas of Puget Sound.[21] A glance at Table 4.1 shows that the Republican reapportionment plan had radically altered the balance of power in the House. Districts that were once competitive became solidly Republican and formerly Democrat districts were found to be competitive. There was a net shift of seven districts from the solidly Democratic column into the solidly Republican column. The extensive redrawing of district lines had created districts not only equal in population but Republican as well. As a consequence, Republicans gained control of the House and this, combined with a Republican governor, gave the Republicans a whip hand in state politics. Equally as important, the 1966 election demonstrated that with solid Republican control

TABLE 4.1

Control of Legislative Districts,
by Party, 1964 and 1966

	Number of Districts	
	1964	1966
Solidly Republican*	18[a]	25[d]
Split Control	8[b]	8[e]
Solidly Democratic	23[c]	16[f]

*Solidly Republican or Democratic means that either party won all seats in the district.

[a]15 two-member districts and 3 single-member districts.
[b]6 two-member districts and 2 three-member districts.
[c]4 three-member districts, 12 two-member districts, and 2 single-member districts.
[d]25 two-member districts.
[e]7 two-member and 1 three-member districts.
[f]16 two-member districts.

Source: Compiled by the author.

147

in the majority of legislative districts it would be difficult, but not impossible, for the Democrats to regain control of the House. In those districts that elected one Democrat and one Republican, the Republicans wisely marshalled their resources and ran strong candidates, with adequate campaign funds expended against the weaker of the two Democratic candidates. As a result, at least four of the districts with split control are nominally Democratic.

Reapportionment had had its first impact. The Republicans had gained solid control of one house of the legislature. The Democrats, recognizing they would not be able to control both houses after re-apportionment, were willing to trade control of the House for continued control of the Senate, the bailiwick of Senator Grieve, chief Democratic negotiator.

RECRUITMENT

With the surprising Republican legislative victories in the House in the 1966 elections, an abnormally large freshman class entered the House in 1967. Whereas the preceeding session had yielded an average of twenty-eight freshmen, 1967 found thirty-four newcomers. To what extent were these people different in background from those who had served in 1965? Had reapportionment brought different kinds of people to the legislature?

Table 4.2 indicates that the reapportioned sessions of 1967 and 1969 were not appreciably different in age distribution from the mal-apportioned sessions of 1963 and 1965. The 1965 and 1967 sessions

TABLE 4.2

Distribution of House Members, by Age, 1963-69

Age	1963	1965	1967	1969
21-30	5	7	4	1
31-40	29	26	21	23
41-50	29	32	37	37
51-60	14	11	18	21
61-70	18	19	10	10
70+	1	0	1	5
No Data	3	4	2	0

Source: Compiled by the author.

have substantially more people in the 41-50 and 51-60 age cohorts. But what of the differences between those entering the House after reapportionment compared with those leaving the House? Were not the people recruited for the reapportioned legislature younger than the people leaving? The answer is "yes, but." The average age for freshmen is two to eight years younger than that of last termers, as Table 4.3 reveals, but the data from 1963 indicate that the phenomena are not unique to reapportioned legislatures; people who leave the legislature are replaced by younger people, reapportionment or not. And even though there is a constant circulation of younger people replacing those a little older, the average of the legislature varies imperceptibly over the three sessions. The data indicate that young people are recruited to the legislature, some of whom stay for extended periods but many of whom depart after two or three terms, to be replaced by younger legislators.

While there may not be much difference in age between the 1963-67 legislatures, there is a world of difference in the accumulated experience they could bring to bear on state problems. As Table 4.4 shows, the average length of service for each of the legislative sessions varies, with 1963 and 1969 having legislators with the greatest experience. The lack of experience in the House for the 1965 and 1967 sessions can be traced to two traumatic events in Washington political history, the Goldwater debacle of 1964, which led to the defeat of many incumbents (it will be remembered that the Democrats increased the margin in the House greatly from 1963 to 1965), and reapportionment, which created even more turnover of personnel. The people who did

TABLE 4.3

Average Ages for Freshmen, All Members,
and "Last Termers,"* 1963-67

Average Age	1963	1965	1967
Freshmen	40.1	40.1	41.0
All members	46.3	45.6	46.4
Last termers	45.6	48.6	43.9

*Last termers refers to those who served their last term in the House during those years. Data for 1969 were unavailable at the time this was written.

Source: Compiled by the author.

149

TABLE 4.4

Average Length of Service for All Members and
Those Leaving the House, 1963-69

Average Length of Service (in terms)	1963	1965	1967	1969
All members	2.6	1.5	1.9	2.6
Last termers	2.7	2.9	1.7	*

*Because this study was conducted during the 1969 session and before the 1970 elections, it was impossible to tell which legislators would not, for one reason or another, return.

Source: Compiled by the author.

not return for the 1967 session were experienced, having served an average of almost six years in the legislature. This left proportionately few "old-timers" to knock off in the 1968 election, but a number lost bids for reelection. Consequently, the fact that the average number of terms for all members for 1963 is 2.6 is grossly misleading; in 1963, thirty-seven members had served less than three terms while in the 1969 session that number had risen to sixty-one. The 1964 election and reapportionment in 1965 had created a House membership that, by 1969, had become curiously bifurcated. Almost two-thirds of the membership had not served prior to the 1964 election and forty-eight had not endured the reapportionment battle of 1965. Thus, the average of 2.6 terms for all members in 1969 is composed of a large number of members who are "newcomers" and a small number of those who have had extensive legislative experience. Reapportionment, combined with the 1964 election, resulted in a House of Representatives different in membership, if not composition, from the 1963 House.

As we noted, the high turnover between 1963 and 1969 did not lead to a noticeable shift in the average age of the House. When we examine occupational distributions for the House during the 1963-69 period, it is evident that there was little change in the occupational profile of the legislature. In fact, as Table 4.5 reveals, despite the enormous turnover during this period, the 1969 House differs from its 1963 predecessor only in having a few less farmers (the result of reapportionment), a few more people involved in commerce, and more professional people.

TABLE 4.5

Distribution of House Members, by Occupation, 1963-69

Occupation	1963	1965	1967	1969
Attorney	15	17	18	16
Agriculture or cattle	16	15	11	13
Insurance, real estate	9	7	7	10
Business and industry	15	13	12	18
Blue collar	7	6	3	3
White collar	4	5	7	3
Professional	23	26	27	29
Retired	4	1	1	3
Other	6	9	6	4

Source: Compiled by the author.

The impact of reapportionment, then, in Washington State has been to bring a great many new people to the legislature, but people with backgrounds very similar to the people they replaced. Whites replaced whites, professional men replaced professional men, and attorneys replaced attorneys. They might come from different parts of the state from their predecessors, but in occupation and age they differed little. Nevertheless, the infusion of new blood into a legislative body must bring some changes; old alliances are changed or broken and new ones must be created. And if the people elected to the legislature since reapportionment are little different in background from the people they replaced, do they bring different perspectives and orientations to the legislature? To that question we now turn our attention.

METHODOLOGY

In order to obtain data about the perceptions and orientations of people who had served or were currently serving in the House, mail questionnaires were sent to members who had served in the 1963, 1965, and 1967 sessions and had not returned, and interviews with ninety-seven of ninety-nine members of the 1969 House. Table 4.6 gives the response rate for each group.

It is clear that the more recently a person had served in the legislature the more likely we were to receive a questionnaire from

151

TABLE 4.6

Response Rates for Former and Current Legislators

| | Last Session Served | | |
	1963 or 1965	1967	1969
Total number of legislators	68 (58)*	20	99
Number of respondents	28	14	97
Percentage	41.2	70.0	97.9

*Only 58 could be located; the others were deceased or had moved.

Source: Compiled by the author.

him or to have interviewed him. Subsequently, those who served in the malapportioned legislature only (1963 or 1965) provided us with the lowest response rate. Those who responded to the questionnaire, however, are typical of the total group in age and education and we will assume, with some hesitation, that the twenty-eight respondents are representative of those who served in the malapportioned House and did not return. The low response rate, however, suggests that we be hesitant in using these data to say something concrete about people who served in the malapportioned House. With this caveat in mind we can analyze the data.

To analyze the impact of reapportionment on the perceptions and role orientations of the legislators, we have classified the legislators into three categories:

1. Old legislators: those people who last served in the House in 1963 or 1965 and who have not returned. This group represents the legislators from the malapportioned House (twenty-eight respondents).

2. Transitional legislators: those who served in both the malapportioned and reapportioned Houses. This would require that they be elected to the House by at least the 1965 session and to have served until 1967 or later (sixty-three respondents).

3. New legislators: those people who served only in the reapportioned House, in either the 1967 or 1969 session or both (forty-eight respondents).

These three categories enable us to compare those people who left the malapportioned legislature with those who replaced them, and to compare these two groups with that hardy group of legislators who were elected under two different districting plans.

EXPERIENCE AND MOTIVATION

While the people newly elected to the House are not very different in background from those they replaced, are there differences in community-role and prior political experience? Has the creation of new districts and the combination of old ones resulted in the recruitment of people less central to their community, less involved in community affairs, and with less prior political experience? Has reapportionment resulted in replacing experienced community influentials with community novices?

The literature in political science is replete with evidence that political activists—congressmen, lobbyists, party workers—are joiners; the number of community organizations to which these people belong is quite substantial. Members of the Washington House certainly fit this picture, as Table 4.7 documents. Only 9 of the 140 members for whom we have data were not involved in community organizations of one sort or another. Not only are they involved in community organizations, but they are heavily involved; the average

TABLE 4.7

Membership in Community Organizations
(in percent)

No. of Community Organizations	Old	Transitionals	New
None	7.1	9.5	2.0
One	10.7	12.7	10.4
Two	35.7	22.2	14.6
Three-five	28.6	34.9	52.1
Over five	17.9	20.6	20.8
	100.0	99.9	99.9
N=	(28)	(63)	(48)
Average	3.0	3.1	3.6

Source: Compiled by the author.

number of organizations for all members, regardless of when they served, is more than three. These are men and women who have played and continue to play an important role in the organizational life of their community.

Comparing the three groups of legislators reveals that the new members participate substantially more than either the old or transitional members. More than half of the new legislators belong to three to five community organizations, compared with only a quarter of the old legislators who belong to as many organizations. The difference is reflected in the average number of organizations to which they belong; the average for old and transitional members is 3.0 and 3.1, respectively, while the new members average 3.6 organizations. Reapportionment apparently opened up substantially new channels of participation for people who were already active participants. When new seats were created or old seats became vacant, people well known and visible in the community were recruited. In some districts, in which boundaries had been substantially altered, the incumbent found himself in a new district where he was not well known and challenged by someone more active and better known to the voters. This was certainly the Republican strategy in some districts; in two-member districts they ran well-known Republicans against the weaker of the two Democratic candidates.

While the new members belong to comparably more organizations, does this necessarily mean they play a more central role in the life of their communities? In response to a question about the extent to which they are (or were) consulted on community affairs and community decisions, we find that legislators, as a group, are critically involved in the political life of their communities. Only 6 of 159 legislators said they were never consulted on local matters, while approximately 40 percent are (or were) consulted "very frequently." Reapportionment apparently has had some impact on the recruitment of local influentials to the legislature. A comparison of the old and new legislators, summarized in Table 4.8, indicates that more new legislators play a more central role in community decision-making. Only one out of six of the new legislators is consulted only "once in a while," while one of four of the old legislators played that marginal a role. At the same time, more new members are consulted "moderately frequently" than old members. By combining these data with those on organizational membership, we can see that the new legislators are more important in their communities, as measured by participation in organizational life and consultation on community decisions, than the people they replaced. If the function of a legislator is to represent the interests of his constituents, the new legislators may be in a better position to do this than the old ones.

TABLE 4.8

Consultation on Community Affairs
and Community Decisions
(in percent)

Extent Consulted	Old	Transitionals	New
Never	7.1	23.2	4.0
Once in a while	25.0	22.2	16.6
Moderately frequently	32.1	30.2	41.8
Very frequently	35.7	44.4	37.5
	99.9	100.0	99.9
N=	(28)	(63)	(48)

Source: Compiled by the author.

The transitional members are the most frequently consulted of the three groups. This raises a chicken/egg dilemma, however. Did the transitionals make the change from the malapportioned to the reapportioned House because they played a crucial role in their community and were highly visible, or do they play an important role in community affairs because they have served at least three terms in the legislature, a fact that confers visibility upon them within the community? These two alternatives are not mutually exclusive. It is possible that the community influentials were initally elected to the malapportioned House because they were visible. Their position in the community allowed them to retain their legislative seat in the face of redistricting, and their subsequent legislative experience has made them even more visible and indispensable to their communities. Community influentials are recruited to the legislature, and legislative experience can help a man maintain his position in the community by providing a community with access to other kinds of resources to help solve community problems. Transitionals also play a crucial role in the legislature because they have the experience and seniority to occupy influential roles in the legislature. Community influentials can then use their base in the community to gain access to the legislature, to maintain themselves there, and to build a power base within the legislature as well as within their own communities.

While legislators, past and present, are central to the organizational life of their communities, to what extent do they actively participate in governmental or party activities? Participation in community organizations is of a kind in which the participant can control the quality and quantity of his participation. Recognizing this, community organizations make infrequent demands on their members; Elks, Moose, and Lions, for example, generally meet weekly for a luncheon or dinner, with any further participation at the discretion of the individual member. Participation in government and politics calls for a different quality and quantity of participation. Party activity demands very intense participation at infrequent periods, such as elections and political conventions. Governmental service, on the other hand, calls for a nearly total commitment of time and energy for stipulated periods of time; a person is a city councilman, meeting twice a week for four hours, for a two-year period.

Given the fact that legislators are men and women of status in their communities, with many demands on their time, it is not surprising that many of them come to the legislature with only party experience, as noted in Table 4.9. Party work can be fitted into and around already busy schedules and, in some cases, can be beneficial for one's professional career. Lawyers and insurance men in politics often find it difficult to unwind their political from their professional activities. At the same time, substantial numbers come to the legislature without any prior governmental or political experience. These people are not unprepared, however. Participation in community organizations and unofficial participation in community affairs has given them sufficient visibility to be elected to the legislature. Government provides a third source of personnel, although it must be

TABLE 4.9

Prior Political or Governmental Experience
(in percent)

Prior Experience	Old	Transitional	New
None	28.6	17.7	25.0
Party only	42.9	44.4	52.1
Governmental only	25.0	21.0	10.4
Party and government	3.8	16.1	12.5
	100.0	100.0	100.0
N=	(28)	(62)	(48)

Source: Compiled by the author.

noted that three-fourths of those who had served in governmental posts had served in part-time administrative posts rather than full-time elective positions. Once again, the involvement is limited. Only a very small proportion of the legislature could be called "professional" politicians in the sense of having served in both party and government prior to coming to the legislature.

When political parties look for candidates for the state legislature, they must look within their ranks and those of the community organizations. Those recruited to the legislatures from within the party may view the legislature as a reward for loyal and faithful party service,[22] those recruited from community organizations may find the legislature a means of expanding their horizons and their personal spheres of influence. In fact, the picture that emerges from the data is that of the "citizen-legislator," organizationally and politically active in his own community, who takes time from his home life and career to serve in the legislature.

The pattern is not consistent, however. The new members have more party experience and less governmental experience than the old members. Reapportionment seems to have altered channels of recruitment to the legislature. Whereas government was an important source for potential legislators in the malapportioned House, it is substantially less important now. Faced with the necessity of filling a great many new or recently vacant seats, the political parties responded by nominating party faithful. As a result, there were correspondingly more positions available in the party structure. Reapportionment, then, has had its impact in two ways: it created new seats and made others competitive which the parties filled from the party ranks which, in the second step, opened the party structure to the recruitment of new people, largely from urban and suburban areas whose district boundaries experienced great changes.

The transitionals differ from the new and old legislators in their greater political experience prior to the legislature; less than 20 percent of the transitionals had no political experience prior to the legislature. Legislative service, for the transitionals, is not a unique experience but a continuation of a life style started before election to the legislature. The resultant legislature is composed of "citizen-legislators" with a small cadre of "professionals" who have had prior governmental and party experience. Reapportionment has not altered that pattern, it has reenforced it.

If legislators are individuals with high status who play an important role in their own communities, why did they run for the legislature in the first place? Salary is not an adequate explanation. Prior to the 1969 session, legislators received $1,200 per year and $25 per day living expenses, hardly a munificent sum, given the status and occupational expertise of the members. What other reasons were important?

Responses to a question about why they ran for the legislature
the first time were coded as opportunity—either a new seat was created
or an incumbent retired; sponsorship—was asked to run for the legislature by friends, local organization, or political party; issue—felt
strongly about a particular issue; psychic—saw the legislature as a
change in life style or a challenge; and interest—expressed a long-
standing interest in politics or the legislature.

There is some difference in motivation for running for the legislature between the old and new legislators as indicated by Table 4.10.
For both groups interest in politics was a salient fact for at least half
the members. For one member, interest stemmed from a political
science course he had taken in college while another "had become
acquainted with the legislative process many years earlier when my
father was a member and I a page and committee clerk." Opportunity
and sponsorship were comparably important for the two groups. Opportunities for the two groups varied, however; for the old legislators,
opportunity involving a vacant seat was the result of retirement or
death while for the new legislators it was often the result of redistricting. Sponsorship was common to both groups. One schoolteacher was
asked by school people and those interested in education to run. For
many others, the party requested them to run for a vacant seat. The
largest difference between the old and new legislators is the higher
level of psychic motivation for the new legislators. One old legislator

TABLE 4.10

Reasons for Running for the Legislature
(in percent)

Reason for Running	Old	Transitionals	New
Opportunity	17.9*	30.6	21.3
Sponsorship	28.6	32.3	21.3
Issue	10.7	22.6	17.0
Psychic	17.9	22.6	38.3
Interest	50.0	25.8	55.3
N=	(28)	(62)	(47)

*Columns total more than 100 percent because respondents could
give more than one response.

Source: Compiled by the author.

stated he ran for the legislature "because I was young—24 years old—
and I had ambition and egoism." A new legislator responded, "I had
been pretty successful in my business and I was looking for something
new to do. I was looking for a new challenge." Reapportionment not
only altered the channels of access to the state legislature but recruited people who viewed the legislature as a challenge and an opportunity to do something new.

The transitionals, on the other hand, have a far more diffuse
motivational pattern. No one motive predominates. As a result,
opportunity was more important and interest in politics less important
for the transitionals than for the old or new legislators. This latter
point may well indicate that interest in politics may be enough to get
people to run for the legislature but not enough to return them time
and time again.

Thus far we have examined the social and experiential backgrounds of those recruited to the House to determine whether reapportionment has had any noticeable impact on the type of people
recruited. The answer is clearly yes. The new legislators are more
active in their own communities and are contacted more frequently
on community affairs and community decisions than the people they
replaced. Reapportionment apparently changed the channels of recruitment to the legislature; party has become far more important as
an experiential base for running for the legislature. It will be interesting to see whether party work is as important a prerequisite in the
future once the legislative districts have become stabilized. The new
legislators also differ from their predecessors in their motivation to
run; new legislators have been more prone to run for the legislature
because it is a challenge or for a change in pace. The challenge and
the opportunities provided by reapportionment resulted in the recruitment of legislators who differed in some significant ways from the
people they replaced and those who made the transition from the old
to the new legislature.

PERCEPTIONS AND EVALUATIONS

A person elected to the legislature brings with him to that body
a set of expectations as to what legislative service is all about and a
corresponding set of perceptions as to how he should act.[23] Of basic
importance is his perception of whether he feels he should represent
his constituents or act as a free agent, voting his own convictions.
The legislator's perception will influence the role he plays in the
legislature and his chances for reelection. Related to this perception
is the legislator's expectation of representing the people of his district or the wider constituency of the state. The person who perceives

his role as one of representing his district and the wishes of his constituents will have a very narrow view of his role in the legislature. His initial question about any issue will invariably be, "how does this affect my constituents?" His answer will heavily influence his behavior in the legislature. Bills that are favorable or unfavorable to his district will elicit active response, all others will not be relevant. This narrow role perspective has the one advantage of helping insure reelection, but it excludes the legislator from much of the legislative process. The legislator who views himself as operating independently of his constituents and representing the broader interests of the state will find himself able to play an active role in the legislative process, on a wide range of issues, unbounded by the concerns of his constituency. Such a field of operation, however, bears with it the cost of possible electoral defeat. A third set of role perspectives are available. They call for the legislator's listening to his constituents on some issues and voting his conscience on others, representing his district on some matters and the state on others. A mixed role allows the legislator a maximum amount of freedom at a minimum cost. He can choose to represent his constituents when he is aware of their wishes or when the issue is salient for them, and ignore them all other times. He may choose to place his district before the state but recognize that there are few issues that affect only his district.

The mixture of role orientations in a legislative body may well determine how that body to policy questions. Legislatures dominated by district-oriented legislators will neglect statewide problems to solve district problems first. Constituency-oriented legislators will seek to determine public opinion in their district on issues before they act, being unable to act on issues for which there is no vocal opinion or which require action before public opinion can coalesce. For these reasons, it is important to know whether reapportionment had any impact on how state legislators and state legislatures perceive their roles.

All respondents were asked, "Some people say that a legislator should represent what the majority of his constituents want, while others argue that he should vote his personal conviction. What do you think?"[24] From Table 4.11, it is clear that there is no significant difference between the old and the new legislators about which role to play; both old and new legislators endorse the mixed role. Given the flexibility and latitude of the role, the data are not surprising. What is surprising is the difference between the old and new legislators, on the one hand, and the transitionals on the other. While the majority of the transitionals opt for the mixed role, a sizable percentage (27 percent) choose to represent their constituents' views. The data cause one to ask whether a constituency orientation is the result

TABLE 4.11

Constituency versus Conscience Role Orientation
(in percent)

Role Orientation	Old	Transitional	New
Vote constituency	11.1	27.0	13.0
Vote conscience	22.3	19.0	26.1
Both	66.7	54.0	60.9
	100.0	100.0	100.0
N=	(27)	(63)	(46)

Source: Compiled by the author.

of having served in the legislature for some time or whether it is a prerequisite for being reelected. It should be noted that voting the way one's constituents want is a function of the length of service in the legislature; the more one has served in the legislature, the more likely he is to recognize the wisdom of heeding his constituents' desires. Even within the transitionals' group, the legislator is more likely to wish to represent his constituent if he has had more legislative service. And conversely, the more one heeds his constituents, the more likely it is that he will return to the legislature. Although the new legislators, like the old, are less prone to perceive their role as representing their constituents, that role becomes more important through time, and we may find that new legislators become increasingly constituency-oriented. Those who do not fail to return.

While reapportionment had no apparent impact on the constituent-conscience role dilemma, it had a decided impact on the areal role orientation. In response to the question, "Some people say that a legislator should be dedicated to advancing the interests of his own district while others say that he should work for the interests of the entire state. What do you think?," new legislators were substantially more willing than old ones to perceive themselves as representing the state, according to responses summarized in Table 4.12. While the majority of the new legislators perceive themselves as playing both roles, there is a sizable minority (35 percent) who view the state as the more important referent. This fact, combined with the small proportion of new legislators who perceive themselves as representing their constituents' views, might well mean that the reapportioned legislature would be more willing to discuss issues of broader scope than the malapportioned House. Discussion and action are not synonymous, however.

TABLE 4.12

State versus District Role Orientation
(in percent)

Role Orientation	Old	Transitional	New
Represent district	3.7	14.3	6.3
Represent state	22.3	31.7	35.4
Both	74.0	54.0	58.3
	100.0	100.0	100.0
N=	(27)	(63)	(48)

Source: Compiled by the author.

The role orientation of the transitionals is also of interest. As one would expect, some transitionals who desire to represent their constituents' views also feel they should represent their district. They are a distinct minority, however. In role orientation, the transitionals are far closer to the new legislators than they are to the old; while the majority feel they should represent both their district and the state, a sizable minority feel that the interests of the state (31 percent) should have priority. Length of service may give concern as to how constituents feel on issues, but it also leads to a recognition that on some issues the interests of the state are paramount to those of the district.

The combination of data from the transitionals and the new legislators—those making up the reapportioned House membership—reenforces the conclusion that the new legislature should be far more willing to discuss issues of a broad nature, whose impact extends beyond the boundaries of any one legislative district. Whether this would mean increasing concern for urban legislation is a question that will be discussed later.

One predicted impact of reapportionment was the destruction of old coalitions based on similarity of interests, experience, and party, and the creation of new ones. What was to be the basis of the new coalitions? Experience? No. Similarity of interests? If a correspondence of interests occurred, it would become relevant in later sessions when combined with experience. Party, then, provides a ready basis for structuring legislative coalitions if the new legislators are willing to accept party leadership. Given that the only prior experience for many new legislators was within the party, one would expect them to look to party leaders for leadership. To what extent is that true? To what extent did the old and new legislators differ in following party leadership?

Respondents were asked, "Some people feel that a legislator should follow party leaders and party policy when voting on legislation, while others feel that he should be independent of party. What do you think?" Almost no old legislators felt any obligation to follow party leaders on policy matters. Instead, they preferred the mixed role of adhering to the party when it stood to benefit them most and remaining independent on other occasions. This unwillingness to follow party leadership may be one reason why some of the old legislators did not return to the House; it was the party leadership that drew the district boundaries and the party leaders have notoriously long memories. It is apparent, however, from the data summarized in Table 4.13 that party was not a relevant dimension of coalitions that existed in the malapportioned House.

The new legislators, on the other hand, were substantially more willing to follow the lead of the party, although the majority of them wished to play a mixed role. One wonders whether party is salient for new members of the legislature primarily because it provides them with a ready-made set of cues for finding their way through an otherwise confusing process. After a while, does party become less salient as legislators develop power bases independent of the party?

The data on the transitionals would seem to argue that the answer to that question is no. In fact, the longer one serves in the legislature, the more salient party becomes as a cue. The transitionals are far more willing to follow party leaders than either the old or new

TABLE 4.13

Party Role Orientation
(in percent)

Role Orientation	Old	Transitionals	New
Follow party	3.8	31.7	20.8
Be independent	15.4	22.2	18.8
Both	80.8	46.1	58.3
	100.0	100.0	99.9
N=	(26)	(63)	(48)

Source: Compiled by the author.

163

legislators. It must be remembered, however, that the transitionals, because they have served longer than the old or new legislators, are rapidly moving into positions of leadership within the party and in the legislature. Their perception that legislators should follow party leaders may be the expression of a desire that other legislators follow them.

Once again, it is clear that the combined data on the transitional and the new legislators would indicate that party will be far more salient a factor in constructing legislative coalitions in the reapportioned House than it was in the old House. There is enough slack in the party orientations to indicate that there should also be substantial opportunity for interparty coalitions, particularly on issues on which the party does not take a stand.

Equally important as whether the legislator feels he should represent his constituents or follow his party is his perception of his own expertise. It is the subject matter experts in any legislative body who hold positions of influence. With the large turnover in personnel between 1963 and 1969, what impact did that turnover have on the distribution of specialists and generalists in the House? Did reapportionment eliminate a large number of specialists who might have given stability and continuity to the reapportioned House? Or was the reverse true—were the specialists the ones to survive? And what levels of competence did the new legislators bring to their job?

While two-thirds of the old legislators were specialists, they were replaced by new legislators with nearly as great a specialist orientation, as indicated by Table 4.14. Thus, there was little loss of specialization from the malapportioned to the reapportioned Houses. What is surprising is the large number of specialists who made the transition from the old to the new House to act as committee chairmen

TABLE 4.14

Specialist versus Generalist Orientation
(in percent)

Orientation	Old	Transitional	New
Specialist	66.7	75.8	63.3
Generalist	33.3	24.2	36.6
	100.0	100.0	99.9
N=	(27)	(62)	(29)

Source: Compiled by the author.

164

and subject matter specialists. The reapportioned House will be characterized by a high level of specialized competence, led by members who combine expertise, experience, and formal position within the legislature.

Thus far, we have talked only about legislators' perceptions of the roles they play. What expectations do they have of legislative service? What do they like or dislike about serving in the legislature? How important to them is serving in the legislature? Once again, did reapportionment have any significant impact on the expectations that legislators have about serving in the legislature?

Legislators currently serving in the House were asked, "If you had to leave the legislature and not return, what would you miss most?" and those who had served but not returned were asked, "Since leaving the legislature, what have you missed most?" Their answers indicated a set of identifiable rewards for legislative service; political rewards—respondents mentioned working for specific issues or work on the legislative process, committees, floor debate, etc.; social rewards—respondents mentioned the fellowship and camaraderie of serving in the legislature; psychic rewards—respondents assessed their service in emotional terms, i.e., "the excitement of it all," "being in the center of things," "the color and drama."

There are surprisingly large differences between the three groups of legislators, as noted by Table 4.15. A large percentage of old legislators (almost two-thirds) received political rewards; they enjoyed the "nitty-gritty" of the legislative process. Social and psychic

TABLE 4.15

Rewards of Legislative Service
(in percent)

Rewards	Old	Transitionals	New
Political	61.9*	50.9	30.8
Social	23.8	37.7	34.1
Psychic	23.8	66.0	45.5
N=	(21)	(53)	(44)

*Columns total more than 100 percent because some respondents gave more than one answer.

Source: Compiled by the author.

rewards were important for substantially fewer old legislators.* Political rewards may have been more attractive to old legislators because their length of service in the legislature insured them access to the legislative process. If we compare the political rewards of the transitionals and new legislators, it appears that length of service is a factor. Transitionals, whose length of service is similar to the old legislators, have a correspondingly high proportion of members mentioning political rewards. Since committee chairmanships and party leadership posts are disproportionately held by the transitionals, it is not surprising that so many receive political rewards. They are in an optimal position to do so. New legislators, on the other hand, having served two terms or less, are only now beginning to play an important enough role in the legislative process to derive political rewards.

In addition to political rewards, a large proportion of the transitionals receive psychic rewards. Seniority allows them to participate in the legislative process and to derive emotional satisfaction from such participation. The quality of the psychic rewards for the transitional and new legislators differs in quality; transitionals receive psychic rewards from their ability to manipulate and participate in the legislative process, while the psychic rewards for the new members are derived from being allowed to watch rather than participate in the process.

The new legislators, denied access to influential participation in the legislative process, must opt for social and psychic rewards. Like freshmen in Congress, the new legislators must sit quietly and learn the rules of the legislative game before they can begin to gain political rewards.[25] Subsequently, their rewards can be only those rewards of the spectator—social and psychic.

If the data from the old legislators are accurate reflections of their rewards during their period of service, then the old and new legislatures will differ radically. If age data are accurate, the old legislature was composed of a large proportion of members seeking political rewards—working hard on issues of interest to them, being active in committees, and speaking freely and frequently on the floor— the prototypes of James David Barber's "Lawmakers."[26] If the old legislature was composed of like-minded men, it might have accomplished great legislative feats because men with experience and interest could agree to act in concert. If composed of unlike-minded men,

---

*It must be remembered that former legislators were asked to think back four to six years, and it may be that memories of the legislative process linger long after memories of the friends and excitement have faded.

the old legislature would have resulted in discord, rancor, and legislative immobility as men with experience and interest acted in conflict with one another. The new legislature, on the other hand, will be largely controlled by the transitionals—they have the experience to make the legislative machinery operate smoothly. As the new members return to the legislature for further experience, the new legislature will gradually look more like the old. But the first few sessions of the reapportioned legislature should find the transitional legislators in command.

Membership in the legislature entails costs as well as rewards. To determine the costs of legislative service, members of the 1969 session were asked, "If you had to leave the legislature and not return, what would you miss least?" and those who have served but did not return were asked, "Since leaving the legislature, what have you missed least?" Their answers were categorized as: political costs— respondents mentioned floor debate, committee hearings, political campaigning; social costs—respondents universally mentioned social engagements promoted by lobbyists; and psychic costs—respondents mentioned the frustration and time involved in the legislature and being away from home, family, and work. While being away from work is an economic cost, it has a psychic dimension because the legislator's work provides him with a basis for comparison between his work in the legislature and his occupation.

Approximately equal numbers of old legislators paid political and psychic costs, as evidenced in Table 4.16. The "nitty-gritty" of the process and the personal strain of the legislative role imposed

TABLE 4.16

Costs of Legislative Service
(in percent)

Costs	Old	Transitionals	New
Political	40.1*	33.9	32.5
Social	13.7	30.2	35.0
Psychic	45.5	47.2	55.0
N=	(21)	(53)	(40)

*Columns total more than 100 percent because some respondents gave more than one answer.

Source: Compiled by the author.

comparably high costs. Social costs were remarkably low. This distribution of costs among the old legislators may be the result of fading memories of what they disliked about the legislature, and a redefinition of why they did not return; lobbyists' parties had little to do with their not returning, while endless floor debate and being away from wife and job can be rationalized as reasons for not returning. Social costs are forgotten and political and psychic costs are remembered.

Transitionals are more likely than old legislators to encounter social costs and less likely to pay political costs. Being in positions of power within the legislature, the transitionals are in a good position to limit the political costs of legislative service. For those in a position to influence the legislative process, participation in the process is a reward rather than a cost. The comparably high social costs for the transitionals may be the result of the transitionals' currently serving or having recently served in the legislature and being aware of the time demands made by parties. This can best be seen by comparing the social costs of new and transitional legislators; there is very little difference between the two groups.

In fact, the new legislators differ from the transitionals mainly in the psychic costs they encounter. The newness of the legislative role may make the new legislators far more aware of alternative roles available outside the legislature than the transitional member who has served for some time and adapted to the "citizen-legislator" role.

SUMMARY

What impact has reapportionment had on the kinds of people serving in the legislature? There has been an enormous turnover of personnel between 1963 and 1969, attributable to the 1964 election and reapportionment in 1965. But the social composition of the legislature has changed very little. With reapportionment, white, Anglo-Saxon lawyers and businessmen from small towns have been replaced by white, Anglo-Saxon lawyers and businessmen from the suburbs. While no different socially, the new legislators differ interestingly from the people they replaced in experience, role orientations, and attitudes toward legislative service.

Comparing the old and new legislators, we find the new legislators far more central to the communities they represent; they are members of more organizations and they are consulted more frequently on community affairs. Reapportionment also opened up the legislature to people who had worked faithfully in the party and community organizations, who were looking for some sort of change, and who were interested in politics. While party work was an important source of recruitment for the old legislators, prior service in the government was also important—far more than for the new legislators.

While there is very little difference between the old and new legislators on whether to represent their constituents or vote their conscience (both groups overwhelmingly favor doing both), there are substantial differences about whether to represent the interests of the district or the state and whether to follow party leaders. Although both new and old legislators favor playing a mixed role—representing both district and state and only occasionally following party leaders—proportionately more new legislators favor representing the interests of the state and following party leaders on policy.

The expertise that the legislature lost as a result of reapportionment was replaced by comparable expertise. Roughly the same proportion of old and new legislators view themselves as expert in some legislative field.

There are also significant differences between the old and new legislators in terms of what they like and dislike about serving in the legislature. Old legislators liked the nuts and bolts of the legislative process while the new members respond to the legislature as an emotional experience in which they are observers rather than participants. The difference, of course, could very well be the result of different terms of service in the legislature, with substantial service in the legislature necessary before one can appreciate the nuts and bolts of the process and become a participant rather than an observer. Thus, this difference in expectation may be less the result of reapportionment and more the result of experience. The differences between the old and the new legislators on what they like least are less startling. Old legislators are more critical of some dimensions of the legislative process—debates, political campaigning—while new legislators are more critical of the party dimension of the job and of being away from home, family, and work. As with things they like most, these differences may be the result of different lengths of service. One had to serve in the legislature for a period of time to appreciate the negative dimensions of the job, while new legislators, fresh from home and job, are most aware of being away from them.

The differences between the old and new legislators, combined with the characteristics of the transitionals, indicate that the reapportioned House should approach its task somewhat differently from its malapportioned predecessor. The transitionals will provide the formal leadership and expertise, and they will find the new legislators willing to follow their lead, paying close attention to problems confronting their districts, but also willing to consider issues of broad, statewide concern. To what extent has that been true?

REAPPORTIONMENT AND
LEGISLATIVE POLICY

Have these changes in personnel and attitudes had any impact
on the output of the state legislature? Changes in structure, procedures, personnel, and attitudes will be irrelevant if they do not produce changes in the product of the legislative process. If there is no
change in legislative process, then innovations are nothing more than
games people play to feel that they are accomplishing something
substantive. The magnitude of change in attitudes and perceptions in
the reapportioned Washington House of Representatives indicates that
changes in policy should follow.

There are two ways to measure the impact of reapportionment
on legislative output. First, one can examine the kinds of bills the
legislature passes and compare the types of bills passed by the old
and new Houses. This would give an indication of the relative emphasis
the two Houses placed on certain policy questions, particularly urban
problems. A second mode of analysis would be to compare the expenditure of funds for state services under the old and new Houses.*
If reapportionment has had any impact, it should be seen in a shift in
the kinds of bills that the legislature considers and the kinds of expenditures that it approves. The reapportioned House, for example,
should give increasing emphasis to urban legislation and give a corresponding shift in expenditures to urban-related services, especially
education and welfare.

What impact has reapportionment had on substantive policy
matters? Has reapportionment meant that urban problems now receive a fairer hearing and more concrete action? Have political and
attitudinal changes in the legislature meant a different policy output
for the House?

To answer these questions, we must look at the introduction and
disposition of urban-oriented bills in the Washington House for the
1963, 1965, and 1967 sessions. These three sessions will enable us,
as before, to contrast the 1963 and 1965 malapportioned House with
the 1967 reapportioned House. Urban-oriented bills were bills listed
in the Topical Index of the Legislative Record under "Cities and
Towns" for the three sessions. While this definition may be simple
and ignore some urban-oriented legislation that may be otherwise

---

*A substantial amount of research has compared state expendi-
tures for states that were malapportioned in varying degrees, with
the conclusion that malapportionment made no difference in expenditures. There has been virtually no comparison of expenditure patterns before and after reapportionment.

classified, e.g., an educational state aid formula that benefits cities, it has the virtue of being simple and inclusive. Such bills include those that affect zoning, mass transportation, school districting, annexation procedures, municipal employee regulations and benefits, and garbage disposal, for example.

It is clear from Table 4.17 that while the number of bills introduced during the three sessions has increased by more than 25 percent, the number of urban oriented bills introduced has remained comparatively constant, declining from 11 to 8 percent of all bills introduced. Reapportionment has not led to a noticeable flood of new urban legislation as some critics feared it would. Instead, reapportionment's impact is best measured in the number of urban-oriented bills that have passed the House; the number rises from eleven in 1963 (13.5 percent) to sixteen (26.7 percent) in 1965, and thirty (36.6 percent) in 1967. Urban-oriented legislation was more than twice as successful in 1967 as it was in 1963 and one-third again as successful as in 1965. The increasing success in the passage of urban legislation is matched by an increase in the percentage of bills introduced by

TABLE 4.17

Urban-Oriented Bills Introduced in
Washington House of Representatives,
1963, 1965, and 1967

	1963	1965	1967
Total number of House bills introduced	720	716	982
Total number of urban-oriented bills introduced	80	60	82
Percent of all bills which are urban-oriented	11.1	8.4	8.4
Number of urban-oriented bills passed	11	16	30
Percent of urban-oriented bills introduced by urban legislators*		81.7	90.2
Percent of urban-oriented bills passed	13.5	26.7	36.6

*Legislators from King, Pierce, and Spokane counties, the three most urban counties in the state.

Source: Compiled by the author.

171

urban legislators that, coupled with increased representation for urban areas, means that urbanites have greater access than ever before to the legislative process—access that they are using with increasing effectiveness.

The type of bills has also varied from 1963 through 1967. The bills introduced in 1963 were primarily concerned with annexation, streets and highways, and municipal housekeeping details. The urban-oriented bills that passed that session mirrored those concerns; they focused on the crucial problems of providing fire protection for cemeteries, placing some municipal police under civil service, establishing uniform cost accounting for municipal street systems, and defining population minima for town incorporations. The 1965 session shows increased awareness of urban problems through bills calling for urban mass transportation, reallocation of state sales tax revenue to the cities, and land use planning; the only major urban legislation that passed, however, allowed cities to participate in the construction of sports stadiums (a bill needed for Seattle to construct a domed stadium), the establishment of a regional planning agency, and the funding of land use planning at the local level. The 1967 session, the first after reapportionment, saw the introduction of a number of new bills. The governor's office recognized that a new spirit permeated the legislature, particularly the House. Governor Evans and his advisors felt the new legislature would be more willing to consider different types of legislation and they moved accordingly, sponsoring new legislation. In addition to the traditional housekeeping legislation, bills relating to tourism, urban transportation, urban renewal, financing off-street municipal parking, municipal industrial development, and the creation of state and community affairs agencies within state government were introduced. The bills that passed the 1967 session, however, were only marginally different from those that had passed earlier sessions. Once again, the successful legislation tended to be housekeeping legislation, with an occasional major urban bill passing if it involved little or no expenditure of state funds. In addition to the creation of badly needed new municipal court judgeships and legislation permitting the adoption of a uniform municipal code, the House also passed bills allowing state funds for the planning of urban mass transit, the creation of comprehensive community health centers, and the allocation of funds to promote local tourism. Perhaps the legislature's most drastic policy change was the authorization, for the first time, of state funds for cities and counties on a block-grant basis. The 1967 session authorized the expenditure of $23,815,000 for the 1967-69 biennium for cities, and a maximum of $3,000,000 for the counties. Funds were to be allocated to cities on a population basis, meaning that western Washington cities would get the bulk of the money available.

If we compare the number of bills introduced and passed in the old and new House, we must conclude that reapportionment has had substantial impact on policy. Urban-oriented legislation is being introduced with greater frequency and with a higher probability of success in the reapportioned House. If we compare the quality of legislation, the picture looks different. The kinds of bills that passed the reapportioned House are only marginally different in kind from those that passed the old. The appropriation for cities and counties is a striking exception. More important than the kinds of bills that are passed are the kinds of bills now being introduced. It is now legitimate to talk about rapid transit, urban renewal, and fair housing in the House, while it once was not. Although introducing and debating urban-oriented bills is not the same as passing that legislation, it is an obvious and necessary first step. Recognizing the legitimacy of an issue is an important first step toward its solution.*

Equally as important, old priorities in legislation may no longer be operative. Traditionally, the Highway Department has had virtually no opposition on its appropriations and long-range plans for highway construction. During the 1969 session, for the first time in the memory of many, the Highway Department was defeated in its bid to gain legislative approval of and funding for the construction of new bridges across Lake Washington, connecting Seattle and its eastern suburbs. Antifreeway forces on both sides of the lake combined to form a potent force, representing a large enough constituency, to forestall action on the issue. Success in this instance may mean that urban legislators will increasingly be able to get what they want and prevent what they do not want.

Legislation is only one measure of the impact of reapportionment on policy, however. As mentioned earlier, the reapportioned House has not been prone to fund large capital investments in the cities. And without money, legislation is meaningless. To what extent has reapportionment made a difference in patterns of state expenditure?

We have examined state expenditures for six services—public safety and regulation, education, human benefits (health and hospitals, corrections, and welfare), natural resources and recreation, agriculture, and transportation—for the period 1961-71.† As noted in Table 4.18, all six services experienced dollar increases in expenditures for the ten-year period, with education, human benefits, and

---

*It is also noteworthy that an abortion bill was introduced in the House for the first time in 1969; it was killed in committee.

†The figures for 1969-71 are proposed figures from the governor's budget.

transportation experiencing the greatest dollar increases. These three services also accounted for more than 80 percent of all state expenditures for the period. Expenditures for education and human benefits more than doubled and those for transportation more than tripled. The increases for public safety and regulation, natural resources and recreation, and agriculture are for smaller dollar amounts, but the percentage increase in expenditures for natural resources and recreation is only slightly less than that of education in magnitude. Natural resources and recreation has become an increasingly salient issue in Washington, as more and more people have moved into the state with the expansion of Boeing and the aerospace industry, and long-time residents have become increasingly concerned about the preservation of open spaces, natural areas, and recreational facilities. The growth rates of expenditures for public safety and regulation and agriculture are the lowest of the six services examined. Federal support of agriculture and the diminishing importance of agriculture in the state's economy are explanations for the modest increases in agriculture expenditures; public safety and regulation is the only service that suffered a loss in expenditures from one biennium to the next, the result of efforts to provide services without raising taxes.

Expenditure growth rates are uniform for all services during this ten-year period. Some, such as public safety and regulation and agriculture, grow less slowly for a biennium and then spurt ahead the next biennium. Natural resources and recreation expenditures, on the other hand, spurt ahead to establish new expenditure levels and then the growth rate levels. For the three largest expenditure items, however, there is a progressive growth in percentage increase. Expenditures for high-demand services, including education, welfare, and transportation, must progressively grow to meet increased demands.

Has reapportionment made any difference in these expenditure patterns? By comparing expenditures for these six services for the periods 1961-63 to 1965-67 and 1965-67 to 1969-71, we should be able to see the changes in expenditures before and after reapportionment.* If reapportionment has had an impact, the dollar and percentage increases in expenditures for some services should be greater after reapportionment than before.†

---

*The 1965-67 biennium expenditures were used as a base point because these expenditures are based on the last budget developed by the malapportioned House.

†It must be recognized that inflation plays a factor in differences that may occur in expenditure patterns before and after reapportionment.

TABLE 4.18

State Expenditures for Six Selected State Services

Service	Expenditures (in 000's of dollars)									Percent Increase 1961-71
	1961-63	Percent Increase	1963-65	Percent Increase	1965-67	Percent Increase	1967-69	Percent Increase	1969-71	
Public safety and regulation	58,872	11.6	65,728	-17.2	54,393	40.5	76,443	31.4	100,450	70.6
Education	708,657	12.1	794,355	19.5	949,388	40.0	1,325,859	45.7	1,932,009	172.6
Human benefits (health and Hospitals, corrections, and welfare)	333,268	8.0	360,078	22.1	439,791	32.0	580,427	37.6	798,805	139.7
Natural resources and recreation	44,779	1.9	45,650	19.3	54,470	83.5	99,952	21.7	121,666	171.7
Agriculture	7,380	11.5	8,231	9.4	9,008	26.2	11,367	13.4	12,895	74.7
Transportation	234,246	17.8	276,033	36.4	376,544	37.0	515,905	53.1	789,805	237.2
Total state expenditures (all services)	1,597,352	12.4	1,795,615	19.6	2,146,917	37.4	2,950,697	44.1	4,252,487	166.2

Source: Compiled by the author.

TABLE 4.19

Dollar and Percentage Increases in Expenditures
before and after Reapportionment

Service	Expenditures (in 000's)	
	1961-63 to 1965-67	1965-67 to 1969-71
Public safety and regulation	-$4,479 (-7.6%)	$46,057 (84.7%)
Education	$240,731 (34.1%)	$982,621 (103.5%)
Human benefits	$106,523 (23.0%)	$369,014 (81.6%)
Natural resources and recreation	$9,691 (21.6%)	$67,196 (123.4%)
Agriculture	$1,628 (22.1%)	$3,887 (43.2%)
Transportation	$142,298 (60.7%)	$413,261 (109.8%)
Total	$549,565 (34.4%)	$2,105,561 (98.1%)

Source: Compiled by the author.

It is clear from Table 4.19 that reapportionment has made a difference in expenditures. Spending has accelerated dramatically since the 1965-67 biennium; percentage increases range from -7 percent to 60 percent for the malapportioned legislature and 43 percent to 123 percent for the reapportioned one. These expenditure increases are reflected in corresponding increases in total state expenditures, in dollar amounts and percentage increases. The impact has been differential, however. Expenditures for natural resources and recreation increased only 21 percent prior to reapportionment (the second lowest percentage increase of the six services) but 123 percent after reapportionment (the largest percentage increase of the six services.) Transportation, the fastest growing service area prior to 1967, is the third fastest service growth since that time.

Reapportionment clearly has called for some restructuring of policy and expenditure priorities. If we use percentage increase in expenditures as an indicator of priorities attached to various services by the governor and the legislature, we see the following differences in priorities:

Malapportioned Legislature	Reapportioned Legislature
1. Transportation	1. Natural resources and recreation
2. Education	2. Transportation
3. Human benefits	3. Education
4. Agriculture	4. Public safety and regulation
5. Natural resources and recreation	5. Human benefits
6. Public safety and regulation	6. Agriculture

Natural resources and recreation and public safety and regulation have both improved their relative positions while all other services have declined in importance. The growth in expenditures for natural resources and recreation, as was noted above, is the result of growing concern over these problems in a state abundant in natural resources and recreational opportunities, but that spent very little money in this area prior to 1960. The increase in expenditures for public safety and regulation is a function of two factors, a recovery from a cut in expenditures in 1965-67, and a commitment from the governor and the legislature to control the state's spiralling highway death toll, a commitment that took the form of increased expenditures and tighter driver and safety regulations.

Of those services that lost rank, the most surprising is that of human benefits, the state's budget designation for welfare services. While state expenditures for human benefits increased both in dollars and percentages, its relative increase was less than for the other services and less than the average for all state expenditures. Because welfare is a predominately urban phenomenon, it appears that an urban problem has received comparatively poorer treatment under the reapportioned legislature. Appearances can be deceiving, nonetheless. The welfare dimension of the human benefits classification increased by only 14 percent prior to reapportionment, but 73 percent thereafter. The reapportioned legislature was cognizant of the welfare needs of the cities and responded to them. The legislature was also faced with other welfare demands—the need for special schools for disadvantaged and physically debilitated children and increasing commitments to hospitals for the tubercular and the alcoholic. The competition for scarce state dollars has meant that welfare has had to lose more and more of its share of the total expenditure pie. And within the category of human benefits expenditures, welfare had to compete with increasing demands from hospitals and health and from new welfare services.

Education's position in the priority list has changed very little. Inasmuch as 44 percent of all state expenditures go to education, it is not surprising that education's expenditures continue to spiral upward at a rate comparable to the total state expenditures. The increased expenditures for education since 1965-67 are misleading, however. A large share of that increase arose as a result of the establishment of a statewide community college system and the construction of a number of community colleges throughout the state. The 1965-67 to 1969-71 percentage increase for community colleges is more than 300 percent, by far the largest for any educational category. It is also interesting to note that the vast majority of the new community colleges are located in the urban and suburban areas of western Washington, therefore attractive for new legislators.

Highway expenditures increased 60 percent prior to reapportionment and 109 percent after. The relatively small percentage increase in highway expenditures after reapportionment is owing to the completion of a substantial segment of the state's interstate system before 1967 and a growing disenchantment with highways as a means of moving people in an urban environment. The battle over the Lake Washington bridge is symptomatic of the kinds of problems the Highway Department has encountered recently in dealing with the legislature and the legislature's growing reluctance to give the Highway Department a blank check for highway expenditures. Rapid transit is now viewed by many legislators as an attractive alternative to freeways in urban centers.

It is clear from the data that spending for state services has accelerated enormously since 1967-69, a result of reapportionment, the 1964 election, inflation, and population growth in the Puget Sound area. Not only has spending accelerated, but there has been a shift in priorities, emphasizing natural resources and recreation, public safety, and regulation. Even for those services that increased at a comparable rate, there were differences in how the money was being spent; the creation of a community college system was an important dimension of the increased spending for education, while spending for welfare took proportionately more of the human benefits expenditures. After 1965, the state seemed increasingly willing to spend money on urban-oriented services and services desired by urban constituents.

CONCLUSION

The Washington State League of Women Voters clearly won the legal and political battle it began in 1954 with its first initiative campaign. Although the League initiated the campaign for reapportionment, its subsequent role has been that of unsuccessful participant and interested observer, as the battle was waged at the ballot box, in the courts, and in conferences between the governor and legislative leaders. The process, begun in 1954, officially culminated in the 1956 Redistricting Act and its subsequent approval by the federal court. If we were interested in how reapportionment came about, we could have stopped at that point. But the institution of an innovation does not necessarily bring about its intended consequences. The 1965 redistricting plan was not the end of the reapportionment battle, but the beginning; it provided the opportunity to recruit new people to the legislature, and the opportunity for the governor and party leaders to form new legislative coalitions with the newly recruited legislators. Would the opportunities be used and to what end? The critical question was not whether reapportionment would occur—Baker v. Carr and Reynolds v. Simms guaranteed it would—but what its impact would be.

This study has provided some indicative answers to that question. There was an enormous turnover in personnel, the result of reapportionment and the 1964 election. New people were recruited to the legislature, people who viewed the legislature and the job of being a legislator differently from the people they replaced. Changes in personnel meant a new spirit, a new set of expectations that permeated the House. Lobbyists discovered that they had an entirely different clientele. As one lobbyist noted:

> The freshmen who came into the House in 1967 thought they knew as much but really knew as little as the people before them. Rather than relying on the Fourth Estate (the lobbyists) for counsel, they went to their own ways. We had to establish contacts all over again and show these people what we could do for them.
>
> Question: What effect did this have on your activities?
>
> You couldn't tell how votes were going to go and you didn't know who to talk to. Until things got organized it was pretty rough. Every member was important.

Party leaders were also cognizant of the change in personnel. The new members were reluctant to follow party leadership but, lacking the political experience to operate alone, most had to rely on the party for advice. The solid core of legislators who made the transition from the old to the new House must have played an important role in establishing procedures and mood for the new House.

The lack of legislative experience on the part of the new members gave effective control of the House to the senior Republicans who controlled the party and committee chairmanships and who, in conjunction with the Republican governor, were faced with the task of promulgating a legislative package. Because the Democrats controlled the Senate, the House leadership-international coalition had to define a program that would satisfy the new urban and suburban legislators in the House and gain sufficient support from urban Democrats in the Senate to insure its passage.

The package that emerged from the 1967 and 1969 sessions included legislation establishing and funding community colleges around the state, funding feasibility studies for rapid transit in Seattle, and allocating state funds to cities and counties, to name a few. Not only was the reapportioned House willing to hear urban bills, but it also passed and funded some of them. The result was an acceleration of spending for all state services, particularly those of interest to urban and suburban voters.

The reapportioned House, however, was not a total change. Some bills, such as the abortion bill, received a hearing for the first time but failed to be reported out of committee. Others, such as tax reform, required 117 days of work to fashion an acceptable package.

It must be remembered that reapportionment, per se, was not the immediate cause of those changes in policy that did occur. Altering district boundaries created a political situation in which changes could take place, provided the political actors could make use of the opportunities. New districts are meaningless unless they attract new people to the legislature. Both parties seized the opportunity, running candidates for the legislature who were local notables but who had little or no prior political experience. Many of them won. This change in personnel provided an opportunity for senior legislators and the governor to fashion new coalitions and initiate new programs in a legislature no longer bound by many of the old constraints. Less burdened by its legislative past, the reapportioned House was in a position to, and did, initiate some policy changes. The changes were not as broad or dramatic as some would have hoped or liked, but within the range of what was possible they comprised a substantial difference.

Creating an opportunity and climate for change does not guarantee that change will occur. In another state, reapportionment may have produced no significant change in policy. In Washington, reapportionment created the opportunity for change, and the political actors used that opportunity.

NOTES

1. See Gordon Baker, Rural Versus Urban Political Power
(New York: Random House, 1955); Malcolm Jewell, The Politics of
Reapportionment (New York: Atherton Press, 1962), The State Legis-
lature (New York: Random House, 1962), and "Legislative Reappor-
tionment," Law and Contemporary Problems, Spring 1952; and Paul
T. David and Ralph Eisenberg, Devaluation of the Urban and Suburban
Vote, 2 vols. (Charlottsville: University of Virginia, Bureau of Public
Administration, 1961).
2. Royce Hanson, The Political Thicket (Englewood Cliffs, N. J.:
Prentice-Hall, 1966), p. 22.
3. See Roscoe Martin, The Cities and the Federal System (New
York: Atherton Press, 1965).
4. See Robert A. Goldwin, ed., Representation and Misrepresentation (Chicago: Rand McNally, 1968) and Alfred de Grazia, Apportionment and Representative Government (New York: Praeger, 1963).
5. Jewell. The Politics of Reapportionment, p. 3.
6. William J. D. Boyd, "Reapportionment: Problems, Prospects,
Probabilities," in Goldwin, Representation and Misrepresentation,
p. 131.
7. Thomas Dye, Politics, Economics and the Public (Chicago:
Rand McNally, 1966).
8. Ira Sharkansky, Spending in the American States (Chicago:
Rand McNally, 1968), and Thomas J. Anton, The Politics of State
Expenditure in Illinois (Urbana: University of Illinois Press, 1966).
9. For an excellent description and analysis of the 1956 battle,
see Gordon E. Baker, The Politics of Reapportionment in Washington
State (New York: Holt, Rinehart, and Winston, 1960).
10. State ex rel O'Connell v. Meyers, 51 Wash. (2d) 454 (1957).
11. Thigpen v. Meyers, 211 Fed. Supp. 826 (1962). For an excellent description and analysis of the case see William B. McDermott,
"The Impact of Baker vs. Carr in the State of Washington: The Relationship of Constituency to Compliance" (Ph.D. dissertation, Department of Political Science, University of Washington, 1965).
12. McDermott, "The Impact of Baker vs. Carr," p. 61.
13. For a discussion of the coalition and the reasons behind its
formation, see Hugh A. Bone, "The 1962 Election in Washington,"
Western Political Quarterly, 16 (June 1963), 469-70, and McDermott,
"The Impact of Baker vs. Carr," pp. 104-111.
14. McDermott, "The Impact of Baker vs. Carr."
15. Hugh A. Bone, "Washington," in Eleanor Bushnell, ed., Politics
of Reapportionment in the West (Salt Lake City: University of Utah
Press, forthcoming).

16. McDermott, "The Impact of Baker vs. Carr," pp. 176-180.

17. Richard Neustadt, Presidential Power (New York: Science Editions, 1962).

18. Bone, "Washington."

19. Boyd, "Reapportionment," p. 117.

20. Bone, Washington."

21. See Bruce M. Haston, "Impact of Reapportionment on Election of 1967 Legislature," Quorum, I (Fall 1966), 1-2.

22. See Frank J. Sorauf, Party and Representation (New York: Atherton Press, 1963).

23. See John C. Wahlke, Heinz Eulau, William Buchanan, and Leroy C. Ferguson, The Legislative System: Explorations in Legislative Behavior (New York: John Wiley, 1962).

24. This question was used because it presented the role dilemma clearly to each respondent and forced him to make a choice. For a more indirect method of ascertaining this role perception, see ibid.

25. See Donald R. Matthews, U.S. Senators and Their World (Chapel Hill: University of North Carolina Press, 1960).

26. James David Barber, The Lawmakers (New Haven: Yale University Press, 1965).

PROFESSIONAL STAFF
AND LEGISLATIVE INFLUENCE
IN WISCONSIN
Alan Rosenthal

The need for improvement in state legislatures is by no means new. People have been criticizing legislative performance for years. What is new is that concerted action is now taking place. Throughout the nation, real efforts are being made to modernize legislative organization, operations, services, and facilities. Legislatures in almost all states are undergoing change and improvement. As a result, legislatures are probably better today than ever before. It may not seem so, however, because the problems facing them are worse than ever before.

Among the many reform proposals being considered and adopted, there is one on which agreement is overwhelming. Legislatures need and must have greater professional assistance in gathering, processing, and assessing information. Without staff, the reform argument goes, legislators cannot possibly arrive at competent judgments. Without staff, there is little hope of redressing the imbalance between the power of the legislature on the one hand and that of governors and administrative bureaucracies on the other.

Probably more than anything else, staff is what both attentive citizens and legislators themselves now demand. A recent report of the American Assembly, for example, recommends professional staff for majority and minority leaderships, legislative councils, major standing committees, and central services such as bill drafting, law revision, and library and reference. A recent compilation of recommendations from various national and state reports, published by the Citizens Conference on State Legislatures, devotes more space to staff than to any other subject. Studies conducted by the Eagleton Institute of Politics at Rutgers University for legislatures in Rhode Island, Maryland, Wisconsin, Connecticut, Florida, and Mississippi propose the establishment and/or expansion of various types of staff.

My own surveys of several legislatures indicate that increased staffing is considered to be essential by most members. In New Jersey, Connecticut, Florida, and Mississippi, representative samples of legislators were asked whether their legislatures needed major improvement, some improvement, or little improvement at all. In these states the percentages believing there was a need for major improvement were 44, 54, 51, and 52 percent respectively. Legislators were then asked to suggest the most important types of improvement that they felt should be made. In New Jersey and Florida, half the members volunteered that increased staffing was essential. In Connecticut, three-fifths and in Mississippi, almost two-fifths felt the same way.

Knowledgeable people, then, acknowledge the importance of legislative staff. But the specific effects of particular staffing patterns have been virtually ignored. A recent president of the New York Senate expressed things well when he stated: "To help us in decisionmaking, we need not just more staff, not just full-time staff, not just better-trained staff, so glibly urged by the traditional reformers." Even more important, he continued, "we need to know what kinds of staff we need."[1] Different species are likely to have effects that differ in direction and character. One species may affect certain people and aspects of the legislative process, another species may strike alternative targets. Some effects are anticipated, others are unexpected. Some may produce radical change, most will probably reinforce traditional habits. Certain results are desirable, others less so. These are the considerations I shall explore by concentrating on the establishment and effects of two particular types of staff in the Wisconsin legislature.

THE POLITICS OF STAFFING

In the 1965 session, four full-time research analysts, one assigned to each party caucus in the Assembly and Senate, and a central fiscal staff, intended to serve the joint finance committee, began work for the Wisconsin legislature. These pilot projects were aspects of a larger movement toward legislative improvement that had its beginnings several years before. In order to assess the effects these staffs had on the legislature, it is necessary first to consider the context in which reform began and the factors that appear to have impelled reform efforts.

Generally, legislative reform may result from any number of factors. Some are relatively remote and others are more proximate. Among the most important are pressures from outside the state, citizen demands from within the state, political leadership, legislative deprivation, critical events, and a tradition of institutional reform.

Several of these were significant during the early 1960s when the Wisconsin legislature embarked upon its modernization program.

Perhaps the most important conditions facilitating or retarding legislative reform are to be found in the political cultures of the states. In some states, such as Pennsylvania, New Jersey, and Connecticut, a tradition of governmental or political reform is absent. In others, such as Wisconsin, reform is habitual. At least since the beginning of the century, people in Wisconsin have conceived of politics as a worthwhile endeavor, tending to promote the public good. Less cynical than people elsewhere, citizens in this progressive state believe in the efficacy of political action, the importance of voting and other forms of participation, and the ability of people through government to control their environment.

In Wisconsin, citizens and politicians are not reluctant to innovate; rather, they have been willing to undertake governmental programs that were new and daring at the time of their adoption. Wisconsin was the first state to enact a modern, enforceable income tax. It provided for generous programs in social welfare, even before the New Deal, and it embarked upon one of the most ambitious conservation programs in the nation. Compared to other states, it has traditionally maintained a high level of public services and exerted great effort—as indicated by per capita taxes in relation to per capita personal income—to pay for them. Citizens in the state are not only concerned about services, they are also extremely conscientious about the conduct of government. Patronage barely exists and lobbying is severely controlled. People expect government to be run honestly and politics to be uncorrupt. To a remarkable degree their expectations have been fulfilled.

Such a public climate was conducive to legislative improvement. It was hardly sufficient, however. A supportive climate did not absolutely require change in legislative institutions in the sense that public expectations were translated into demands by citizens, the press, and civic and interest groups. Unlike in some other states, such as Maryland and Washington, where outside groups exerted pressure, in Wisconsin the impetus for improvement came mainly from within the legislature itself. It came in response to certain critical events.

Often a drive to strengthen a legislature follows upon the heels of a critical event, or cluster of events, such as the turnover caused by reapportionment, a constitutional convention, or a change in control of government. In Wisconsin, the major impetus was a shift in party control of the executive and legislative branches. During the period from 1959 to 1964, when the legislature was developing a number of potentially important changes, its motivation to modernize was stimulated primarily by the sharp alteration in state politics. Wisconsin had traditionally been dominated by Republicans. They controlled every legislature from 1939 to 1959 and held the governorship during these two decades as well. Not until the period after 1945 did the contemporary Democratic party begin its development, and not until 1958 did it elect a governor and simultaneously gain control of the state Assembly. Since then, partisan politics in the state have been highly competitive. Democrats reelected Gaylord Nelson governor in 1960, and elected John Reynolds in 1962. The Republicans won in 1964, 1966, and 1968 with Warren Knowles. Throughout this period, the Senate remained safely in Republican hands, while division in the Assembly was quite close, with Democrats in the majority in 1959-60 and 1965-66 and Republicans in the majority during 1961-62, 1963-64, and 1967-68. This change in the party system, and especially the confrontation between a Democratic governor and Republican legislature from 1961 through 1964, prompted the drive for a stronger legislature.

Even at this time, the legislature was not weak. In fact, compared to legislatures in other states, it was well endowed. Neither attempts at modernization nor professional staffing were new. As early as 1901, a legislative reference bureau was established to assist members. In 1947 a legislative council, with a legal staff, was created. The council's origins owed nothing to a lack of auxiliary aides for the legislature, as was the case in many other states. Instead, in establishing the council, Republican legislative leaders hoped to gain some initiative from the executive and thereby exercise greater influence over state policymaking.[2]

By the early 1960s, the Wisconsin legislature was hardly in a condition of urgent need. It benefited from staff assistance in bill drafting, legislative reference and some research, continuous statutory revision, as well as legal help in matters pertaining to uniform laws. Nevertheless, in view of reform orientations that prevailed in the state and the changing nature of party control, legislators were willing to go further, if the circumstances were propitious. In one important respect, they were indeed propitious. A major foundation was ready to pay half the costs of a program of legislative improvement.

The idea of the Ford Foundation's contributing to Wisconsin's efforts was first raised at a meeting of the National Legislative Conference at Oklahoma City in 1957.* At that time, Earl Sachse, the

---

*The National Legislative Conference is an organization that includes legislators and legislative staff. Many ideas on modernization are exchanged at its meetings. Organizations such as the Legislative Conference, the Citizens Conference on State Legislatures, and the Eagleton Institute have played an increasingly important role in the reform movement, because they offer opportunities for legislators from the states to meet together and discuss common problems, needs, and remedies.

executive director of Wisconsin's legislative council, and William
Pincus, a representative of the Ford Foundation, discussed ways in
which the foundation could be of assistance. The next year Sachse
and Pincus exchanged correspondence, and shortly thereafter negotiations began with members of the legislature taking a leading part.
On the basis of a proposal drafted by Sachse, in October 1959 Ford
approved a six-year grant of $240,000, to be matched by a like amount
from state revenues.

The initial plan contemplated three phases—the first concentrating
on fiscal review and budget analysis, the second on intensive research
in the most important general fields of law, and the third on legal
research and bill drafting. During the next two years, however, negotiations among legislators led to substantial modification. By early
1962, when the legislature enacted an authorizing bill, objectives and
methods had shifted considerably. No longer were legal research
and bill drafting, designed principally to assist the legislative council,
major components. Instead, the three-phase program included: (1)
budget review and fiscal analysis, aimed at the development of new
techniques in the field; (2) review of legislative organization and
procedures, aimed at the development of procedures leading to better
informed legislators, higher quality legislation, improved services,
and shorter sessions; and (3) demonstration projects, to determine
the value of staff services to the legislature and its committees.

To accomplish the phase relating to organization and procedures,
Paul Mason, a parliamentary expert from California, was hired as a
consultant late in the year. Many of his recommendations led to
changes in legislative rules and statutes, which were adopted in the
1963 session. To accomplish the phase relating to fiscal analysis,
W. Donald Knight, an economics professor at the University of
Wisconsin, was hired early in 1963. His study was completed two
years later. In addition, Dale Cattanach, who later became director
of the fiscal bureau, was engaged in late 1963 to work on budget review
aspects of legislative improvement. These initial phases are of no
immediate concern. Rather, we are interested in legislative decisions
to establish demonstration staffs, legislative anticipations regarding
their purposes, and legislative assessments of their effectiveness.
In late 1964, a committee of legislators directing the Ford Foundation
program concluded that several types of staffing should be undertaken
as a demonstration phase at the beginning of the 1965 session. The
types of staff decided included student interns, fiscal analysts, and
caucus analysts.

The intern project was designed first, to satisfy the Ford Foundation's original plan that the legislature work closely with the state
universities, and second, to assist the standing committees of both
houses in issues other than finance. In view of the experimental nature

of the program, legislators decided to start with only four part-time
university students, who began work the second month of the 1965
legislature. Two of them served Assembly committees and the other
two Senate committees. The first year of the project was far from
successful. Within a few months, there was agreement that the interns
had not been properly prepared for the duties they were supposed to
assume. Legislative leaders felt that they had not been given adequate
direction by committee chairmen or members. One intern reported
that he and his colleagues had no idea of what they should do, where
they could get a desk, or for whom they were to work. He described
his experience:

> After some remarks about the lack of direction, I was
> assigned principally to the Assembly Judiciary Commit-
> tee. Although I do not believe that I was ever formally
> introduced to the entire committee, I did meet the chair-
> man and kept in touch with him. I began keeping files of
> all the bills that came through the committee and I at-
> tended all the hearings and executive sessions. . . . Al-
> though I continually asked the chairman for assignments,
> he was usually too busy to channel to me the problems on
> which the committee might need information. . . . Much of
> the research I did was unused and the committee made many
> decisions without the benefit of information I could easily
> have obtained for them if only I had been assigned the
> task beforehand. As time has gone on my working re-
> lationship with the committee has become closer, but all
> along that relationship has been characterized more by
> drift than by conscious direction.

In only one case did members of a committee actually seem satisfied
with an intern's services, but even here the intern would have welcomed
closer supervision and direction.

Despite these problems, the legislature decided to continue the
program, although with several modifications. The Senate majority
leader insisted that primary responsibility for the interns be with the
executive secretary of the legislative council. Sachse himself suggested that the interns be employed the year prior to the session to
assist council interim committees and continue their work with standing
committees during the session. It was agreed, therefore, that four
university students would be awarded internships in 1966. Under the
supervision of the executive secretary, they would work with interim
committees of the council until the 1967 session commenced, at which
time they would be assigned to standing committees and receive specific projects from the chairmen.

During the 1967 session, the program appeared to be working somewhat better, but it still was less than effective. The interns themselves were not satisfied. One felt that his chairman was not fully aware of what the program was about, although the chairman had supervised an intern in the previous session. Another felt his chairman "didn't really want help" and used him only for minor tasks. A third, by contrast, believed that he had an ideal working relationship with his chairman, an individual who in his previous career had been accustomed to using staff. All but the latter agreed that supervision was inadequate and their services were not being efficiently used. Legislators also agreed that the internship program was lacking in essential qualities. Three-quarters of the seventy-four members we interviewed (out of a total membership of 133) during 1967 responded that interns were only somewhat effective or not very effective at all. It was certainly not envy that caused these rather critical response, inasmuch as a similar proportion of members of committees to which interns had been assigned responded the same way as did those whose committees had no interns. Although only one out of four lawmakers thought that student interns were doing a very effective job for the legislature, the program was retained. In 1969, legislative interns, now working full time, were serving the legislature through still another session.

Interns had not really been of intense concern to those legislators who decided on the demonstration projects. What they were most concerned about was budget review and fiscal analysis. A staff to perform such functions, in fact, had been recommended to the legislature from time to time. Legislators and their consultants, however, had somewhat different ideas about what a fiscal staff would do. The former hoped to redress the imbalance between gubernatorial and bureaucratic power on the one hand and legislative power on the other. By establishing staff, they intended also specific improvement in the legislature's budget-review performance. The consultant, on the other hand, hoped that staff would also help the legislature conduct a rational-comprehensive review of the budget—providing the legislature with a better understanding of the total budget, furnishing information on fiscal alternatives, coordinating the work of several groups possessing fiscal authority, and engaging in long-range fiscal analysis and planning to ensure that limited funds were appropriated to those areas of greatest need.

Fiscal staff began operating under the direction of Dale Cattanach in 1964. When the following session began, the new director was authorized two full-time and two part-time employees. During the year, the fiscal staff worked closely with the joint finance committee, submitting, in addition to verbal information, approximately fifty written reports to the chairmen or members. Apparently, the legislature was satisfied with its demonstration project. The allotment of $36,000 for personnel during 1965 was increased to $63,500 for the following year. Cattanach's request for five full-time analysts, as well as clerical and secretarial help, was endorsed by the legislature.

There is little doubt that legislators thought highly of the fiscal staff. In our interviews during 1967, we found that about two out of three members were of the opinion that their fiscal agency was very effective, and nearly all of the remainder thought it at least somewhat effective. Members of the joint finance committee, who might be expected to have the most reliable judgments on the question, were practically unanimous. Nine out of ten of those we interviewed, who served on the fourteen-member committee, reported that fiscal staff had been very effective. Hardly anyone in the legislature would have been willing to dispense with its services, and within a few years the fiscal bureau became a permanent legislative agency.

While the continuation of fiscal staffing was never really in question, the experiment with caucus analysts proved both venturesome and controversial. Staff for the parties in the two houses was actually an afterthought. Such a plan had not been broached during the early stages of negotiations with the Ford Foundation; nor was it developed easily. Even in late 1964, legislative leaders were divided. A few believed that existing research groups were sufficient to provide all the information the legislature needed. One pointed to possible duplication of effort and potential adversary relationships among caucus analysts working for the different party groups. Moreover, there was a question, raised by the executive secretary of the legislative council, as to whether partisan staffing faithfully complied with the terms of the Ford matching grant. The Senate majority leader, however, was determined. His caucus had on its own employed an analyst in the 1963 session, and the experience had proved worthwhile. As long as the caucuses were treated equally, he maintained, the terms of the grant would be fulfilled. The Senate would hire caucus assistants in any event, so the Assembly might as well follow suit. It was finally decided that there should be no restrictions regarding the employment by each party caucus of one analyst, to serve for the length of the next session, from January through July 1965.

The session during which staff operated was a trying one and the position of analyst was indeed precarious. In Wisconsin it had been a bold step to require the state to contribute to the salaries of people employed by political parties in the legislature. As a result, analysts were conscious of negative public and press attitudes and, as one stated, "much of the work we do has to be hidden in desk drawers when a reporter walks in to chat with us." In addition, the nonpartisan staffs in the legislature did not welcome any competition from partisan people, who threatened to come between them and legislators. And legislators themselves were unaware of how analysts might help. The analyst hired by the Senate Democrats described things: "When I first reported to the job, the minority leader was very apprehensive. . . . And he didn't quite know what to do with me. He told me I would sit in on caucuses but not all of them, because some of them got pretty sensitive, and they wouldn't want an outsider sitting in." At the end of the trial period, leaders expressed opinions that because of a lack of direction the project remained in flux. They decided, nonetheless, to continue it for three additional months. Then, as the year drew to a close, they agreed that caucus analysts would be useful during the interim as well as the session, "securing information relative to pending legislation and assisting in answering requests from individual citizens and organizations regarding state government." So, they made the four positions full time.

However uncertain the beginnings, within a relatively brief period caucus staffing had become fully accepted. By 1967, the state had assumed responsibility for financing the project and the number of analysts for each Assembly caucus had been increased from one to three. Legislators appeared quite satisfied. Our survey of members found that three-fifths rated the caucus staffs as very effective, and nearly all of the remainder rated them as somewhat effective.

THE EFFECTS OF STAFFING

If survival is an adequate test, then each of the three demonstration projects conducted by the Wisconsin legislature proved successful. Each has persisted in one form or another. Survival, however, is not a sufficient criterion. Legislators themselves think highly only of the fiscal and caucus staffs, and these are the ones we shall consider further. Acknowledging their reputations for effectiveness, it is necessary to ask what kinds of effects they have and on whom they have such effects.

Staff may well be effective in diverse ways. And, of course, different types of staff may have quite different effects. It would be a mistake, for example, to presume that a central bill-drafting agency and administrative aides serving individuals affect legislators in the same manner. It would be foolish, for instance, to assume that professionals serving committee chairmen and those serving elected party leaderships produce similar results. It would be incorrect to regard all effects as substantially the same, with none more important than others.

At the outset, we require some means of conceptualizing effects, selecting theoretically significant ones for additional examination. There are, I suggest, four extremely important dimensions of possible effect. First, there is the dimension that relates primarily to individual legislators and how they adjust to legislative life. Staff may facilitate adjustment, easing the burdens of members or enhancing their feelings of security and gratification. Second and third are dimensions relating to legislative organization, including how the legislature is structured to make decisions and how such structures are maintained. Staff may lead to a redistribution of influence in the making of legislative decisions. It may also encourage integration, or disintegration, within the legislative parties or within the two houses. Fourth is the dimension relating to the legislature's performance in the governmental process, notably its ability to share in the formulation of state policies and exercise general control over the administration of programs by the departments and agencies of the executive branch.*

Having postulated conceptual dimensions, the next question is how we determine whether staff have any effects within each. The best way is to adopt a research design that will enable us to evaluate each dimension both before and after staff. This method permits measurement (at time 1, in 1961 and/or 1963, before the existence or development of staff, and at time 2, in 1967, after staff is fully operative) of differences in a number of dependent variables, which serve as operational indicators of legislative adjustment, legislative decisionmaking, legislative integration, and legislative performance. The design is illustrated in the diagram, in which X_1 is the legislature during 1961 and/or 1963, X_2 is the legislature during 1967, and d is the difference in measurements between these two periods. Depending

$$\boxed{\quad X_1 \quad | \quad X_2 \quad} \qquad d = X_2 - X_1$$

on the specific type of dependent variable we use, the difference between X_2 and X_1 can be attributed to the impact of one or the other independent variable, caucus or fiscal staff.† This is the general

---

*These dimensions, although conceptually distinctive, empirically overlap. If staff have effects in one respect, these effects are likely to be felt at least indirectly in some others as well. For example, if staff serve to promote feelings of efficacy on the parts of individual legislators, this in turn may well have impact on decisionmaking.

†For the latter period it has been possible to collect some data that were not available for the earlier one. Thus, the cross-section at time 2 is denser than at time 1, and in some instances inferences are made although comparison between periods is not possible.

192

logic, but there are problems that should be noted before we proceed to an assessment of staff effects.

In our study, it is naturally difficult to control extraneous variables or to identify factors other than caucus or fiscal staffing that may have contributed to a change in the dependent variables. The introduction of staff was not the only factor differentiating the legislative environments of 1961 and 1963 from that of 1967. A number of other changes inevitably occurred. In the earlier sessions Democrats served as governor; in the later one a Republican held office. Although in each of these sessions party control in the legislature was almost precisely the same,* individual members and the composition of party leaderships naturally changed. There were other differences also, including among the most important the varying salience of particular state issues from one period to the next.

In short, it is conceivable that something other than staff may account for an alteration in the decisionmaking structure or changes in legislative performance. It would be delightful to have a control group—another and identical legislature—in which caucus and fiscal staffing were not introduced. None, however, exists. In the present study, confined to a single state (or even in a study that ranges wider), it is not possible systematically to hold constant the few factors noted above or the large number of others. We have tried, as far as possible, however, to take them into account in the analyses below.

Another problem deserves mention. This research, like any other, is no better than the data and measurements on which it relies. In social research there is inevitably a gap between conceptualization and operationalization. An indicator that is susceptible of some type of measurement is never quite the same as the characteristic it is supposed to measure. People, for example, may question whether responses to an interview item legitimately reflect the structure of legislative decisionmaking or whether conflict between the parties on a budget bill is an adequate surrogate for legislative integration. No perfect linkage can be devised, but the challenge must be met.

Reliance on a single research method or one type of data may be hazardous, as is illustrated by the divergent results of studies making exclusive use of roll-call votes to demonstrate the importance of party in the legislature. As a safeguard, we have used a number of methods and a variety of data, which are unlikely to share the same weaknesses. They will be described in the context of analysis. Some

---

*The split in the Assembly was 55 Republicans to 45 Democrats in 1961 and 54 Republicans to 46 Democrats in 1963 and 1967; the split in the Senate was 20, 22, and 21 Republicans to 13, 11, and 12 Democrats in 1961, 1963, and 1967 respectively.

data pertain to attitudes and evaluation, others to observable behavior. Some are intended to suggest the effects of caucus staff, others the effects of fiscal staff. These relatively hard data are supplemented by "focused interviews" with members and employees of the legislature, my own observations in Wisconsin, and academic studies conducted previously. All of this information should provide a fair evaluation of the effects of caucus and fiscal staffs on legislative adjustment, decisionmaking, integration, and performance.

Adjustment

Nearly everywhere rank-and-file members of a legislature comprise the lumpen proletariat of government. As a rule, people expect little of many of them and many of them expect little of themselves. Despite occasional exceptions, legislators as a class suffer from impoverished egos and low self-esteem. This is not surprising, in that service in a legislature reminds them constantly of how insignificant an individual is and how small a difference he makes. Whatever may be said abstractly about the importance of their jobs, legislators are rarely given the help they need in order to contribute very much.

Wisconsin lawmakers were always better off than their counterparts in most other states. For many years they have enjoyed assistance from a legislative reference bureau that renders invaluable aid in drafting bills and providing basic information. They have also been helped by the competent professional staff of the legislative council, which concentrates on assisting interim and session committees. Because more strategic members inevitably commanded the largest portion of staff attention, the rank and file have lacked adequate support. This was something legislative leaders sought to remedy when they initiated pilot projects in fiscal and caucus staffing.

One of the original purposes of fiscal analysts was to furnish all legislators relevant information on budget and tax policy. Quickly, however, the bureau sensed that its overriding obligation was to the joint finance committee, the locus of legislative power over appropriations and revenue, and especially to its cochairmen. In 1967, for example, practically all of the memoranda drafted by the fiscal bureau were directed to the cochairmen or members of the finance committee. Hardly any work at all was undertaken for rank-and-file members of the Senate or Assembly. As a consequence, fiscal staffing had little effect on the material well being of individual legislators.

Caucus staffing was quite different. It was designed to combine service to leaders, caucuses, and individual members of the legislative parties. In practice, the mix of services varied among the four staffs.

In the Senate, the Republican analyst functioned primarily as an administrative assistant to the majority leader and paid less attention to the needs of the other twenty members of the caucus. The Democratic analyst split his time more equally. In the Assembly, the Republican staff divided its efforts during 1967, although during the session before it had principally served the leadership. By contrast, the Democratic staff, while assisting both leaders and followers, focused relatively more attention on the needs of the former.

Unlike administrative assistants who serve individual legislators in Congress or states such as California and Florida, caucus staffers in Wisconsin ordinarily do not involve themselves in district or constituent problems. They perform such services for leaders, but rank-and-file members handle their own constituency affairs. Nonetheless, Wisconsin's analysts provide both tangible and symbolic benefits to individual party members. By furnishing members with information and publicity and enhancing their sense of security and self-esteem, staffers facilitate the adjustment of many individuals to the trials of legislative life.

First, they help to educate members. Party decisions depend not only on a recognition of the political and partisan implications of issues, but also on some understanding of the technical questions involved. This is where staff has been useful. During legislative sessions, the caucus meets almost every day to discuss bills that have been reported by standing committees and are ready for floor consideration. Before staffing, the burden of understanding and explaining bills at caucus meetings fell on party leaders, who had little free time to do the job properly. In the minority caucus, where no committee chairmen were represented, the task was extremely difficult. Analysts took over much of the burden, reviewing bills and reporting to the caucus. In one situation, for instance, before the minority caucus in the Assembly could take a position, it was necessary for members to make sense of a very complicated issue. Few people in or outside the legislature were able to comprehend a provision proposed in the governor's budget. The Democratic analyst, who was concentrating on the budget, spent hours explaining it to party members until finally a majority emerged with some understanding as well as a party position.

The educational function of staff is not confined to formal meetings of the party. Information is also communicated informally, in staff offices and at other places in the capitol. It is not at all unusual to find legislators sitting around an analyst's desk, drinking coffee, exchanging political news and legislative gossip, and receiving tactfully prefered advice and encouragement. Questions, such as "Where do I go to get this?" and "What do I say in a letter to a constituent?" are raised by legislators, and helpful answers are supplied by staffers. In addition, the Assembly minority staff and the speaker's administrative assistant convey information by means of periodic newsletters.

Despite the pervasiveness of partisanship in the legislature, the overwhelming proportion of content in each party's newsletter has been factual, objective, and descriptive, serving to inform members as to the content and status of legislation and to give them materials to use as a basis for publicity.

One of the major reasons why analysts perform the educational function successfully is that they maintain—varying according to the individuals involved in an exchange—the confidence of party members. In large part this confidence is built on the direct publicity assistance they render to legislative rank and file as well as legislative leaders. Caucus staffs were not originally intended to engage in public relations activity, but this rapidly became one of their most important functions. From the very beginning, the general need for public relations assistance existed, and legislators had only to be encouraged by analysts in order to request specific help. One analyst described the situation when staffs first came into being: "When I arrived in '65 many of them didn't know how to put out a press release. They just did not put out press releases. They invited reporters from the local paper to a big meeting or else they put in a paid advertisement. The ones that did put out releases didn't know where to send them." By the next session, almost half the time of analysts was spent on publicity for party members.

Each staff provides such help. In the Senate, for example, the Republican analyst contacts daily and weekly newspapers, arranges for photographs to be taken of all members, and furnishes a list of media to everyone. In the Assembly, even greater attention is spent on publicity. Filed copies of press releases permit some assessment of how Republican and Democratic staffs handled public relations during 1967-68. Republicans were slightly more oriented toward press work than were Democrats. In the first year of the biennium, the Democrats issued twice as many releases as the Republicans; in the second year, the proportions were reversed, mainly because Assembly Republicans hired a staffer whose major skill and principal interest was public relations.

The two groups in the Assembly allocated their work differently. Both favored the party leaderships. However, the allotment of press-release work by Democrats to leaders was disproportionate. This is evidenced by the fact that of the releases produced by Republicans, 5 percent related to the speaker and majority leader, but of those produced by Democrats 25 percent related to the minority leader and assistant minority leader. The two groups differed in attention given to the needs of members from marginal electoral districts. Unlike the Republicans, the Democrats focused overwhelmingly on marginal rather than safe district members. This is evidenced by the average number of press releases prepared for each type of rank-and-file member during 1967-68. Republicans issued an average of fifteen releases for members from safe districts, nineteen for ones from moderately safe districts, and eighteen for those from marginal districts. By contrast, Democrats issued an average of only eight releases for legislators from safe and moderately safe districts and twenty-nine for those from marginal districts.

In view of the amount of concern given publicity, it is relevant to inquire whether press releases drafted by the staff were actually used by Wisconsin newspapers. Urban dailies are disinclined to publicize local legislators' statements or activities, however conveniently packaged. Suburban, small town, and rural dailies and weeklies, however, take legislator press releases seriously. One analyst, for example, commented: "I do see newsletters we prepare mailed out, and I do see the Wisconsin Press Association's clipping service that shows our material is being reproduced in newspapers."[3] Another mentioned that between 75 and 80 percent of the press releases turned out were actually published by the weekly press. Still another noted that staff work had made it possible for the Assembly minority leader to have a regular column published in a suburban weekly paper.

It is not necessary to rely on the evaluations of staffers themselves. There is another means to see just how members have been helped in achieving greater publicity than before. In order to provide at least indirect data on staff effectiveness, the contents of sixty-six different newspapers in a sample of sixteen Assembly districts were examined for the periods of January through June of 1963 and 1967.* Although the amount of overall space devoted to news did not change substantially during this period, there was a tremendous rise in the coverage given local legislators. Total column lines expanded from about 6,000 in 1963 to about 12,500 in 1967, more than 100 percent. The number of articles increased by almost 150 percent. Separate articles on members, legislator names appearing in headlines, and first-page placement all doubled. Certainly, much of the increased and improved coverage was attributable to the publicity endeavors of the two Assembly staffs.

Even if press releases are translated into newsprint, there is still a question of whether additional publicity makes any difference to the electoral prospects of incumbents. Improving one's chances for reelection is, after all, what a legislator chiefly cares about and

---

*These districts included some in which the same and different Republicans held office in each year, some in which the same and different Democrats held office in each year, and some that switched not only incumbents but party control as well. Among the newspapers were eight dailies and fifty-eight weeklies.

what a political publicist seeks to accomplish. Press releases and publicity can make voters aware of who their representatives are and how effective a job they are doing.

State legislators in Wisconsin, as a recent study shows, had special need of public relations assistance for campaign purposes. Men running for the legislature felt state voters were much less interested in their races, less informed about their campaigns, and less aware of the issues and candidates than were those running for congressional or statewide office. They believed that campaigns for higher-level offices were more in the public eye and were reported more extensively in the press. As John Kingdon states, "Unlike the congressman, he [the candidate for state legislature] feels that voters are not involved in politics at his governmental level and that the media do not cover his activities as fully."[4]

Although caucus analysts worked on campaigns in 1966, it was not until the 1968 elections that their actions could possibly prove meaningful. How meaningful, in terms of electoral outcomes, is a matter that merits discussion. In order to discover just how much of the vote their publicity efforts shaped, we have used regression analysis.* In this analysis independent variables are the numbers of press releases in 1967 and 1968, the percentages of the 1966 vote for incumbents and their party affiliations, and the percentages of the 1968 vote won by their party's gubernatorial candidate. The dependent variable is the percentages of the 1968 vote for incumbents running for reelection to the legislature.† By means of multiple regression, we can determine how much each independent variable contributes to variation in the dependent variable.

The results, as expected, indicate that press releases account for an extremely small proportion of the variation in the 1968 vote. Far more significant is the electoral success in each district of either

---

*A multiple regression equation—

$$Y' = a + b_1 (X_1) + b_2 (X_2) + \ldots + b_n (X_n),$$

where X_1 represents the first independent variable, X_2 the second, and the letters represent regression constants—is used to measure the combined effect of a number of independent variables on a dependent variable. It is also useful to assess the relative importance of each of the independent variables in predicting the dependent variable.[5]

†A total of sixty-three assemblymen have been examined. Press release data on several incumbents running for reelection were unavailable, and these cases were omitted from analysis.

Warren Knowles or Bronson LaFollette, the Republican and Democratic gubernatorial candidates in 1968. More significant also is the
1966 vote received by assemblymen, which partly reflects the general
popularity of individual candidates and the general characteristics
of district constituencies. Yet, press releases did influence electoral
margins in certain districts. Whereas in safe districts the amount
of publicity hardly mattered, in marginal districts it had some effect.
In a sharply contested race, some effect may make the difference between winning and losing. For politicians, such a difference is a big
one.

In any case, legislators think that press releases matter, particularly when they face difficult election challenges. And what they
think is probably more important in terms of adjustment than how
much press releases actually count. As long as press releases appear
to be critical, politicians will continue to believe the publicity pays
dividends. Their beliefs are reinforced by visible illustrations of
impact. In the 1968 elections, for instance, minority Democrats in
the Assembly picked up two seats, having expected to lose five or six
in a Republican year. Party members were elated, attributing much
of their success to caucus staff. Their gratitude was expressed in
the comment, "What a great job!" and the remark, made in jest, "If
you worked harder we could have won the Assembly."

Not only the material but also the less tangible benefits of staff
have to be taken into account. The services of caucus analysts are
used directly by many legislators. The fact that they are available
is known by all. The very existence of staff affects the atmosphere.
Legislators feel that someone cares, someone is there to help if help
is needed. Thus, staff tends to reduce the anxieties of legislators.
"Their job is made easier; the business of survival comes easier,"
is the way a Republican Assembly staff man put things. Staff also
tends to increase legislators' self-confidence. "They like the attention
I give them," commented an employee of the Senate majority party.
"Just your presence builds their egos," said another staffer, describing
one particular senator who boasted to constituents that he had his own
assistant and speechwriter. An analyst for Assembly Democrats
summed up the effects on rank-and-file members as follows:

> If you supply them with an independent source of infor-
> mation and press releases, they're pretty happy. . . .
> You fight with the party organization and the adminis-
> trative branch of government on their behalf. . . . They
> love this. They're also impressed with the idea that
> you're theirs, they have an administrative assistant, and
> you show interest in their problems—which often is one
> of the most difficult jobs, because many of them are
> really insignificant problems.

Whether or not staff reduces work load or provides material comfort, it is still appreciated. In the case of the fiscal bureau, direct benefits are more important. Members of the joint finance committee to whom it responds are more inclined to express satisfaction with fiscal staff than nonmembers who receive minimal aid. In the case of caucus staff, direct benefits are not as important. Members who receive comparatively little public relations assistance are just as likely to rate their staff highly as members who receive comparatively more.

If any factor discriminates among orientations toward fiscal and caucus staff, it is seniority or length of service in the legislature. One analyst explained why new members find it easier to use staff: "They don't feel that you have to be approached with trepidation, as the oldtimers sometimes do. They take you as a matter of course, which is very nice. They work with you." In addition, senior members in Wisconsin, as elsewhere, are more inclined to pursue traditional habits and extol the virtues of citizen legislatures. They are less inclined to support legislative modernization. They are less likely to rely on staff and less likely to evaluate either fiscal or caucus analysts very positively.

Nevertheless, to the large and undoubtedly increasing majority of members, professional staff provides satisfaction. It makes legislators feel that they count. It gives them the agreeable sense of having trustworthy information and being in control. It encourages increased self confidence and greater pride in legislative service. It provides some degree of stability and security in an arena characterized by reversal and frustration.

Decisionmaking

In some legislatures power is relatively centralized, with important decisions made by party leaders and caucuses. In others power is relatively decentralized, with important decisions made by standing committees or members on the floor. A familiar example of the latter pattern is the U.S. Senate, in which each member has prestige and opportunity, leadership tends to be passive, and members of standing committees often see their bills amended on the floor. A familiar example of the former is the U.S. House of Representatives, in which individual members have few opportunities to express personal initiative, the leadership somewhat more, and standing committees are practically authoritative within their assigned jurisdictions. Typically, power in most state legislatures is even more centralized than in the House, inasmuch as members serve only part time, committees hardly function regularly, and leaders—often in collaboration with the governor and his aides—exercise predominant control.

Centralized decisionmaking has been characteristic of the Wisconsin legislature for a number of years. In comparison to other states, power in the legislature is concentrated. It is held mainly by party leaders and caucuses.[6] On matters of revenue and appropriations, the Joint Finance Committee, dominated by the speaker's appointments, has also traditionally been strong. Although the pattern of decisionmaking in any state legislature tends to remain relatively constant even over long periods of time, some alteration did take place even during the brief span between 1963 and 1967. Legislative leaders perceived a decline in the influence of standing committees and committee chairmen. So did chairmen, one of whom commented: "In the past, in my ten years here, the committee recommendation and the chairman's ability to persuade and succeed in his recommendations was strong. In the last session and this session, committee recommendations are often reversed. The committee chairman function is weakening. . . ." This chairman explained the decline in terms of the increased sophistication of younger legislators, who no longer took their cues from standing committees. Another chairman explained the decline in terms of the new caucus staffs, which provided alternative sources of information to party members.[7]

This development is understandable, given that, as legislators realize, any change is likely to affect somebody's prerogatives, someone's power. Staffing is no exception. Although a number of factors contributed to a change in the structure of legislative decisionmaking, staffing was a major one. The creation of fiscal staff surely strengthened the finance committee and the creation of partisan staff certainly strengthened leaderships and caucuses. Meanwhile, standing committees became weaker than before.

The strengthening of leadership, caucus, and joint finance is evidenced by survey data that reflect the orientations of legislators. Although the evidence is indirect, it clearly supports our argument. Members of the Senate and Assembly were asked to assess the effectiveness of each of these groups as well as that of all standing committees. Approximately three out of four thought joint finance very effective; about two out of three considered leaders and caucuses to be very effective; but substantially less than half felt this way about standing committees. Did staff have anything to do with these assessments? The answer, I believe, is yes.

If staff made a contribution to leadership and caucus, we would expect to find evaluations of one group linked to those of another. In other words, a legislator's assessment of staff should influence his assessment of leadership and caucus. The first set of cross-tabulations in Table 5.1 indicate that this is so. Evaluations of staff, on

TABLE 5.1

Linkages between Evaluations of Staff and Evaluations of Legislative Groups

Legislator Evaluations of Caucus Staff and of Leadership, Caucus, and Standing Committees

Evaluations of Leadership, Caucus, and Standing Committees	Evaluations of Caucus Staff (in percentages)		Strength of Relationship (gamma)
	Very Effective	Only Somewhat Effective	
Party leadership			
Very effective	76	61	+.35
Only somewhat effective	24	39	
Totals	100 (42)	100 (28)	
Party caucus			
Very effective	70	46	+.45
Only somewhat effective	30	54	
Totals	100 (43)	100 (28)	
Standing committees			
Very effective	46	41	+.11
Only somewhat effective	54	59	
Totals	100 (41)	100 (27)	

Legislator Evaluations of Fiscal Staff and of Joint Finance Committee and Standing Committees

Evaluations of Joint Finance Committee and Standing Committees	Evaluations of Fiscal Staff (in percentages)		Strength of Relationship (gamma)
	Very Effective	Only Somewhat Effective	
Joint finance committee			
Very effective	81	55	+.56
Only somewhat effective	19	45	
Totals	100 (42)	100 (22)	
Standing committees			
Very effective	46	37	+.19
Only somewhat effective	54	63	
Totals	100 (41)	100 (19)	

Source: Compiled by the author.

the one hand, and leadership and caucus, on the other, are related, while those of staff and committees are not. The more positively members evaluate staff, the more positively they evaluate both party leaders (gamma = +.35) and party caucuses (gamma = +.45).* But there is no similar relationship between attitudes toward staff and committees (gamma = +.11). Similarly, if fiscal staff made a contribution to the finance committee, we would expect to find some linkage, with evaluations of staff effectiveness influencing those of finance committee effectiveness. The second set of cross-tabulations in Table 5.1 show a strong relationship (gamma = +.56). Of those who rate the staff most positively, 81 percent consider the finance committee very effective; of those who rate the staff less positively, only 55 percent think the committee very effective. Yet, attitudes toward the fiscal staff and those toward standing committees other than joint finance are not linked. The relationship is much weaker (gamma = +.19).†

During the period under investigation, a variety of factors helped strengthen the finance committee. A number of organizational and procedural changes, designed to enable it to concentrate on major policy issues, were made. A bifurcated or split legislative session, which permitted the committee to review the budget unhampered by general legislative meetings early in the year, was tried. Subcommittees were used; written statements supporting budget requests were sought from department and agency witnesses; and a program budget was instituted. At the start of the 1967 session, the speaker appointed a number of hard-working conservatives to the committee. The fiscal bureau, however, was probably most important, because it supplied persuasive information and advice to the cochairmen and members. Until its creation, the joint finance committee had no independent assistance in budget review. Staff aid had been provided the committee by the budget analysts in the bureau of management of the department of administration. While advising the legislature,

---

*Gamma (G) is an ordinal measure of association, showing the amount and direction of the relationship between variables. The formula is $G = \frac{f_a - f_i}{f_a + f_i}$, where f_a = the frequency of agreements and f_i = the frequency of inversions between two scales or sets of rankings.[8]

†In these analyses, it is impossible to ascertain causality, particularly since the time order of the variables cannot be specified. Thus, it is conceivable that positive evaluations of leaders and caucuses lead to positive evaluations of staffs, instead of vice versa. Information obtained from focused interviews, however, does not support such an interpretation.

these employees of the executive branch were also responsible for the formulation, presentation, explanation, and defense of the governor's budget recommendations. Legislative fiscal staff changed this state of affairs.

Since 1965, and especially in 1967 when five full-time professionals staffed the fiscal bureau, the finance committee could call on experts of its own. The bureau worked first and foremost for the committee, responding to specific or broad requests from the chairmen and members. Its support is significant. Turnover of membership on the committee had been extremely high; in the sessions from 1959 through 1967 it averaged 57 percent, as compared with a 27 percent turnover in members of the entire legislature. This meant that most members were new, serving apprenticeships, and much in need of the information staff could furnish. We shall see later that staff guidance has demonstrable effect on the work of the committee.

Caucus analysts function differently, but they too strengthen the legislative groups to whom they are responsible. As we have already mentioned, they help individual legislators and enhance their independence from committee recommendations. Members are educated by the party caucus and caucus staff as much as they are by their committee experience. Thus, committee recommendations become less important in the determination or enactment of legislation. Even more important, caucus analysts buttress party leaders, providing them with tools to increase their influence over the caucus.

Because of their public relations skills, analysts could be depended on to communicate relevant information through newspapers to both the general public and the membership of the legislative party. Day-to-day life in a legislature is chaotic and each member's direct information is usually fragmentary. Therefore, legislators, like outsiders, tend to rely on the press, not so much for ideas and insights, but rather for convenient and comprehensive information and standards of significance. Caucus staff have been instrumental in helping leaders use the newspaper press to convey their messages. When the legislature is in session, the Madison Capitol Times is read by nearly all lawmakers. Since the institution of caucus staff, this newspaper's coverage of the statements and activities of legislative party leaders has increased greatly.

From 1961 to 1967 the total number of column lines reporting leadership statements or activities almost doubled. There were notable differences, however, among the four party leaderships, as are shown in Table 5.2. The increase of Assembly Republicans was slight, mainly because they had received so much press in 1961. If we examine coverage based on the issuance of press releases, as is also reported in the table, it is possible to obtain an idea of the impact of caucus analysts. In the Senate, there was hardly any increase

TABLE 5.2

Caucus Staff Support of Party Leadership,
as Indicated by Press Coverage
from 1961 to 1967

Chamber and Party	Percentage Increase in Press Coverage, 1961 to 1967		
	Press Release Source	Other Source	Total Coverage
Assembly Republicans	59	03	10
Assembly Democrats	213	108	137
Senate Republicans	02	177	162
Senate Democrats	15	173	128

Source: Compiled by the author.

in the number of lines based on press releases, and the growth in
leadership coverage was attributable to other factors. In the Assembly, coverage generated by press releases rose demonstrably for
Republican leaders and even more markedly for Democratic leaders.
In the 1961 session 13 percent of the total coverage received by Republican leaders and 28 percent of that received by Democratic leaders
derived from press releases. In the 1967 session the proportions
had risen to 19 percent and 37 percent respectively. The growth is
surely a product of the publicity endeavors of the Assembly analysts.

Effects were not only direct, they were indirect as well. Staff
helped familiarize leaders with techniques designed to capture the
attention of reporters. One analyst, in particular, taught leaders for
whom he worked how to approach capitol correspondents and how to
be aggressive rather than passive in communicating the news they
wanted printed. Since he served the Senate Democrats in 1965 and
the Assembly Democrats in 1967, his instructional abilities were
partly responsible for the greatly increased coverage, which resulted
from the individual efforts of leaders rather than from staff releases.

Analysts make other contributions to leadership. The minority
staff especially "fronted" for party leaders, performing the more
obnoxious tasks and taking the heat from the rank and file for unpopular
decisions or mistakes in timing. It also functioned as a channel for
complaints, which members were reluctant to bring personally to
their leaders. In the words of one analyst, "the caucus staffer could
become very invaluable to the leadership in letting them know when

storms were brewing in the caucus and what types of revolts were coming on what types of bills." Thus, analysts acted as the "eyes and ears" of the leadership, informing it of the mood of the legislative party and preventing miscalculations due to ignorance of individual or factional views within the caucus. As a result of their close relationships with rank and file, they could let leaders know "when things were going smoothly," so that advantage in scheduling could be taken at an especially felicitous time. On the basis of their experience, they could advise leaders as to who needed persuasion and what persuasive techniques would work best.

In Wisconsin, staffing a fiscal bureau and party caucuses led to an increase in the centralization of decisionmaking influence. One arrangement strengthened an already strong finance committee; the other aided individual legislators, but also increased the control of leaders over party caucuses. Both staffs, at least indirectly, contributed to a decline in the power of substantive committees in the legislature. This may not have been precisely what legislators who originally decided on the caucus and fiscal staff experiments wanted, but this is the way things turned out.

Integration

If the structure of decisionmaking is affected by caucus and fiscal staffing, so are patterns of legislative integration. Whatever Wisconsin's legislative leaders had in mind, certain potential effects of staff on integration were overlooked. The most significant was the promotion of greater intraparty unity and interparty conflict. Here, the contribution of the fiscal bureau was minor while that of the caucus staffs was major indeed.

Fiscal staff reinforced the joint finance committee, but its work had extremely little impact on the integration of either the committee or the legislature. Committee members divided along approximately the same lines, before and after staff became available. Cohesion and partisanship neither increased nor decreased. The primary reason for such stability was that staffers limited their intervention to relatively noncontroversial matters. Although the staff director retained considerable discretion, he used it gingerly, insisting that it was the legislature's prerogative to define his office's role and refusing to expand unilaterally or interpret broadly the legislature's definition. Given his limited resources, he exercised caution before devising tasks for which there was no immediate need, offering services when there was no particular request, or undertaking jobs that were virtually impossible to accomplish.

Like everyone else at the state capitol, the director of the fiscal bureau was conscious of the pervasiveness of partisanship in the legislature. In such an atmosphere, the bureau's effectiveness appeared to depend on nonpartisanship and neutrality. This necessitated avoidance of the political thicket and brambles of partisan, controversial issues. The adoption of such a strategy meant the renunciation of opportunities, however attractive, to suggest alternatives to the major policies proposed in the governor's budget or to become involved in disputes between majority and minority parties in the legislature. As far as fiscal analysts were concerned, competing party leaderships, caucuses, and partisan staffs could fight their battles, but the fiscal bureau would remain as aloof as possible.

By contrast, partisan staff, in strengthening party leadership and caucus, inevitably increased the salience of party as a reference group in the legislature. It helped to increase cohesion within the parties and conflict between the parties.* In Wisconsin, years before the establishment of caucus staffs, one of the norms of special significance was adherence to party. Almost a decade earlier, for instance, it was found that members of the Assembly were expected to vote with their party on procedural motions and on party platform legislation. If they could not go along, owing to the nature of their constituencies, they were obligated to announce the reasons for their deviance to the caucus or party leadership.[9] Voting with the party frequently was accompanied by conflict between the parties on the floor, mainly because the majority of assemblymen in each party represented conflicting district organizations or reference groups and had perceptions of opposing partisan interests.[10] In comparison to other states, intraparty conflict was low and interparty conflict was high in the Wisconsin legislature.[11] Caucus staffing is obviously not responsible for the norms that previously existed, but in a number of ways it has reinforced them.

To promote cohesion within the legislative party, leaders pursue a number of strategies. First, they try to convince members that

---

*This does not mean that staff was a principal independent cause of cohesion or conflict. Party orientations and party voting, in Wisconsin as elsewhere, are related primarily to constituency factors. Cohesive parties and partisan conflict are usually associated with competitive states in which legislators of either party represent similar, relatively homogeneous constituencies. Occasionally, cohesion and conflict are also affected by state party organizations that dominate legislative decisions. Yet, groups in the legislature count because they communicate party positions and reinforce—rather than enforce—conformity to these positions.

their individual fortunes and party fortunes are linked together. Second, they try to provide members with substantive arguments for following the leadership, especially on platform bills or other legislation that may affect the party's prosperity. Third, they try to prevent members from being embarrassed or attacked and endeavor to stave off intraparty disputes and factional disagreements. In each of these respects, analysts have been of assistance.

Members make their own judgments as to the effects of legislation on their constituencies, but often they rely on staff for an assessment of its effects on their own party. The staffer tends to communicate leadership views (or on occasion imputes views to the leadership) and tailors the argument to the dispositions and needs of the individual member. At times he discourages the introduction or support of bills by individuals, mainly to keep them from embarrassing themselves and damaging the party. One caucus analyst explained: "One of my impacts on policy is to stop our own people from putting in crazy bills that the party can be hurt by." The analyst also helps reduce potential sources of strain by shifting responsibility for unpopular decisions. At the end of a session, for example, many bills await floor consideration but time is severely limited. The staff then has the task of obtaining bipartisan agreement on a calendar of particular bills that will be brought to the floor. If individual members object because their bills have not been chosen, analysts blame the elimination on the opposition party. "They won't go along" is the reason given to disgruntled legislators.

The tasks of caucus analysts include the formulation of party amendments and the mobilization of support through the cosponsorship of introductions and the promotion of member unity in voting on the floor. Staff impact on legislative integration can easily be discerned if we examine legislative consideration of the governor's budget bills, as reported by the finance committee in 1963 and 1967.

In the 1967 session the strategy of minority Democrats was to attack the Republican budget, create issues that would receive notices in the press, and increase their chances against the opposition in the following year's elections for the legislature. A Democratic analyst in the Assembly reviewed the budget thoroughly and formulated about a hundred amendments proposing increases that would unbalance the administration's budget. These were reviewed by the leadership, reduced in number, and later presented to the minority caucus. Many were introduced in the Assembly, which acted on the budget bill first, and a number were subsequently introduced in the Senate. According to the staff's own assessment, of the forty-two Democratic amendments introduced in the Assembly, the contents of about one-third directly reflected staff initiative, while the contents of another third reflected the ideas of caucus members. Responsibility for the remaining third was shared.

Within the limits set by leadership and caucus sentiment, the minority staff innovated in the campaign against the 1967 budget bill. Its major function, as well as that of other caucus staffs, was to foster party unity by broadening support for the party position. This meant encouraging members to join in sponsoring amendments that had been agreed to by the leadership and caucus or else recruiting leadership and caucus to support amendments of concern to individuals with common interests. In either case, caucus staffs served to bring larger numbers of party members to together. Their performance in this respect is evidenced in a comparison of multiple sponsorship of amendments to the budget bills of 1963 and 1967. If staff actually contributed to the broadening of support, there should be a higher proportion of amendments with several sponsors in the period after staffing than in the period before. Table 5.3 indicates that this is the case for Democrats in both houses and Republicans in the Assembly. In 1963, only 15 percent of Assembly and 7 percent of Senate amendments introduced exclusively by Democrats were sponsored by three or more party members. In 1967 the proportions were far higher— 64 percent in the Assembly and 67 percent in the Senate. The increase in multiple sponsorship was dramatic indeed, at least for the minority party.

TABLE 5.3

Caucus Staff Promotion of Party Unity,
as Indicated by Multiple Sponsorship of Amendments
to the Budget Bill in 1963 and 1967

Sponsorship, by Party	Percentages of Amendments Having Three or More Sponsors					
	Assembly			Senate		
	1963	1967	Change	1963	1967	Change
Republican amendments	12	21	+09	27	12	-15
Democratic amendments	15	64	+49	07	67	+60

Source: Compiled by the author.

Staff members also served to promote party unity when amendments came to a vote, helping leaders round up support on the floor in the Senate and Assembly. Their efforts were successful, as is shown by a comparison of party cohesion in 1963 and 1967.* Not all of the amendments introduced were accorded roll-call votes, but a majority were. The cohesion scores in Table 5.4 show an increase in party unity from 1963 to 1967 on the combination of amendments, procedural motions, and final passage of the budget bill. Average Republican cohesion increased from 59.0 to 97.1 in the Assembly and from 43.1 to 91.1 in the Senate; average Democratic cohesion increased from 70.9 to 89.2 in the Assembly and from 54.3 to 76.1 in the Senate. Scores are also reported for amendments sponsored exclusively by each party. In seven out of eight comparisons between 1963 and 1967, cohesion rose. In the 1967 Assembly, for instance, both parties were virtually unanimous in voting on the nineteen Democratic amendments, as the minority attacked and the majority united to defend the governor's tightly balanced budget. There was less unity on the nine Republican amendments, because these had not been designed to put the minority on the defense and were consequently less controversial. It appears, therefore, that the work of the Democratic staff had the effect not only of mobilizing the minority party but also of promoting counterbalancing unity within the majority party. Largely because of staff efforts, first the minority coalesced, and then the majority closed ranks in response.

The result was harmony within the parties and conflict between them, as they united in opposition to one another. Larger proportions of Republicans opposed larger proportions of Democrats in 1967 than in 1963. This is shown by the average indexes of likeness in voting on the budget bill in Table 5.5.** On total roll calls, scores designating voting agreement between the two parties decline from 44.9 to 19.3 in

---

*The index of cohesion measures the extent of agreement within groups, by showing how much an actual distribution of votes deviates from the distribution that would be expected if all influences operated in a random fashion. In terms of a legislative party, the cohesion score is the difference between the percent voting "yea" and the percent voting "nay." If all members vote in the same direction, cohesion is at a maximum and the index value is 100. If members split evenly, half voting one way and half the other, cohesion is at a minimum and the index value is 0.[12]

**The index of likeness measures the difference between two groups in their distributions of votes. It is the complement of the difference between the respective percentages voting "yea" in the two groups. If all members in each group vote "yea," likeness is at a maximum and the index value is 100. If all members in one group vote "yea" and all those in the other vote "nay," likeness is at a minimum and the index value is 0.[13]

TABLE 5.4

Caucus Staff Promotion of Party Unity, as Indicated by Party Cohesion on
Roll-Call Votes on the Budget Bill in 1963 and 1967

Average Indexes of Cohesion[a]

Sponsorship, by Party	Assembly			Senate		
	1963	1967	Change	1963	1967	Change
Republican amendments	(N=38)	(N=9)		(N=52)	(N=6)	
Republican cohesion	52.1	90.6	+38.5	45.6	76.5	+30.9
Democratic cohesion	80.5	78.3	-02.2	55.6	80.5	+24.9
Democratic amendments	(N=23)	(N=19)		(N=8)	(N=35)	
Republican cohesion	72.0	99.6	+27.6	55.5	94.4	+38.9
Democratic cohesion	65.2	94.9	+29.7	75.0	76.1	+01.1
Total votes[b]	(N=82)	(N=32)		(N=72)	(N=51)	
Republican cohesion	59.0	97.1	+38.1	43.1	91.1	+48.0
Democratic cohesion	70.9	89.2	+18.3	54.3	76.1	+21.8

[a]The higher the index of cohesion, the greater the party unity.
[b]Total includes votes on amendments sponsored exclusively by Republicans and Democrats and also votes on amendments sponsored jointly, procedural motions, and final passage of the budget bill.

Source: Compiled by the author.

the Assembly and from 60.1 to 18.0 in the Senate. The decline is especially evident for minority amendments in the Assembly. In 1967, for example, the two parties in the Assembly stood in virtually unanimous opposition in voting on the nineteen Democratic amendments.

One cannot generalize from the budget bill to other issues considered by the legislature. There were many problems on which caucus staff had no partisan effect. At times, analysts of opposing

TABLE 5.5

Caucus Staff Promotion of Partisan Conflict,
as Indicated by Disagreements on Roll-Call
Votes on the Budget Bill in 1963 and 1967

| Sponsorship, by Party | Average Indexes of Likeness[a] | | | | | |
| | Assembly | | | Senate | | |
	1963	1967	Change	1963	1967	Change
Republican amendments	47.0	60.0	13.0	58.3	35.3	-23.0
Democratic amendments	32.4	02.8	-29.6	38.3	14.7	-23.6
Total votes[b]	44.9	19.3	-25.6	60.1	18.0	42.1

[a]The lower the index of likeness, the greater the conflict between the two parties.

[b]Total includes votes on amendments sponsored exclusively by Republicans and Democrats and also votes on amendments sponsored jointly, procedural motions, and final passage of the budget bill.

Source: Compiled by the author.

parties cooperated, such as when legislative or staff prerogatives were in question. At times, issues simply did not divide members along party lines, but instead bipartisan coalitions, with different bases, opposed one another. On balance, however, the establishment of staff did tend to increase partisanship. This can be seen if we again examine press coverage of legislative leaders in 1961 and 1967, looking specifically at newspaper reports of partisan statements and behavior.

Since there was an absolute increase in leadership press, as noted previously, there was also an absolute increase in reports of partisanship. This was true for all groups except Assembly Republicans. For Senate Republicans, the number of column lines with partisan content increased by 74 percent; for Senate Democrats, by 57 percent; and for Assembly Democrats, by 247 percent. Even more indicative, partisan coverage based on press releases increased even for Assembly Republicans, and rose by as much as 364 percent for Assembly Democrats. In the case of the minority leaders in the Assembly, almost half the press in the earlier session was concerned with partisan statements or behavior; in the later session, with a Democratic caucus staff at work, about two-thirds involved partisanship. This coverage reflected real controversy. Although it did not independently cause controversy, it did add fuel to the fires and contribute to the vigor of legislative partisanship. For Assembly Democrats, especially, staff press efforts were instrumental in the leadership's strategy of unifying the minority and criticizing the majority.

Performance

Legislative leaders did not intend to foster partisanship when they decided on fiscal and caucus staffing. Rather they hoped that additional aid would lighten the legislative burden, increase legislative efficiency, and improve legislative performance. Staff disappointed their first two hopes. Fiscal and caucus analysts actually made more work for legislators—by uncovering problems, perceiving opportunities, and passing on information and research to their patrons. Nor did analysts make for greater efficiency, if efficiency means getting the job done more quickly and with less effort and fewer resources. With regard to the third hope—the improvement of legislative performance—staff was responsible for considerable gains. Both the fiscal bureau and caucus analysts helped, although the two types of staff contributed to improved legislative performance in somewhat different ways.

It is possible to assess the achievement of the fiscal bureau if we bear in mind the limits of legislative control of state expenditures. In Wisconsin, as in other states, the legislature theoretically has power to alter spending programs of any type. Yet, in practice it controls a relatively small portion of total expenditures, because the financing of several costly programs is specified by formulae and continuing appropriations and the financing of others is politically sacrosanct. Ordinarily the budget bill enacted by the legislature is not very different from the one proposed by the governor.[14] In relation to the magnitude of state spending, the effects of legislature, committee, and fiscal staff must be considered slight.

Gross dollar changes in the governor's 1967-69 budget recommended by the finance committee to the Senate and Assembly amounted to only 4 percent, and those recommended by the fiscal staff to the committee amounted to only 1 percent.* Despite original anticipations, few old programs were eliminated. This is because the staff devoted most of its energies to new and expanded programs and because political and constituency considerations outweighed technical arguments to the contrary. Furthermore, despite leadership desires, the budget resulted in a deficit for 1968, as spending exceeded revenues.

Nevertheless, the staff had an absolute impact, reinforcing the legislature's customary budgetary role and contributing to legislative economizing. One important state facility was closed down, largely because of staff work. In evaluating budget requests, the Joint Finance Committee was no longer completely dependent on agency justifications. It now had what it considered to be more objective information, and it responded affirmatively to staff suggestions for budget cuts. Of seventy written recommendations, twenty-nine were accepted in precisely the form proposed by the staff and another fourteen were accepted with some modification by the committee. Savings of approximately $3.8 million could be directly attributed to the fiscal staff, and an additional $5.7 million in budget reductions was certainly an indirect consequence of its suggestions.

Of obvious interest is whether these or comparable cuts would have been made even without the advice of staff. Examination of the budget action of the finance committee both before and after it had the services of an effective fiscal staff helps answer the question. In 1965 and 1967, a Republican governor submitted a program budget to the legislature, whereas in previous years a program format had not been used. In 1965, legislative control was divided, and Democrats had a majority on the finance committee; in 1967, Republicans controlled both houses and the committee as well. During the first budget review, the fiscal staff was new and extremely small; during the second, the staff included a director and three analysts.

If staff had an impact, we would expect the finance committee to have made greater changes in the second budget than in the first. This was not the case. Differences in the total number and dollar amounts of changes made in these budgets were quite the reverse. In the 1965-67 budget, the committee altered sixty-eight items; in

---

*My analysis of staff recommendations, here and below, is based on written memoranda and studies prepared by the fiscal bureau in 1967 and submitted to the Joint Finance Committee. Documents considered include only those that either explicitly make recommendations or present alternatives in such a manner that staff preference is evident. It has been impossible to account for advice communicated verbally. Thus, whatever bias exists would tend to understate the impact of staff.

the 1967-69 budget, it altered fifty-nine items. In the earlier budget, it cut about $31 million; in the later budget it cut about $24 million. These findings are misleading, however, because the fiscal staff did not review the entire budget. Instead it concentrated attention on higher education and public welfare. If staff had an impact, it should have been on these budgetary items rather than others. This, in fact, is what happened, as the data in Table 5.6 show. In 1965, the number of changes in higher education and welfare constituted about 16 percent of the total made by the finance committee; in 1967 they constituted about 29 percent. In 1965, the dollar decrease in these budgetary areas amounted to 9 percent of the total cut by the committee; in 1967, they amounted to approximately 77 percent.*

The fiscal bureau contributed in less direct ways also. It served as a deterrent, cautioning the governor and executive departments and agencies against excessive budget demands. One aim in estab-

TABLE 5.6

Fiscal Staff Impact on Legislative Budget
Review, as Indicated by Changes Made by the
Joint Finance Committee in Higher Education and
Public Welfare Items of 1965-67 and 1967-69 Budgets

| | Higher Education and Public Welfare | |
Changes by Finance Committee	1965-67	1967-69
Number of changes as percent of total number of changes	16.2	29.1
Gross dollar change as percent of total gross dollar change	9.5	67.4
Dollar increase as percent of total dollar increase	13.1	55.6
Dollar decrease as percent of total dollar decrease	9.0	77.5

Source: Compiled by the author.

---

*These differences may in part be attributable to a change in committee control. However, they are too great to be explained completely, or even largely, by the disinclination of the 1965 Democratic-controlled committee to cut education and welfare expenditures. In general, no matter who controls—Republicans or Democrats—the committee's first concern is to reduce state spending.

215

lishing a staff had been to promote greater fiscal alertness and responsibility by the administration. The very existence of legislative fiscal analysts, it was hoped, would stimulate departments and agencies to budget more stringently. The results seem to conform to expectations. Today, agency representatives check with fiscal analysts prior to formulating their budget requests. They take greater pains than previously in preparing and justifying agency proposals in order to minimize their vulnerability. The behavior of the governor and his budget advisers has also changed. Even before executive budget hearings, the bureau of management cautions agencies to cut items in anticipation of legislative staff scrutiny. During executive hearings, the governor's advisers devote particular attention to those areas most likely to receive critical staff examination.

The fiscal staff's role is still limited, but its presence is felt. Executive officials at first were extremely critical of the new legislative arrangement and refused to cooperate. Still remembered is the early threat by the bureau of management: "Stay in line or we'll wipe you out." Since then, executive officials have gradually and perhaps grudgingly come to regard legislative fiscal staff as a force with which they must reckon. Their behavior has changed. Once the staff had considerable difficulty obtaining information from the executive, especially copies of agency requests for the internal transfer of appropriated funds. By 1967, it was encountering fewer difficulties acquiring information from agency heads and was actually gaining informal cooperation from lower-level personnel who had originally questioned the authority of the staff to even ask. Thus, as a result of staff activity and executive response, control by the legislature had slowly increased.

As far as legislative performance is concerned, caucus staffing also makes a difference. It has fostered improvement in two interrelated respects. First, it has helped the legislative parties, and especially the minority, exert continuous pressure on the executive branch, and thereby has enhanced legislative control. Second, it has enlarged the number of alternatives that can be considered by the legislature, and thereby has contributed to legislative modification of proposals advanced by the governor and the executive departments and agencies.

Increased independence of the executive is demonstrated in the press coverage accorded legislative leaders. Recall that in 1961 a Republican majority stood in general opposition to a Democratic governor and in 1967 a Democratic minority opposed a Republican governor. Other things being equal, we would expect the distribution of legislative endorsement and criticism of the governor to be about the same in each of these sessions. Yet, a comparison of leadership press in these two periods shows a relative decline in endorsement and an increase in criticism. This was owing in part to factionalism among the 1967 Republicans, split into "moderates," who led the Senate party and supported the governor, and "conservatives," who led the Assembly party and desired to maintain maximum independence. It was attributable in larger part to staff.

As has already been mentioned, total coverage and partisan coverage rose substantially from 1961 to 1967. There was also a rise in content pertaining to administration policies and actions. Reports of leadership statements and activities favoring the administration increased, by 66 percent in the Assembly and 120 percent in the Senate. But reports critical of the administration increased more, by 109 percent in the Assembly and 294 percent in the Senate. Taken together, the number of column lines with proadministration content almost doubled, while the number with antiadministration content practically tripled.

The impact of minority analysts during the 1967 session attacks on the administration is especially evident. Reflecting Democratic party leaders, their aim was to oppose the Republican governor. Of the press devoted to criticism by Assembly minority leaders, the staff prepared releases on which approximately half was based. By contrast, the majority staff in the Assembly contributed to only about one-third of Republican proadministration coverage, and only occasionally prepared releases critical of the governor and the executive branch. The main burden of Republican staff criticism was borne by the speaker's administrative assistant. He kept tabs on administration activities and made use of the speaker's weekly report, which he drafted, to question the administrative bureaucracy periodically. In fact, almost one-fifth of the content of the weekly report contained criticism of the administrative bureaucracy. By 1967, then, both legislative parties had become more inclined to attack the administration, if not the governor himself. Bureaucracy was regarded as fair game whoever was in power.

The mimeograph machines operated by staffers helped the parties articulate and communicate their positions. The releases that were cranked out both reflected and engendered a critical attitude toward the executive. Caucus staffs, however, did more. They helped to fashion alternatives for legislative consideration, and thus encouraged legislative independence. One legislator described their role: "Staff men have a great deal more influence on legislators than you would believe resulting from the fact that they sit down with us and discuss possible alternatives."[15] A Republican analyst explained: "During the session the leadership is concerned with a limited number of bills, and as the session progresses our bill analyses lead to the drafting of amendments." A Democratic analyst went into the difference made by having staff available to legislators:

You get the situation, when they are on the floor and in a
fight on a fairly complex subject, say a fair housing bill
. . . they want an amendment very quickly. Before, they
had two alternatives. One would be to write it up themselves. They just didn't have the inclination or the time,
because they might be right in the middle of a debate.
Secondly, they could call the Reference Bureau, but it
quite often was backlogged on work. There was just nobody else they could turn to.

Now, he concluded, they turn to caucus analysts, and as a result
amendments to bills have increased considerably. This is true, as
scrutiny of amendments to those bills enacted into law during the
1961, 1963, and 1967 sessions indicates. The data in Table 5.7 show
that the ratio of amendments to bills rose markedly in both the Assembly and Senate between the earlier periods and 1967. The alternatives placed before the legislature were greater in number than they
had been before.

Although proportionately few alternatives were adopted in 1967
as compared to prior years, staff did more than create partisan
issues. Attempts to alter policy outcomes, particularly by minority
analysts, were also made. The 1967 Democratic leadership sought
to advance counterproposals to those initiated by the majority and
the Republican governor. But on some issues the minority could not
hope to win or even exert a modifying influence. The budget, which
we have already discussed, was one of them. Republicans held firm.
Another was a comprehensive air pollution control measure. A
standing committee reshaped a bill introduced by several Democratic

TABLE 5.7

Caucus Staff Impact on Legislative
Alternatives, as Indicated by Amendments to
Enacted Bills in 1961, 1963, and 1967

Chamber	Average Number of Amendments Per Bill		
	1961	1963	1967
Assembly	0.72	0.81	1.97
Senate	0.75	0.60	1.39

Source: Compiled by the author.

assemblymen, and repeated minority attempts on the floor failed to alter the committee bill in any important way. On another measure, dealing with consumer credit, the Democrats made amending efforts on the floor and forced a few minor compromises, but no major ones. In these endeavors, the staff played a role, but, like the minority party, had practically no effect on the final outcome.

In a number of instances, however, staff made a real difference. On several measures, such as an executive reorganization program, minority staff formulated amendments that were later adopted by the legislature. On others, which were anathema to Democrats, staff efforts led to minority victories. One of these was a joint resolution proposing a national convention to amend the U.S. Constitution in order to modify the Supreme Court's decisions on legislative apportionment. After passing by a single vote in the Senate, the resolution was opposed by Assembly Democrats who had been mobilized by staff. They threatened to disrupt proceedings if the resolution were brought up in the Assembly. It was never brought to a vote and died as the session ended. Another bill, to merge three Wisconsin counties in one legislative district and potentially eliminate a Democratic assemblyman, was also stopped before a vote, thanks to a campaign by minority staff.

The strategy of the minority staff was to attack an administration proposal, provoke public response, and force the Republicans to shift their position. According to a Democratic analyst: "They have policy x. You attack the hell out of x. If the public is responsive to that attack, they modify x." In a number of important instances, the strategy worked, and Republican proposals were compromised as a result. On one complicated measure, intended to balance the state budget by increasing costs to the counties, the minority staff pounded away incessantly. Finally, the Republican administration retreated and agreed to a provision that levied less on the counties. On another measure, a highway safety bill, both Assembly parties dissented from the governor. Probably more staff energies were devoted to this legislation than to any other during the 1967 session. With Republicans divided, and some opposed to the governor's plan, the Democrats had a good chance to affect the outcome. They helped the Republican leadership defeat one provision, then led a fight that led to the defeat of another and a substitute proposal of their own.

A precise calculation of staff effects on policy outcomes is impossible. Staff were not responsible for all of the dimensions of policy emerging from the 1967 legislature. But they did render vital assistance to those who had a part in shaping the contours of policy. The minority staff, in particular, were of critical help, enabling Democrats in the legislature to develop new ideas, raise issues, force compromises, veto those proposals most unpalatable to them, and fashion a party program to campaign for in the state's next election.

CONCLUSION

In Wisconsin, staffing did not make a weak legislature strong; rather it made a strong legislature stronger. This, of course, is what the leaders had in mind when they decided to experiment with several demonstration projects. Just how the legislature would be strengthened was quite another matter. Leaders hoped that caucus and fiscal staffs would lighten the legislative work load and increase legislative efficiency. What they expected did not happen. They did not intend to encourage the minority party, increase partisanship, and heighten conflict by creating caucus staffs. What they did not expect did happen. They agreed that staff would not be a panacea or a revolutionary agent, since they had neither need nor desire to engender radical change. They hoped merely to reinforce existing institutional patterns, and this is just what happened. Both caucus and fiscal analysts make a difference, but it is a difference well within the limits of legislative tolerance.

Caucus staffers helped rank and file, party groups, and party leaders do a little better what they had already been doing before. Although they may have encouraged, they did not create publicity needs or partisan inclinations. Mainly, they tried to respond to these needs and inclinations. The job was difficult. It is a challenge to work for one politician, and a greater one to have to satisfy a large number. Yet, the challenge could be met, if staffers were careful to stay within the bounds of leader and member expectations. As one analyst explained:

> Legislators are beset by a thousand insecurities every
> day. . . . On the other hand, they're jealous of their
> prerogatives and think that they're pretty important,
> but are surprised when somebody pays attention to them.
> So if you can establish some trust, gain their confidence,
> you can really have an impact on the legislative proc-
> ess. But all it takes is one legislator vehemently against
> you to poison the entire caucus, because it's quite easy
> for him to do . . . as an elected official to other elected
> officials.

Trust and confidence are conditions of staff effectiveness, and this minimizes the danger of ambitious young men leading those whom they are employed to obey.

The fiscal bureau operated under similar restraints. Because the staff desired to achieve effectiveness, it was sensitive to the needs of the finance committee, as members saw their needs and not as professional analysts might unilaterally define them. Therefore, it has not attempted any drastic alteration of legislative review of the budget. Although the fiscal bureau may have informally collaborated with an agency on program development, it never suggested to the finance committee a program that had not been proposed by the executive. Occasionally it recommended against a particular cut that the committee intended, and from time to time it supported an agency request denied by the governor. For the most part, however, it sought to eliminate fat from the budget. This behavior should occasion little surprise. Staffers adopt the orientations of committee members. They share the budget-cutting goals of the men for whom they work, because this is what is expected, what is most convenient, and what produces results.

Some fiscal analysts are concerned because committee consideration of the budget is rather irrational, ignoring priorities and comparisons among programs. Some might like to wrestle with major policy alternatives. Some might like a more rational-comprehensive consideration of the state budget. But the fiscal bureau is primarily intent on having an impact. Brief experience, at least, has indicated that payoffs come from giving the committee what it specifically wants, can easily understand, and can conveniently exploit. During the 1967 session, it is clear that the form and scope of fiscal staff work influenced the committee's response. The briefer the analysis and the more explicit the proposal, the likelier adoption. Even more indicative was the strong relationship between the subject of staff recommendations and committee response. The more limited in scope the recommendation, the likelier adoption. Three out of five proposals concerning resource allocations (involving personnel, equipment, or operations) and only one out of three proposals concerning program changes (involving the level and nature of a major activity) were accepted by the Joint Finance Committee.*

Both types of staff adopted the colors of the legislature; they did not gallop into battle with standards of their own. The legislative process was reinforced, but by no means transformed. Staff impact was nevertheless considerable, although the effects of one staff agency were not the same as those of the other. In the case of caucus staffing, specific effects were not even uniform from one party to another.

---

*The relationship between the scope of a proposal and its acceptance by the committee is indicated by a gamma coefficient of +.46.

Staff impact was channeled mainly through the minority party in the Assembly.* Other caucus staffs had similar influence on legislative adjustment, providing party members with political and technical information, public relations assistance, and assurances that people were there to help them with their problems. Other staffs had lesser direct impact on decisionmaking, integration, and performance. But the effects of the minority in the Assembly were felt, at least indirectly, by legislative parties in both houses.

Despite variation among staffs, several general conclusions emerge from this study of institutional effects. In a legislature characterized by competent professional services, fiscal and caucus staffing added substantially to both the material and psychological well-being of individual members. As a result, the adjustment of rank and file to the uncertainties of legislative life was made easier. In a legislature characterized by centralization, fiscal staff enhanced the decisionmaking capability of the finance committee and caucus staff enhanced that of party leaderships. As a result, the standing committee system became weaker and the caucus system became stronger. In a legislature characterized by partisan controversy, fiscal staff intentionally avoided issues that might stimulate partisanship, while caucus staff engendered greater cohesion within the parties and conflict between them. As a result, attacks by the minority and defense by the majority became more vigorous and also more informed. In a legislature characterized by effective performance and relative independence, caucus staff promoted alternatives to executive proposals, fiscal staff buttressed the budget-cutting behavior of the finance committee, and both encouraged criticism of the conduct of programs by administrative agencies. As a result, legislative participation in determining state policy expanded somewhat and legislative control of administration increased gradually.

----

*There are several reasons for this. First, minority Democrats, lacking the ability to draw on the resources of the governor and executive agencies, were more motivated to seek the type of help staff could provide. Second, minority Democrats, unrestrained by loyalty to the executive, conceived their principal role to be one of opposition, and therefore had particular need for partisan assistance. Third, unlike in the Senate, the minority in the Assembly had the opportunity to affect legislative outcomes, primarily because the parties in the lower house were rather evenly divided. Fourth, Assembly Democrats were especially advantaged by the services of aggressive analysts, who willingly and skillfully worked to promote conflict.

Whether these effects are desirable can be disputed. Evaluation will vary, according to one's view of what the legislature is all about. Few people, I suspect, will argue against staff contributions to legislative adjustment. Some may question the concentration of staff effort on publicity. But this appears necessary, if the principal needs of rank-and-file members are to be satisfied and their confidence won. Perhaps increased partisan conflict is unhealthy, particularly in a system where partisanship is already a way of life. Most legislatures, however, can tolerate conflict, especially when the majority party is aligned with the executive branch. Perhaps greater economizing makes less sense than a comprehensive comparison of all existing programs and available alternatives. It is rather doubtful, however, that the latter can be done. Moreover, supporting the capacity for stinginess of an appropriations committee may be quite functional, since practically everyone else—the governor, departments and agencies, interest groups, and even substantive standing committees—is expansionist, program-oriented, and disposed to spend money by increasing demands on the state's purse.

The only undesirable effect of staffing, in my opinion, has been the alteration of a precarious balance of power within the Wisconsin legislature. Any change, and particularly creation of a new staff or augmentation of an old one, will no doubt result in some redistribution of internal power. In Wisconsin, the problem is that caucus analysts helped weaken already weak committee systems and strengthen already strong party groups. To redress this imbalance, an appropriate remedy would be to strengthen standing committees, probably by providing professional staff to the most important ones. This remedy may be simpler to prescribe than apply, since groups who have power are likely to get staff, and staff, in turn, is likely to confer greater power on those who are already powerful.

Whatever the specific drawbacks, caucus and fiscal staff serve well in Wisconsin. It is dangerous to generalize, but staffing does seem to strengthen a state legislature. This is what I have found in Maryland, Connecticut, New Jersey, Florida, and Mississippi—the five states, in addition to Wisconsin, in which I have recently conducted research. Other factors, such as salaries, facilities, and the length and timing of legislative sessions, may also affect legislative strength. It is difficult, however, to isolate the effects of any one, because legislatures that have made a single improvement usually have made others as well. Yet, of all the factors over which a legislature has some measure of control, staff is probably the most important. Therefore, state legislatures should improve their staffs, if they hope to improve themselves. This can be done, but it requires that account be taken of the potential advantages and disadvantages of one arrangement in comparison to another and that hard consideration be given to staffing priorities. Only then will state legislatures be able to get the types of staff which will serve them most effectively.

NOTES

1. Earl W. Brydges, "New Frontiers in Legislative Staffing," State Government, 39 (Autumn 1966), 227.

2. James M. Roherty, "The Legislative Council as Legislative Institution: A Study of the Wisconsin Joint Legislative Council (Ph.D. dissertation, University of Wisconsin, 1957), pp. 192, 233.

3. Warren R. Wade, "The Adequacy of Legislative Staffing in the Wisconsin Legislature" (M.A. thesis, University of Wisconsin, 1968), p. 30.

4. John W. Kingdon, Candidates for Office: Beliefs and Strategies (New York: Random House, 1968), pp. 52, 140-41.

5. For an introductory explanation, see Hubert M. Blalock, Jr., Social Statistics (New York: McGraw-Hill, 1960), pp. 326-58.

6. In 1963, Wayne L. Francis found the party caucus to be a central locus of power and, on the basis of a mail survey of state legislators throughout the nation, ranked Wisconsin ninth (tied with Pennsylvania) on an index of centralization. See his Legislative Issues in the Fifty States (Chicago: Rand McNally, 1967), pp. 72-76. Observing the Wisconsin Assembly four years later, Douglas Camp Chaffey also observed a relative concentration of power. See his "Legislative Party Leaders: A Comparative Analysis" (Ph.D. dissertation, University of Wisconsin, 1967), pp. 321-26.

7. These interviews were conducted by Chaffey, ibid., p. 308.

8. For an explanation of Goodman and Kruskal's gamma, see Linton C. Freeman, Elementary Applied Statistics: For Students of Behavioral Science (New York: John Wiley, 1965), pp. 79-88.

9. Samuel C. Patterson, "The Role of the Deviant in the State Legislative System: The Wisconsin Assembly," Western Political Quarterly, 14 (June 1961), 462-63.

10. Wilder W. Crane, Jr., "The Legislative Struggle in Wisconsin: Decision-Making in the 1957 Wisconsin Assembly" (Ph.D. dissertation, University of Wisconsin, 1959).

11. According to a survey of the 1963 session, the Wisconsin legislature ranked thirty-fourth on an index of factional conflict and was tied for fourth on an index of partisan conflict. Francis, Legislative Issues in the Fifty States, pp. 43-45.

12. See Lee F. Anderson, Meredith W. Watts, Jr., and Allen R. Wilcox, Legislative Roll-Call Analysis (Evanston, Ill.: Northwestern University Press, 1966), pp. 31-40.

13. See ibid, pp. 43-45.

14. Ira Sharkansky's analysis of nineteen states, including Wisconsin, demonstrates how close the legislature's final appropriation is to the governor's recommendation. "Agency Requests, Gubernatorial Support and Budget Success in State Legislatures," American Political Science Review, 62 (December 1968), 1223-24. In addition to Sharkansky, Rufus P. Browning, on the basis of a study in Wisconsin, stresses that both governors and legislatures make little use of the budget for policy purposes. "Innovative and Non-Innovative Decision Processes in Government Budgeting," paper presented at annual meeting of the American Political Science Association, September 1963.

15. Quoted in Wade, "The Adequacy of Legislative Staffing in the Wisconsin Legislature," p. 29.

CHAPTER

6

THE OHIO GENERAL ASSEMBLY:
A DEVELOPMENTAL ANALYSIS
Thomas A. Flinn

There are, of course, two well-known, contrasting images or
models of the American state legislature. One is the part-time,
"citizen" legislature; and the other is the more nearly full-time, "professional" legislature. They are usually distinguished by differences
in formal structure. For example, the professional legislature has
annual sessions, regular staff, and respectable salaries for members
in contrast to the citizen legislature with its biennial sessions, lack
of staff, and minimal compensation.

Each has its advocates. The citizen legislature is most often
defended by the aging veterans of the state legislative process itself.
The professional legislature has a variety of friends, some in the legislature, others in academia, and still others in the "good government"
environs of state politics. Each set of protagonists must certainly
be assumed to have more than a little competence in their subject.

This being the case, then one must suppose that they are not
arguing merely about formal arrangements since these are not likely
to affect performance directly. The arguments presumably turn on
the proposition that contrasting formal arrangements are associated
with contrasting conditions that do have an effect on performance.

A brief illustration may help clarify the preceding comments.
Advocates of a professional legislature want annual, unlimited sessions
and professional staffing. But why should they seek these strictly formal arrangements that in and of themselves are only likely to cost
more money? The answer, or one possible answer, is that these
formal arrangements will produce greater specialization among legislators for the reason that they will spend more time at the public jobs
and with the assistance of people who are already expert. Specialization, in turn, may be thought to affect performance, notably the ability
of legislatures to solve complex problems. So certain formal arrangements are urged, because a condition—specialization—is associated

with them. And specialization is thought to have a desirable effect on performance.

There are then these two contrasting models of the state legislature, each with its advocates. They are often delineated in only formal terms, but are obviously much more than that. They are competing sets of formal arrangements with associated conditions or informal arrangements.

Perhaps it should be emphasized that the informal arrangements in these models are often left vague if their presence is noted at all. One unfortunate consequence is that much of the argument about the relative merit of citizen and professional legislatures loses intellectual status because it appears to be merely formal. Another unfortunate consequence is that the argument does not get ahead because it does not deal with the real issues. This study attempts to get beyond formalities and down to real issues.

The method used is developmental analysis,* but it is not common in political research. As it is conceived here, it involves a statement of two models of legislature and the "developmental hypotheses" that one is being replaced by the other. To be more specific, the models are, of course, citizen and professional; and the hypothesis is that the citizen type is being replaced by the professional type. Neither the method in general nor its particular form, especially the developmental hypothesis, may seem to be very startling; but, as will be shown, they have their usefulness.

Application of the method requires as the first step statement of the models in the hypothesis. In this case, the formal elements in the two models, citizen and professional, can be stated easily, because it is only a question of stipulating what should be put in. Not only that, it can be done without fear of much disagreement; the formal outlines of citizen and professional legislatures are agreed upon by most everyone who pays attention to state legislative institutions.

Stating the informal elements in the two models is quite a different problem since, as was said before, these elements are often ignored. The principle of inclusion to be used is that informal elements must be associated with the stipulated formal elements, and several kinds of association will be allowed. One is causal; that is, an informal arrangement will be considered if it is thought to be caused by some formal arrangement or set of formal arrangements. Informal arrangements will also be considered if it is believed that they are associated with formal elements in the legislative models in the sense that they

---

*Harold Lasswell's writings provide the inspiration for developmental analysis, but nothing he has written should be taken as responsible for the particular form it takes in this study.

both spring from some underlying variable. And finally, informal arrangements will be considered if they are associated with formal arrangements in some normative sense, that is, if they both reflect some common norm.

The way in which any given informal arrangement is thought to be associated with a set of formal arrangements will not be given much attention although some suggestions will be offered. The main reason is that the models are at the outset tentative, and their contents will be examined in the light of experience.

Application of a developmental method obviously includes a testing of the developmental hypothesis that is employed, in this case, replacement of the citizen legislature by the professional. And testing requires consideration of both formal and informal arrangements during a period of time. With regard to formal arrangements, it is not specially hard to report whether the characteristics that distinguish a citizen legislature are being replaced by those that distinguish a professional legislature, the reason being that the formalities are a matter of public record.

But tracing changes in the informal arrangements that are thought to go with citizen and professional legislatures is much more difficult since these are often not a matter of public record. There are exceptions with regard to such things as the occupations and tenure of legislators, but these are exceptions. In the case of Ohio, however, the legislature has been the subject of survey research since 1960. Use of these data for developmental analysis presents some problems; but the existence of these data, which is unusual if not unique, is what makes this study possible.

The Ohio data are the basis for two different kinds of analysis of changes in informal arrangements in the state legislature, and of these the first is much the better. It involves measurements at separated points in time, at least two and sometimes more; and the obvious inference is that things have changed or that they have not. The other kind of analysis of informal arrangements permitted by the Ohio data involves measurement at only one or perhaps two points in time in what is roughly the present. Whether any condition to be considered existed in the past is not known; so about all that can be said is that some informal characteristic of the citizen or professional legislature is or is not present right now.

The developmental approach sketched here has utility. One is that it is an alternative to a strictly causal approach to the impact of formal change on legislative systems and performance, which is desperately difficult for many reasons. Among the difficulties are the complexity of the legislative institution, multiple causation, and the likely resistance of the legislative system to change presumed to stem from tinkering with its mechanics. To be sure, seasoned and shrewd observers may make some very well-educated guesses about the effects of formal change, but, if one's methodological preferences are a bit more on the rigorous side, an alternative is essential.

What the developmental method does in general is to allow a disciplined consideration of change. It is disciplined in the sense that not every possible change in an institution or system needs to be considered but only those that are in a given developmental hypotheses. In this particular study, change in a state legislative institution is analyzed with regard to the hypothesis that the citizen type is being replaced by the professional. Elements not in either model are not considered. The hoped-for result is one map of the path of change.

The developmental method is also useful in that it promotes the construction of better models. In the first place, it demands that models be made explicit. Then it involves an attempt to determine when conditions associated in a model thought to be emerging are appearing together. If emergent properties appear, the model may be taken as a reasonable approximation of reality. If they do not, the model may be corrected to eliminate features which by the result of experience and observation seem not to arise when previously predicted.

In the case of this study, one result of developmental analysis may be the better statement of the citizen and professional legislative models.

Finally, an advantage of using developmental analysis, but not an advantage of the method itself, is that it offers a relatively unusual method for consideration. Perhaps some will find it useful for situations in which more rigorous methods cannot be applied successfully, and perhaps some will take what is attempted here in a beginning way as a start for the development of another avenue of research.

The organization of what follows is shaped by what has been said in this introduction. In the first section, citizen and professional legislative models will be described summarily. In the second section, data for testing the developmental hypothesis will be described. In the third, the process of formal change will be reported; and in the fourth, the process of informal change will be analyzed. The concluding and fifth section is a summary of the process of development, if any, of a particular legislative institution and a correction of the models used in the developmental hypothesis if any correction is called for.

LEGISLATIVE MODELS

The citizen and professional models differ, of course, in their formal characteristics. These rather familiar distinctions can be summarized quickly and without much elaboration. It should be recognized that "ideal types" are being formulated and that many actual legislatures will have some characteristics of both the citizen and professional types.

Citizen	Legislative Characteristic	Professional
Unequal	Apportionment	Equal
SMD/MMD/Mixed*	Districts	SMD
Large	Size of legislature	Small
Short	Terms	Long
Biennial limited	Sessions	Annual unlimited
Low	Pay	High
Many	Committees	Few
Little	Staff	Much
No	Offices for members	Yes

As was said before, stating the informal elements in the legislative models is less easy than stating the formal elements. But as was also said before, the method to be used allows for a tentative statement of the models at the outset and for later correction. For the moment, the elements listed below will be taken as the informal components of the citizen and professional legislative models.

Citizen	Legislative Characteristic	Professional
Partisan/Closed	Recruitment	Nonpartisan/Open
Low	Occupational status	High
Low	Tenure	High
Delegate	Representational roles	Trustee
Ritualist/Tribune	Purposive roles	Broker/Inventor
Close	Interest group relations	Distant
Moderate	Policy stand	Expansionist
Low	Specialization	High
Low	Morale/Competence	High
High	Partisanship	Low

There are various reasons for assigning these elements to the contrasting legislative models. As was indicated, some of these reasons will be mentioned in the fourth section as each element receives consideration. But to avoid an appearance of arbitrariness at this point, it is appropriate to note that these models in their

---

*Citizen legislature may have Single-Member Districts, Multi-Member Districts, or a mixture of the two.

informal aspects present two contrasting general images of the state legislature. One is that of the citizen legislature as a locally oriented body, dominated by interest groups, characterized by high turnover in membership, high partisanship, and rather low levels of legislative production for most members. Such bodies certainly have existed; and, no doubt, many still do. The general image of the professional type is, of course, different: less local, less dependent on interest groups, having more experienced members, less partisan, and higher levels of legislative performance from many members. To what extent state legislative bodies like this exist is not known. The image is suggestive of the U.S. Congress; and, if a term is needed other than professional, "congressional" would do.

DATA

Some of the data to be used in the developmental analysis that follows are taken from documents produced by the legislature itself. It is in these documents that a record of formal change may be found. Data for the consideration of some kinds of informal change may also be found in legislative documents. Rosters and journals, for example, are the sources of data for the tenure, occupation, and roll-call studies that will be presented later.

Other data are taken from a series of surveys. The first is the 1957 four-state study by John Wahlke et al., Heinz Eulau being responsible for the collection of the Ohio data.[1] The other surveys were conducted by the author of this study in 1963, 1966, 1968, and 1969. The first three used mailed questionnaires that were sent to all members of the populations being surveyed. Returns were incomplete as would be expected. The 1969 survey involved interviews with a sample of the membership of the legislature.

In the 1957 study, interviews were sought with all members of the legislature and the effort was successful; responses to every item in the interview schedule were obtained from virtually every member. The 1963 questionnaire was sent to all members of the legislature, 170 at that time, and replies were received from 100; Republicans and Democrats were represented proportionately among the respondents. The 1966 questionnaire was designed basically as a study of recruitment; consequently, it was sent to all candidates for the general assembly before the spring primary in which there were 251 Republican candidates and 301 Democratic candidates, 552 in all. Replies were received from 128 Republicans (51 percent), 137 Democrats (46 percent), a total of 265 (48 percent). The 1968 questionnaire was sent to House members only, 99 in all, and replies were received from 60. The 1969 survey involved a 50 percent sample of the membership of both houses of the general assembly. Efforts were made to interview all members of the sample, and 78 percent were actually interviewed. Republicans, Democrats, senators, and representatives responded in about equal proportions.

With regard to each of these surveys, there is, of course, the question of representativeness, "Can the respondents stand for the population from which they were drawn"? In the case of the 1957 study, there is really no sampling problem since there was a virtually complete census of the legislative population. And there is not much question about the representativeness of the 1969 survey. A fairly high response rate was obtained with proportionate representation of subpopulations. Furthermore, failure to achieve an even higher percentage response was owing almost entirely to the difficulty of scheduling interviews toward the end of the session and not to refusals.

The question of representativeness is more serious with regard to the 1963, 1966, and 1968 surveys. Fortunately for the sake of this study, there are reasons for believing the samples obtained in those surveys to be representative. The populations sampled were fairly homogenous in ways relevant to the subjects being explored; that is, it may be assumed that all members of the sampled populations were toward the high end of the scale in terms of political interest, activity, and concern with questions about state government. Furthermore, response rates were fairly good for mailed questionnaires, and the important political party subsets were represented proportionately in each survey.

What may be a stronger arguments for the representativeness of the 1963, 1966, and 1968 samples is the finding of a comparable study.[2] It was done in Ohio in the early 1960s. Questionnaires were sent to a population of county party leaders, another presumably homogenous population. The response rate was just under 50 percent and almost exactly the same for Republicans and Democrats. In order to test the representativeness of this "accidental" sample, a small random sample was drawn also from the same population of county party leaders. Replies from the "accidental" sample and from the random sample were compared item by item, and it was discovered that there was virtually no difference between the responses given by members of the two samples. The larger, "accidental" sample was accepted as representative.

So it may be argued that the 1963, 1966, and 1968 samples are representative and usable; but it must also be conceded that these arguments are not altogether conclusive. Hence, data from these three surveys should be used cautiously. Inferences should be taken as tentative and not too much should be made of small differences.

Another point should be made with regard to the 1957, 1963, 1966, and 1968 data. They were not gathered with the present developmental analysis in view. Hence, data that are desirable for the purpose are missing in some cases because schedules of questions are not as nearly parallel as they might have been. On the other hand, some questions carry through without change; and the 1969 survey was designed essentially to provide continuity to topics and items that had been explored or used in earlier surveys.

FORMAL CHANGE

For many years the formal structure of the Ohio General Assembly persisted without change, but in the late 1950s there were several innovations that were followed by a flurry of others in the middle and the later 1960s. The first of these changes was a shift from two-year to four-year terms for state senators. It was the product of a constitutional amendment that called for election of half of the Senate to four-year terms in 1958 and the election of the other half to four-year terms in 1960. Adjustments connected with the reapportionment plan of 1966 required election of the entire Senate in that year, in effect cutting some four-year terms to two; but the entire membership of the Senate has since assumed four-year terms.

A change that occurred in the 1959 session led to a reduction in the number of Senate standing committees.* Actually, the number of Senate committees had fluctuated from session to session in immediately preceding years, but the 1959 reduction marked the end of the time when Senate committees were ever very numerous. The reduction from 1957 to 1959 was from eighteen to thirteen. Further reductions occurred in later sessions, and in the 1967 session the number was cut to eight. The House did not reduce the number of its committees until 1967 when the number was cut from twenty-one to sixteen. Further data on the number of legislative committees are shown in Table 6.1.

In 1966, the reapportionment revolution struck Ohio. As the consequence of a complicated series of events, major changes were made in legislative representation. Districts were made equal in size in terms of population. Counties were abandoned as units of representation, and new districts were carved out within counties and across county lines. Multi-member House districts that had existed simultaneously with some single-member districts disappeared and were

---

*The general assembly does not use special committees except for studies between sessions; hence, the number of standing committees is nearly always the total number of committees operating in any given session.

233

TABLE 6.1

Number of Standing Committees,
Ohio General Assembly, 1949-69

Year	Number of Committees	
	Senate	House
1949	19	22
1951	11	22
1953	13	22
1955	20	22
1957	18	22
1959	13	22
1961	10	20
1963	13	21
1965	13	21
1967	8	16
1969	8	14

Source: Compiled by the author.

replaced by a system consisting entirely of single-member districts.
At the same time, the size of the House was reduced to ninety-nine
members from the 130 to 140 that had been the size of the old House.
(Under the preexisting system of legislative apportionment, the size
of the House and the Senate also had varied according to formula.)
The size of the Senate was fixed at thirty-three instead of ranging
between roughly thirty and forty members. An additional feature of
the new apportionment system was that each Senate district was made
to consist of three contiguous House districts. Subsequent to the 1966
election, several constitutional amendments were submitted to the
voters in order to make permanent changes effected by the new system
only to be rejected. However, an amendment was accepted finally that
did embody the changes that were part of the 1966 plan.

The reapportioned legislature that assembled in January 1967
went through its regular session until well into the summer and then
recessed rather than adjourning. It reassembled early in 1968 and
continued operations into the spring. A similar procedure was followed
by the legislature that assembled in January 1969. It recessed rather
than adjourning in the summer of 1969 and reassembled early in 1970
according to plan for more work. Ohio had switched to annual sessions.
It was able to do so in the manner just described because the State

Constitution said only that the general assembly should meet in January of each odd-numbered year for a session not limited in length. Crucial factors were the provision for unlimited sessions and the absence of any constitutional inhibition concerning legislative meetings after properly called recesses.

The legislature that assembled in 1967 also took steps to staff itself better. For the first time, Legislative Service Commission personnel were assigned to each standing committee.[3] Also, during this period a legislative intern program was started with the aid of a Ford Foundation grant. When it expired in 1968, the legislature continued the program entirely at its own expense authorizing selection of six or more interns in 1969 and ten or more in 1970. Interns were placed in the Legislative Service Commission and worked under its general supervision. Their principal work assignments were as aides to the majority and minority party leadership in each house.

The 1967 session also saw a substantial strengthening of the Legislative Service Commission itself. Professional staff that had fluctuated between ten and sixteen in 1957 was increased to twenty-four. Later decisions resulted in an increase of the commission's professional staff to thirty-one in 1970, a level more than double what had been typical between 1957 and 1967.

Another change made by the 1967 legislature was to increase substantially the pay of members. This change, together with the switch to annual sessions, was seen by legislators as part of a general move toward a more professional legislature. The pay increases that were made effective for the 1969 session provided that members' salaries would increase from $8,000 per year to $12,750 per year.* Salaries for the president pro tem of the Senate and for the speaker of the House were raised from $10,500 per year to $16,750. Salaries for six other party leaders were also increased substantially, being set at $14,750 for most of them.

The legislature that assembled in 1969 was greeted by several other changes. One was some remodeling done by the House in its section of the State Capitol that provided a room and some desks for members away from the distractions of the floor and corridor. The other innovation was a conference of several days for legislators in a lodge in a state park away from the distractions of the capitol. Some of the board issues likely to face the legislature were discussed by invited experts and assembled legislators. The meeting differed from some orientation sessions offered in other states inasmuch as experienced legislators as well as newcomers attended.

---

*Earlier salary scales fixed pay for members at $5,000 per year effective in January 1957, and $8,000 per year effective in January 1965.

Looking back, it is apparent that change came mainly at two points: the 1966 reapportionment and the 1967-68 meeting of the legislature. The 1966 reapportionment equalized districts in terms of population, abandoned counties as units of representation, eliminated multi-member districts, reduced the size of the House, and stabilized the size of the Senate. The 1967-68 legislature reduced the number of House committees, moved to annual sessions, altered staffing arrangements, made what appears to be a permanent commitment to an intern program that provides additional staff for legislative leaders, increased salaries for legislators substantially, and took a first step toward providing office space for House members.

It is fair to conclude that the Ohio General Assembly is now largely professionalized in terms of its formal arrangements.

INFORMAL CHANGE

In this section, we explore whether the informal structures associated with the professional model have developed with the establishment of the formal dimensions of the model. Various informal aspects of the professional model will be considered in the order in which they are listed in the earlier summary description of the informal features of the citizen and professional legislative models: (1) recruitment, (2) occupation, (3) tenure, (4) representational roles, (5) purposive roles, (6) interest group relations, (7) policy stands, (8) specialization, (9) competence and morale, and (10) partisanship.

First, however, a few words are necessary to describe changing partisan fortunes in state government in Ohio since this is part of the background against which one may wish to place the evidences of change or no change. The governorship from the end of World War II (say the end of 1946) to the end of 1970 has been held as often by the Republicans as by the Democrats, twelve years for each party. The big contributor to Republican success was Governor James Rhodes who held the office for eight years from the beginning of 1963 to the end of 1970. The big contributor to Democratic success was Governor Frank Lausche who held the office for eight years from 1948 to the end of 1956 when he went to the U.S. Senate.

Any quick attempt to characterize either of these complicated and very popular political figures is suspect. Governor Lausche was usually regarded as a Democrat of conservative principles, independent in his relation to his own party and to other organized political forces in the state. Governor Rhodes was a man of restless energy, highly responsive to public opinion, who could be described as a Republican populist if he could be put in any ideological category at all.

The other governors in the 1946 to 1970 period were two Republicans who held the office for two years each and Democratic Governor Michael DiSalle who held Ohio's first four-year gubernatorial term during the years 1959-63. He asked the legislature for action, and got it in 1959 when the Democrats controlled the general assembly. After the 1960 legislative elections, however, he was faced with an opposition Republican majority in the legislature and was voted out of office resoundingly in 1962.

The legislature, unlike the governorship, has been a Republican preserve. From 1946 to 1970, the Democrats controlled the legislature only after the 1948 and the 1958 elections and for two years only in each case. The Senate was evenly divided after the 1964 elections. In general, Republican success must be credited to greater strength at the polls and not to malapportionment or other biases in the election system.

The strength of the two parties in the legislature during the period covered by the surveys that provide the data for this study is shown in Table 6.2.

Recruitment

Advocates of a professionalized legislature certainly hope for the appearance of better legislators, an admittedly hard-to-define condition. They may be the consequence of structural reform or of

TABLE 6.2

Composition of the Ohio General Assembly by
House and by Party, 1957-69

Year	Senate			House	
	R	D		R	D
1957	22	12		97	42
1959	13	20		61	78
1961	20	18		84	55
1963	20	13		88	49
1965	16	16		75	62
1967	23	10		62	37
1969	21	12		64	35

Source: Compiled by the author.

concomitant development, but surely a better legislator to go along
with the better legislature is part of the image. Relevant to quality
in the legislator is the process by which he is recruited. One may
assume that better quality may be achieved if the recruitment process
is broadly open to talent in the community and not confined to the long-
time runners and arrangers in the ranks of the political parties. Of
course, experience in political party organizations may be very good
training; but the likely assumption of reformers is that a more open
recruitment process without the party screen is to be preferred. And
it is their developmental image of the legislature that is to be explored.

To put this a little differently, the openness of recruitment and
the accessibility of office to talent is, of course, a large question; but
here it is narrowed to consider the extent to which party organizations
control the process. Domination by party is taken to be indicative of
a closed and obviously partisan system associated with citizen legislatures, and weaker party control is taken to be indicative of a more open
process associated with professional legislatures.

The role of party in legislative nominations was, as mentioned
before, explored in some length in the 1966 survey that covered candidates in the spring primary when nominees were chosen for the first
reapportioned Ohio legislature. One of the matters considered was
the relation of the candidates to their party at the time they decided
to run. The research strategy was to give candidates a number of
statements depicting alternative relations to party and to ask them
to select the statement that best fitted their own situation. The salient
statements in slightly abridged form with subsequently conferred labels
are as follows:

1. Moat Filler: "There is little chance for a member of my
party in this district . . . but responsible people in my party . . .
appealed to me."

2. Outsider: "I have been interested in politics for a number of
years although I have not been associated closely with the leaders of
either political party in my district."

3. Draftee: "It would be best to say that I was recruited. Some
of the officers of my party or persons close to them suggested that I
run."

4. Party Worker: "I have been active in the affairs of my party
. . . helping it and party candidates. . . . Now . . . there is an opportunity for me to seek a seat in the legislature."

5. Insurgent: "Frankly, the organization of my party in this
district is not what it should be. I hope that my campaign for the
legislature will encourage new people to get into politics and help
create a new attitude among members of my party in this area."

Since candidates who had served in the legislature fall almost
all in one category and were given a follow-on question, data about

them are saved for subsequent analysis. Responses from all "new candidates" are summarized in Table 6.3. The categories into which obvious party candidates fall are moat fillers, draftees, and party workers. They are more than half of all candidates who had not served in the legislature before, which certainly demonstrates a strong party influence. On the other hand, about one candidate in four falls into the outsider category, a fact that suggests that nonparty recruitment may also be significant.

Further information is provided if the relation of recruitment to success in the primary is examined. For this purpose, recruitment process and outcome are cross-tabulated in Table 6.4. Data are based upon the responses of all new candidates and upon the responses of all former members who did not choose the typical incumbent response.

What appears now is much stronger party control. Candidates who one way or another are selected by party organizations, that is, the moat fillers and the draftees, achieve a very high level of primary election success. They are followed by candidates in the party worker category who have a slightly better-than-even chance of winning the primary. Nominations for outsiders and insurgents are not entirely foreclosed, but their road to political success is a hard one.

As was mentioned a little earlier, former members of the legislature described their decision to run in nearly all cases as being expected. Since this was not very informative, they were asked to choose from the statements that have been listed the one that best

TABLE 6.3

Relation to Party at Time of Decision to Run,
New Candidates, 1966

Relation	Percent Choosing (N = 202)
1 Moat filler	3
2 Outsider	26
3 Draftee	9
4 Party worker	44
5 Insurgent	7
NA	10

Failure of column total to equal 100 is due to rounding.

Source: Compiled by the author.

TABLE 6.4

Relation of Recruitment Process and
Outcome of Primary Election, 1966

Recruitment Process	Outcome (percentage across)	
	Winners	Losers
1 Moat filler	86	14
2 Outsider	29	71
3 Draftee	85	15
4 Party worker	56	44
5 Insurgent	22	78

Source: Compiled by the author.

described their decision to run in the year when they were first elected to the general assembly. Results are shown in Table 6.5.

Party workers are clearly the most common; and they are followed by those who were sought out by the parties, that is, the moat fillers and the draftees. Together these three party categories constitute 60 percent of the whole. Outsiders and insurgents are present but in smaller numbers. Once again, the net impression is one of strong party influence although not total party domination, or in other words a closed although not tightly closed recruitment process.

In the 1966 study, candidates in contested primaries were asked about several matters other than their relation to their party when they decided to run. One of these had to do with the role of the party organization in the primary election. Once again, the research strategy was to give the candidate a number of statements describing what a party organization might do in a primary and ask him to choose the statement best describing the role of the organization in his own primary contest. These statements were as follows:

1. The party organization in my district has formally endorsed me, and I am receiving some help from the organization.

2. The party organization has made a formal endorsement, but I am not an endorsed candidate. However, I am receiving some help from people in the regular organization or close to it.

3. The party organization has made a formal endorsement, but I am not an endorsed candidate. Furthermore, I am receiving no help from people in the regular organization or close to it.

TABLE 6.5

Relation to Party at Time of Decision to
Run in Year First Elected, Former Members, 1966

Relation	Percent Choosing (N = 63)
1 Moat filler	3
2 Outsider	17
3 Draftee	19
4 Party worker	38
5 Insurgent	6
NA	16

Failure of column total to equal 100 is due to rounding.

Source: Compiled by the author.

4. The regular organization in my district has made no formal
endorsement. However, my candidacy is acceptable, and in a sense
has been "cleared" by the organization. Some of its members or
people close to the organization are actively supporting me, and I
think that others in the organization are helping me quietly.

5. The regular organization in my district has made no formal
endorsement. However, some of its members are supporting another
candidate (or other candidates) more or less openly.

6. The regular organization in my district has made no formal
endorsement, and its members are pretty much neutral although there
may be an exception here or there.

Results are shown in Table 6.6. Many inferences can be drawn
from these data, but only a few observations will be made here. One
is that candidates reporting themselves to be formally endorsed
(party role 1) or to be party supported in a primary contest with no
formal endorsement (party role 4) constitute exactly half of all the
candidates who are included in the table. Another observation is that
58 percent of the respondents report that they were in primaries in
which there was a formal party endorsement. Furthermore, strict
party neutrality is reported in only 10 percent of the cases. Party
activity is evidently the norm in contested primaries.

The importance of party activity in the primary emerges more
clearly when the relation of party role to outcome is considered—
see Table 6.7.

TABLE 6.6

Political Party Activity in Contested Primaries
as Reported by Candidates, 1966

Party Role*	Percent of Candidates Reporting Role (N = 184)
1	26
2	16
3	16
4	24
5	7
6	10

*Role numbers match the numbers of the statements preceding
the table.
Failure of column total to equal 100 is due to rounding.

Source: Compiled by the author.

TABLE 6.7

Political Party Activity in Contested Primaries
as Reported by Winning and
Losing Candidates, 1966

Party Role	Outcome (N = 184) (percentages across)	
	Winners	Losers
1	81	19
2	7	93
3	3	97
4	52	48
5	23	77
6	26	74

Source: Compiled by the author.

The overwhelming impression from these data are that the party-sponsored candidates win in contested primaries. Considering the primaries with formal endorsements (party roles 1, 2, 3), 81 percent of the endorsed candidates win and hardly any of the others do. Considering primaries without formal endorsements, candidates who enjoy "clearance" (party role 4) have a better than even chance of success; and the chances of those who are not cleared are much less (party roles 5 and 6).

Candidates in contested primaries were also asked a question concerning their strategy in the election. The research procedure was once again to present the respondent with a set of statements describing alternative situations and asking him to pick the statement with the best fit. In this case, there were three statements to choose among. The first described a party-reliant strategy, and respondents choosing it were saying in effect that they were directing their main effort to precinct committeemen, booth workers, or other people who in some way seemed close to the regular organization. The second statement described a group-oriented strategy, and respondents choosing it were saying that their approach to the election was to appeal to identifiable groups other than the party organization. The third statement described an individualistic strategy, and candidates following it were approaching would-be voters on an individual basis.

Without going into all the detail, respondents reported that party-reliant strategies were most common followed by group-oriented strategies and individualistic strategies in that order. More important, the winners were much more likely to have followed party-reliant strategies than were the losers.

The conclusion that emerges from the 1966 recruitment study is that party is a reservoir from which candidates come, a screen through which they must pass, and an object at which their campaigns are directed. This is certainly not the broadly open recruitment process reformers would seem to advocate.

In the 1969 survey, legislators were asked several of the previously mentioned questions having to do with recruitment. These included the question about relation to party at the time of the legislator's decision to run in the last primary and the question about the same relation in the primary when the member was first elected.

In reply to the first question, about two-thirds of the respondents said that they had been incumbents and that their decision to run was the expected thing. Other responses were scattered although party worker was the largest single category. Replies to the second question are shown in Table 6.8. It may be seen that the party worker relation is the most common, but it is followed closely by the outsider relation. Few legislators fall in the moat filler and draftees categories, that is, the party-selected categories.

TABLE 6.8

Relation to Party at Time of Decision to
Run in Year First Elected, Members, 1969

Relation	Percent Choosing (N = 51)
1 Moat filler	4
2 Outsider	27
3 Draftee	8
4 Party worker	31
5 Insurgent	0
NA	29

Failure of column total to equal 100 is due to rounding.

Source: Compiled by the author.

Comparison of these findings from the 1966 study (see Table 6.5) is possible. What such a comparison suggests is that the recruitment process may be changing. The proportion of outsiders seemingly has risen, which finding suggests that the importance of party as a recruiting agency may be weakening. Without better data, however, this should be taken only as the suggestion of a possibility.

Furthermore, some other data serve to weaken even this mild suggestion. In the 1963 and 1969 surveys, legislators were asked whether they had ever held an office in the organization of their party. A majority in each survey replied that they had; and, more to the point, the proportion replying that they had was substantially larger in the later year. Although this finding does not relate directly to the recruitment process, it shows a close relation between legislators and party that could very well extend into the recruitment process.

A similar impression is given by some other data produced by the 1966 and 1969 surveys. In each of these, respondents were asked to evaluate the level of their political party activity in recent years. Comparison of the findings is particularly difficult since the questions were not precisely parallel; but change, if any, would seem to be in the direction of greater political party activity on the part of members of the legislature.

The general conclusion must be that the recruitment process is strongly influenced by political party organizations and to this extent it is not the broadly open recruitment process contained in the postulated model of the professional legislature.

Occupation

Professional legislatures may be characterized by a membership with high occupational status. One factor that presumably contributes to the hypothesized relationship is reapportionment, which tends to shift representation away from rural areas without much change in central city representation. The gain tends to be in suburban areas where occupational statuses are in general higher than elsewhere, and the assumption is that the status of the population will be reflected in the status of representatives. A professional legislature may also attract higher status members because of its higher pay and other factors that presumably contribute to better rewards not only in terms of money but also in terms of prestige.

The record in Ohio for occupational composition of the legislature in the last twenty years is summarized in Table 6.9.

The most obvious thing in the data is the high proportion of attorneys, which is, of course, a common phenomenon in U.S. legislatures. Other professionals including journalists are relatively numerous, comprising about 30 percent of the Senate and about 20 percent of the House in recent sessions.

Coaxing the appearance of a trend out of the data is more difficult. The relative numerical importance of lawyers seems not to have changed very much despite some fluctuation. The category "farmer" is proportionately smaller, but it never was very large at any time in the last twenty years. If the business categories, "insurance and real estate," "business," and "sales and other white collar," are combined, there is in the case of the Senate a decline from the early 1950s to the last two sessions. The largest increase for the same period is in the category "other professional." In the House, there is no decline in the relative importance of the business categories and only a small and perhaps insignificant increase in the "other professional" category. Very tentatively, it may be said that there is some shift from farm and business occupations toward the professions in the legislature as a whole.

Whether this slight trend represents a movement of even smaller proportions toward a higher-status legislature is hard to tell on the basis of existing evidence. The problem is that the occupational categories are not homogeneous. People in business or in the professions do not have the same statuses as other people in these same large categories. As a guess, businessmen legislators are likely to be small merchants and small entrepreneurs, not at the top of the prestige ladder in business. Legislators from the various professions are not likely to be at the top of their professions or close to it either, but they may stand somewhat higher than their business colleagues. Furthermore, their potential upward mobility may be considerable.

TABLE 6.9

Occupational Composition of the Ohio General Assembly, 1949-69*
(in percent)

Session	Attorney	Farmer	Insurance Real Estate	Business	Labor	Sales, Other White Collar	Journalist	Other Professional	Other
Senate									
1949	39	9	12	9	3	0	6	12	9
1951	36	6	12	24	3	0	6	6	6
1953	39	3	12	18	3	3	9	3	9
1955	30	3	9	21	3	6	9	9	9
1957	29	9	6	24	3	6	9	9	6
1959	27	3	15	24	3	6	6	12	3
1961	37	3	11	21	5	3	0	13	8
1963	39	0	9	24	3	3	3	12	6
1965	34	0	9	12	6	0	9	22	6
1967	33	3	12	9	3	0	6	27	6
1969	42	3	9	9	3	0	6	21	6
House									
1949	26	12	8	10	6	16	3	11	8
1951	34	10	13	10	4	12	2	7	7
1953	31	10	11	11	5	11	3	10	8
1955	32	13	10	10	3	10	2	12	9
1957	36	9	13	9	1	9	3	16	4
1959	35	7	15	12	3	6	1	17	4
1961	37	7	16	13	3	3	1	18	2
1963	36	7	16	9	2	7	3	17	3
1965	33	12	15	12	2	8	4	12	2
1967	35	9	12	16	2	2	2	16	5
1969	33	4	11	15	2	6	3	18	7

*Occupational categories are those described by Kenneth Janda, Data Processing, 2d ed. (Evanston, Ill.: Northwestern University Press, 1969), p. 227.

Failure of row totals to equal 100 is due to rounding.

Source: Compiled by the author.

To the extent that this guess is tenable, there may be some shift toward a legislature that is composed of a higher-status membership than has been true in the recent past.

Tenure

Longer tenure is associated with professional legislatures for several reasons. One is that a formal change to longer terms by definition increases the number of sessions to be served per election. The other reason for associating longer tenure with professional legislatures is that annual sessions and higher salaries supposedly create a greater involvement in legislative life on the part of members, and consequently increase their desire to remain.

In Ohio, the upper House of the legislature has moved from two- to four-year terms. The change began in 1958 when half of the members were elected to four-year terms. In 1960, the other half was elected to four-year terms. In 1966, as the result of reapportionment, all Senate seats were up for election, but with half being filled for four-year terms. The other half, filled for two years, reverted to four-year terms in 1968. Annual sessions and higher pay for all legislators were provided in the 1967-68 session. The record with regard to tenure in the last twenty years is shown in Table 6.10. The table indicates, for example, 24 percent of the Senate had no previous legislative experience in 1949 and that this had dropped to 7 percent in 1969. In the House, 41 percent were newcomers in 1949 and only 26 percent in 1969.

It is apparent from these data that there is a considerable movement in and out of the legislature. In the 1951 Senate more than 40 percent of the members were newcomers or had low seniority, and the comparable figure in 1969 was 34 percent. Between these dates the number of newcomers and low seniority members drops, but is never much below 20 percent of the membership. Turnover in the House is even higher. In 1949, 62 percent of the membership was new or had served no more than one previous session. Twenty years later in 1969 session, the comparable figure was 60 percent. In the case of the House as in the case of the Senate, the number of newcomers and low seniority members drops between 1949 and 1969. Thus, high turnover is apparent; but another fact that ought not be lost sight of is the fact that the number of medium tenure members is regularly about one-third of the membership in each house; so there is a body of experienced legislators in every session although they are not high seniority members.

High turnover and the existence of an experienced corps of legislators are not at issue. Is there a trend toward higher tenure?

TABLE 6.10

Tenure in the Ohio General Assembly, 1949-69: Percent of Members by
Number of Previous Sessions in the Legislature

Seniority*	1949	1951	1953	1955	1957	1959	1961	1963	1965	1967	1969
					Senate						
Very high	3	7	3	3	3	13	10	17	9	7	7
High	26	18	25	38	39	23	32	42	33	37	31
Medium	33	33	37	43	42	39	28	20	35	25	35
Low	15	15	24	12	9	3	13	15	9	10	27
None	24	27	12	7	9	24	13	10	12	27	7
					House						
Very high	0	0	0	1	1	1	0	1	1	1	3
High	10	11	11	9	11	14	17	21	20	11	6
Medium	27	32	36	44	42	36	34	30	33	31	32
Low	21	24	30	19	22	15	18	26	19	15	34
None	41	34	24	27	23	34	32	21	28	41	26

*Seniority Legend: Very high = more than 9 previous sessions
High   = 5 to 9 previous sessions
Medium   = 2 to 4 previous sessions
Low   = 1 previous session
None   = no previous sessions

Failure of column totals to equal 100 is due to rounding.

Source: Compiled by the author.

The answer in terms of the figures has to be, "no trend." A fuller answer involves an explanation for the fluctuations that are apparent. Turnover is high at the beginning and end of the period described in Table 6.10, and low in the middle. The obvious explanation for high turnover in the late 1940s and early 1950s is that the Democrats won control of the legislature in the elections of 1948 after many years of Republican majorities (1938 onward) and that the Republicans re-gained control in 1950. Low turnover in the mid-1950s is owing in part, at least, to continuing Republican majorities. Higher rates of turnover occur at the end of the 1950s and in the early 1960s, and the obvious explanation for this is again alternation in party control. The Democrats won the legislature in the 1958 elections, and lost it in 1960. More significant is the rise in turnover in 1967 and 1969, because there was, at those times, no substantial alteration in the partisan complexion of the general assembly. High turnover in 1967 may be attributed to the fact that the districts established for the 1966 election were new as a consequence of reapportionment. But no such explanation will account for the large number of newcomers and low seniority members in 1969. There is no movement toward a higher seniority legislature; and if anything, the movement, in the short run, is the other way.

An explanation for this phenomenon is really not called for in this analysis, and its development would involve generation of another study for inclusion here. However, the question is a challenging one. An impressionistic answer is that high-seniority members tended to be rural members although by no means all of them were. Some were always from higher urban and highly industrialized areas. Re-apportionment cut the number of rural districts, but did not increase the number of central city districts. Surburbs gained in representa-tion, and to date there is, at least, the suspicion that representatives from these areas are not likely to remain long in the legislature. They may have career opportunities open to them that make service in the legislature unattractive in the long run.

Representational Roles

It seems implicit in the image of the professional legislator that he will be less preoccupied with the demands of his constituents, more concerned with giving expression to his own best views of public policy, and more oriented to needs other than and broader than those of his own locality. To put it a little differently, the professional legislator more than the citizen legislator will accept the repre-sentational role "trustee" rather than "delegate," and will have a representational focus that is more nearly state than local.[4]

Questions dealing with representational roles were asked in a number of surveys. One appeared in surveys taken in both 1957 and 1969, and another set of four appeared in 1963, 1968, and 1969 surveys. The item used in the 1957 and 1969 surveys is: "The job of a representative is to work for what constituents want even though this may not always agree with his personal views." Responses are summarized in Table 6.11.

Agreement with the statement suggests acceptance of a delegate role. Data show that legislators in 1957 were very evenly divided between acceptance and rejection of the statement and with about the same degree of intensity shown on each side of the issue. By 1969, legislative opinion had somewhat shifted with almost 60 percent agreeing with the statement as opposed to some 35 percent who rejected it. Interestingly, the trend on the basis of this single item is toward the delegate role contrary to what is expected in terms of the developmental hypothesis.

The four items that appeared in the 1963, 1968, and 1969 surveys permit further analysis.[5] They are as follows:

1. First and foremost, the legislator's job is to represent his constituents, even before the interests of the state.

2. A legislator has his main obligations to the people of Ohio, and he must be careful not to mistake the particular interests of his constituency for the interests of the state as a whole.

3. Even though the legislator is firmly convinced that his constituents are not properly evaluating the issues, it is his job to disregard his own views and vote the way they want.

TABLE 6.11

Responses Showing Degree of Acceptance of
Delegate Role by Session, 1957 and 1969 Surveys
(in percent)

Responses	1957	1969
(N)	(161)	(49)
Agree	16	16
Tend to agree	35	43
Undecided	1	6
Tend to disagree	35	27
Disagree	13	8

Source: Compiled by the author.

4. Because his constituents seldom know all the various aspects of important issues, the legislator serves his constituency best if he is left alone to make careful decisions by himself.

Responses appear in Table 6.12. Agreement with item 1 indicates, of course, acceptance of a delegate role. At no time does a majority of either party adopt that role. There is, however, among the Democrats some noticeable change. It is a steady movement from straight-out rejection of the proposition in item 1 to the position of tending to disagree with the proposition. To this extent, there is some movement toward the delegate role.

Agreement with item 2 indicates a state rather than local focus; and at all times, a majority of each party asserts a state focus. There is some change and among the Democrats, however. In their ranks, there is a substantial and steady decline in the proportion stating agreement with the proposition in item 2 and a corresponding increase in those tending to agree with the proposition. And to this extent, there is some movement to a local focus.

Legislators agreeing with item 3 are stating, of course, acceptance of a delegate role. As was the case with item 1, which also indicates acceptance of a delegate role, there is at no time a majority in either party that accepts this role. But there is some change, and this time in both parties at the time of the 1969 survey. The change is a decline in the proportion of members who simply disagree with the proposition in item 3 and an increase in the proportion who only tend to disagree with the proposition. Again there is some movement to a delegate role.

Agreement with item 4 indicates acceptance of a trustee role but not necessarily a rejection of a local focus. Data are not very clear. Among the Democrats, there is a decline particularly in 1969 in the proportion who state unqualified agreement with the proposition in item 4 and an increase in the proportion who tend to agree. There is also a comparable change in the proportion who disagree and in the proportion who tend to disagree. In general, there seems to be a movement to the middle. Republicans show a similar tendency.

In summary, it is clear that there is no movement toward greater acceptance of trustee roles and of a state focus. On the contrary there may be some movement toward greater acceptance of a delegate role and perhaps of a local focus, which is contrary to the developmental hypothesis.

Purposive Roles

One classification of purposive roles is that of Wahlke et al., and it provides a fourfold classification.[6] The roles are designated

251

TABLE 6.12

Responses to Items Concerning Representational
Roles by Session and by Party,
1963, 1968, and 1969 Surveys
(in percent)

Responses (N)	1						2					
	1963		1968		1969		1963		1968		1969	
	D	R	D	R	D	R	D	R	D	R	D	R
	(35)	(64)	(25)	(35)	(18)	(33)	(35)	(64)	(25)	(35)	(18)	(33)
Agree	14	11	8	6	17	6	54	36	32	40	17	21
Tend to agree	14	23	24	23	17	18	26	41	44	31	67	42
Undecided	0	0	0	3	0	6	3	0	4	3	0	6
Tend to dis-agree	20	38	44	31	56	45	6	14	16	20	11	18
Disagree	43	25	20	34	11	21	6	3	0	6	6	6
NA	9	3	4	3	0	3	6	6	4	0	0	6

Responses (N)	3						4					
	1963		1968		1969		1963		1968		1969	
	D	R	D	R	D	R	D	R	D	R	D	R
	(35)	(64)	(25)	(35)	(18)	(33)	(35)	(64)	(25)	(35)	(18)	(33)
Agree	3	3	0	0	0	6	23	20	16	11	6	9
Tend to agree	6	5	0	6	17	3	17	27	16	17	39	27
Undecided	0	0	0	0	0	6	3	0	4	0	0	12
Tend to dis-agree	23	23	24	31	33	36	26	22	28	37	39	27
Disagree	66	62	72	63	50	42	29	27	32	31	17	18
NA	3	7	4	0	0	6	3	5	4	3	0	6

Failure of column totals to equal 100 is due to rounding.

Source: Compiled by the author.

ritualist, tribune, inventor, and broker. The ritualist is a legislator who concentrates on rules and procedures when describing the norms most acceptable to himself. The tribune sees his purpose in the legislature as giving voice to constituency sentiments. An inventor is a legislator who sees his basic role as being an initiator of policy, and a broker accepts the idea that he should referee "the struggle of interest groups, constituencies, and executive agencies."[7]

It seems plausible to associate a citizen legislature with ritualist and tribune roles. On the other hand, a more professional legislature should be more capable of policy innovation; and there should be, therefore, a higher frequency of inventor roles. Whether brokers are more common in a citizen or professional legislature may be seen as indeterminate.

Eulau in his analysis of the data generated by himself, Wahlke, and others in 1957 considers the frequency with which various purposive roles are mentioned in an acceptable sense by legislator respondents. In the case of Ohio, the findings are: ritualist 67 percent, tribune 40 percent, inventor 33 percent, broker 48 percent.[8] It is obvious, of course, that ritualist roles seem most common and inventor roles least common.

Since these findings were based on an interpretation of responses to an openended question plus probing, replication is very difficult, but efforts were made in the 1968 and 1969 surveys to study these roles. Members were given a set of four statements, each of which was intended to describe one of the four purposive roles defined by Wahlke and his associates. Members were then asked to indicate the statement that they found most acceptable and then the statement that they found next most acceptable. The four statements involved in this inquiry are:

1. The essence of my job is to understand the rules, procedures, and strategies involved in the legislative process—from the introduction of bills through their consideration in committee and debate on the floor to the final vote (ritualist).

2. My primary job is to keep in close touch with my constituents and to find out what they want. Even though I might not always do what they would like, I do want to know what my constituents are thinking on issues that come before the general assembly (tribune).

3. This state is faced with many social and economic problems. I feel that my job is to gain a good understanding of these problems and then work for legislation that will help solve them (inventor).

4. With so many conflicting demands and interests coming before the general assembly, my main job is to listen to the different arguments so that I can understand and evaluate what different groups want (broker).

The frequency with which these statements are accepted as first- and second-choice purposive roles is summarized in Table 6.13.

Looking at first-choice answers, it is readily apparent that there are virtually no interparty differences and that analysis in terms of party is unnecessary. What the data show is that the ritualist role is virtually absent as is the broker role. The most popular role is that of the inventor followed by that of the tribune. In terms of change between the 1968 legislators and the 1969 legislators, there is a very clear drop in the frequency of the inventor role and a corresponding increase in the frequency of the tribune role.

TABLE 6.13

Responses Showing Choice of Purposive Roles by
Session and by Party, 1968 and 1969 Surveys
(in percent)

	First Choice			
	1968		1969	
Role	D	R	D	R
(N)	(25)	(35)	(18)	(33)
Ritualist	0	0	0	6
Tribune	16	11	28	24
Inventor	72	74	56	58
Broker	0	0	0	3
NA	12	14	17	9

	Second Choice			
	1968		1969	
	D	R	D	R
	(25)	(35)	(18)	(33)
Ritualist	16	14	22	9
Tribune	40	43	22	38
Inventor	12	9	17	22
Broker	20	14	22	19
NA	12	20	17	12

Failure of column totals to equal 100 is due to rounding.

Source: Compiled by the author.

Looking at second-choice answers, some rather clear interparty differences appear in 1969 with Democrats accepting the ritualist role more frequently than Republicans and Republicans accepting the tribune role more frequently than the Democrats. The combination role of inventor-ritualist is evidently more common among Democrats, and the combination role of inventor-tribune more common among Republicans, at least, in 1969. In terms of shifts between 1968 and 1969, the clearest change is a decline in the frequency of tribune roles as second-choice selections, which is probably accounted for by the increased frequency of this role as a first choice. Interestingly, inventor makes no corresponding gains.

Comparison of the 1957 findings with those of roughly a decade later is hazardous because of the change in method, but, with due caution, it seems clear that the frequency of the inventor role has substantially increased. For example, it is mentioned more frequently as a first choice in 1968 and in 1969 than it was mentioned at all in the 1957 study. This is a movement in accord with the developmental model of the professional legislature. The frequency of the ritualist role seems also to have declined. It gets less mention as either a first- or second-place choice in the later surveys than mentioned in the earlier study, which is also in accord with the developmental model. Complicated developments in roletaking may be occurring, as is suggested by the decline in the frequency of inventor roles from the 1968 to the 1969 legislature and some increase in tribune roles, neither of which is expected in the developmental model.

Interest Group Relations

The citizen legislature is, of course, somewhat mislabeled. One of its aspects is high partisanship, and its members are more likely to fall in the "political pro" classification rather than in the "amateur." Along with high partisanship is a presumed high affinity for interest group politics. Some indulgence in current and imprecise rhetoric would suggest the citizen legislature is a manifestation or a part of the "old politics" and the professional legislature a manifestation of the "new politics."

A consideration of the position of interest groups and their representatives in the Ohio legislature during at least a dozen years is possible because of the attention they received in the 1957 four-state study and in the 1969 survey that included parallel items. Some other items concerning interest groups were included in the 1968 and 1969 surveys.

One question in the 1957 study had to do with the reliance of members on interest groups for the generation of support for measures they were pushing. It read, "Interest groups or their agents give me valuable help in lining up support for my bills." Members were given a choice of five responses: agree, tend to agree, undecided, tend to disagree, disagree. In 1957, 69 percent of the respondents took one of the affirmative responses, agree or tend to agree. In 1969, 70 percent of the respondents took one of the affirmative responses. Obviously, a large part of the legislature found interest groups helpful; and there was virtually no change in the period covered.

Another item in the 1957 and 1969 surveys also involved help from interest groups. It read: "I get valuable help in drafting bills or amendments from interest groups or their agents." In 1957, 57 percent of the respondents gave an affirmative response; and, in 1969, 52 percent gave an affirmative response. However, a closer look at the data does reveal some changes, as in the following responses in percentages by year:

Year	Agree	Tend to Agree	Undecided	Tend to Disagree	Disagree
1957	28	29	0	27	16
1969	16	36	6	18	24

The number of members who agree has declined, and the number who disagreed has increased. Evidently, legislators were a bit less dependent on interest groups for the drafting of bills and amendments in 1969 than they had been a few years earlier.

A third item appearing in this series concerning interest groups was as follows: "Lobbyists and special interests have entirely too much influence in American state legislatures." In 1957, 33 percent of the respondents agreed to some extent; and, in 1969, 48 percent gave an affirmative response of some kind. In 1957, 67 percent disagreed in some degree; and, in 1969, only 40 percent were in disagreement. Interest groups were evidently losing some of their acceptance by legislators if responses to this single item are accepted as an adequate test.

Somewhat supporting the view that lobbyists are less welcome than formerly are some other data from the 1968 and 1969 surveys that also test attitudes to interest groups. Members were given three statements concerning the place of interest groups in the legislative process, and were asked to indicate the statement with which they agreed most. The statements are:

1. Interest groups are indispensable for the operation of the legislature. They provide legislators with a great deal of information

that helps us make decisions, and after all their members are frequently affected by the decisions we make (positive).

2. I really do not feel one way or the other about interest groups.
They seem to provide some valuable services to many of the members.
I do think, however, that there are certain bad practices connected
with interest groups and with lobbying (neutral).

3. Interest group activity is objectionable to me. Legislators
should make decisions they think are right, and not just try to satisfy
the interest groups that are represented here. Still one cannot deny
the right of interest groups to be heard (negative).

Responses by party by legislature are shown in Table 6.14.
One fact that emerges clearly is that Democrats are less likely than
Republicans to have a positive view of interest groups in the legislative process and more likely to have a negative view. Positive views
declined from the 1967 legislature to the 1969 legislature in both
parties and negative views increased substantially among the Democrats. Whether there is really a trend among Republican members
is hard to know since the changes are not great; but there would appear to be, at least, a short-run trend among Democrats since the
changes are larger.

So reliance on interest groups for drafting bills or amendments
seems to have declined a little. Belief that they are too strong has
grown, and legislators seem to have less favorable views of interest
groups as contributors to legislative performance. These shifts are,
of course, consistent with the developmental hypothesis.

Policy Stands

A professionalized legislature is presumably active in providing
governmental programs. Otherwise the more frequent and longer
sessions and higher pay are a waste of time and money. Lending
credence to the view is the fact that citizens wary of legislative med-
dling in times past prescribed short biennial sessions and low pay.
And if the model of a professional legislature includes greater activity,
then the members should generally support an increase in state
government programs and services.

One question dealing with state government activity was asked
in both the 1957 and 1969 surveys, and another set of five were included in the 1963, 1968, and 1969 surveys. The item included in the
1957 and 1969 surveys is: "The most pressing problems that local
governments face cannot be solved without new state taxes." Responses appear in Table 6.15.

There is obviously a marked shift from 1957 to 1969. In the
earlier year, almost two-thirds of the legislators disagree with the

TABLE 6.14

Percent of Members Holding Indicated Views of
Interest Groups in the Legislative Process by
Session and by Party, 1968 and 1969 Surveys

	Session			
	1967-68		1969-70	
View	D	R	D	R
(N)	(25)	(35)	(18)	(33)
Positive	44	60	33	52
Neutral	36	20	22	27
Negative	16	11	28	9
No answer	4	9	17	12

Source: Compiled by the author.

TABLE 6.15

Responses Showing Support for New Taxes by
Session, 1957 and 1969 Surveys
(in percent)

Response	1957	1969
(N)	(161)	(50)
Agree	17	29
Tend to agree	19	27
Undecided	0	12
Tend to disagree	37	24
Disagree	28	8

Failure of column totals to equal 100 is due to rounding.

Source: Compiled by the author.

proposition that taxes would have to be increased in order to solve local government problems while in the later year almost two-thirds agree with the proposition. Of course, the change in sentiment could well be attributable to factors other than professionalization.

The five questions having to do with state policy that appeared in the 1963, 1968, and 1969 surveys involved a listing of issues with the instructions that respondents were to say whether government support for the issue should increase, decrease, or remain as is. The listed issues were: (1) level of state services, (2) state aids for primary and secondary education, (3) unemployment compensation, (4) mental health program, and (5) state taxes. Results are in Table 6.16.

With regard to the general level of state services (item 1), there is no marked change in the position of the Democrats through the 1960s; but Republicans shift from a restrictive position in 1963 to a mildly expansionist one by the end of the decade.

On the issue of state aid for primary and secondary education (item 2), both parties were expansionist throughout the decade with little change from beginning to end; and as can be seen, the Democrats were a bit more expansionist than the Republicans. The Democratic position on unemployment compensation (item 3) changes from status quo early in the 1960s to a strongly expansionist one. Republicans move in the same direction, but at no point do they match the enthusiasm of the Democrats for this program.

On the issue of the mental health program (item 4), the Democratic position is one of strong support; and it does not vary with the passage of time. On the other hand, the Republican position changes from status quo to strongly expansionist. By 1969, there is little difference in the attitudes of the parties. Finally, on the difficult question of state taxes (item 5), each party shows a growing willingness to increase taxes, although no great enthusiasm for the idea, with the Democrats being more supportive than the Republicans at the time of each survey.

To summarize responses on these five items, neither party moves toward a restrictive attitude on any issue that was examined. Democrats take roughly the same position on several issues throughout the decade, but increase their support for unemployment compensation and state taxes with the passage of time. Republicans maintain an expansionist position on the education issue throughout the decade, and become more expansionist on every other issue.

Adding this summary response to the earlier reported data concerning the need for increases in taxes for the solution of local government problems, it is obvious that the legislature has become more activist in inclination than it was in the past.

259

TABLE 6.16

Responses to Items Concerning State Governmental Services and Taxes, 1963, 1968, and 1969 Surveys (in percent)

	1						2					
	1963		1968		1969		1963		1968		1969	
Responses	D	R	D	R	D	R	D	R	D	R	D	R
(N)	(35)	(65)	(25)	(35)	(18)	(33)	(35)	(65)	(25)	(35)	(18)	(33)
I	63	20	76	60	72	54	83	74	92	69	83	73
D	9	34	0	0	6	6	3	3	0	0	0	3
S	23	43	20	31	17	30	9	18	4	29	6	15
NA	6	3	4	9	6	9	6	5	4	3	11	9

	3						4					
	1963		1968		1969		1963		1968		1969	
Responses	D	R	D	R	D	R	D	R	D	R	D	R
(N)	(35)	(65)	(25)	(35)	(18)	(33)	(35)	(65)	(25)	(35)	(18)	(33)
I	31	2	60	17	78	24	86	48	96	86	89	82
D	11	38	0	9	0	6	0	3	0	3	0	0
S	49	55	36	71	17	64	9	45	0	11	6	12
NA	9	5	4	3	6	6	6	5	4	0	6	6

	5					
	1963		1968		1969	
Responses	D	R	D	R	D	R
(N)	(35)	(65)	(25)	(35)	(18)	(33)
I	54	23	44	34	67	42
D	6	18	0	3	0	0
S	34	55	44	60	17	48
NA	6	3	12	3	17	9

Legend: I = Increase
D = Decrease
S = Remain the same

Failure of totals to equal 100 is due to rounding.

Source: Compiled by the author.

Specialization

As indicated in the introduction, specialization is associated with professionalization. Two reasons that were cited for this association are that the members spend more time in the legislature and, hence, have more opportunity to become specialists in some field. In addition, a full-time staff is available to help them gain specialized knowledge.

Questions concerning specialization were asked in the 1968 and 1969 surveys. The fact that they were not asked in earlier surveys imposes limits on the analysis; but the data will show whether high levels of specialization exist in what is in formal terms a reasonably professional legislature.

The questions and possible responses concerning specialization were:

1. How important do you think it is to specialize on certain subjects?

_____Very Important   _____Generally a Good Idea

_____Not Very Important

2. Is there any particular subject or field of legislation in which you consider yourself particularly expert when it comes to dealing with proposed legislation in that field?

_____Yes   _____No (1968 responses)

_____Yes   _____No   _____Undecided (1969 responses)

Note that allowed responses to the second question are not exactly the same in the 1968 and 1969 surveys. It was felt in 1969 that increasing the range of choice might produce some additional information without destroying comparability. Results are shown in Table 6.17

One quick observation that facilitates interpretation is that increasing the range of responses to item 2 in the 1969 survey evidently had the result only of allowing members who did not feel themselves to be specialists to avoid a straight-out negative response to the question. The relative frequency of negative responses and undecided responses in 1969 are almost exactly equal to the frequency of negative responses in 1968.

Data show that much less than a majority of the legislature think it is very important to specialize. A somewhat larger proportion of the legislature, roughly two-thirds, nonetheless claim to have some specialty although one-third do not. This certainly does not suggest a legislative body in which specialization is very highly developed. Furthermore, if there is any change from the legislature elected in 1966 to that elected in 1968, it is toward a lesser evaluation of specialization, at least, among Democrats.

TABLE 6.17

Responses to Items Concerning Specialization in the
Legislature by Session and by Party,
1968 and 1969 Surveys
(in percent)

	1			
	1968		1969	
Response	D	R	D	R
(N)	(25)	(35)	(18)	(33)
Very Important	36	40	11	36
Good Idea	40	54	83	48
Not Very Important	24	6	6	15

	2			
	1968		1969	
Response	D	R	D	R
(N)	(25)	(35)	(18)	(33)
Yes	64	66	61	64
No	36	31	17	18
Undecided	-	-	22	15
NA	0	3	0	3

Failure of column totals to equal 100 is due to rounding.

Source: Compiled by the author.

Competence and Morale

The professional legislator is thought to have greater competence than his citizen counterpart. This seems plausible given that the professional legislator spends more time at his job and has better facilities at his disposal. The professional is also thought to have higher morale in his role as legislator. One factor that might contribute to this result is higher pay; and if one thinks that a professional legislature is likely to have higher prestige than a citizen legislature, this too could contribute to higher morale among professional legislators.

Three questions relating to competence were asked in the 1957 and 1969 surveys. Another set of three questions relating to competence and morale was included in the 1968 and 1969 surveys as well as another question involving sense of agreement with party caucuses, an indicator of morale.

The relevant questions in the 1957 and 1969 surveys were:

1. There is so little time during a session to study all the bills that sometimes I do not know what I am voting for or against.

2. Many of the bills are so detailed and technical that I have trouble understanding them.

3. So many groups want so many different things that it is often difficult to know what stand to take.

Responses ranged from agree to disagree on a five-point scale and are summarized in Table 6.18. Any kind of disagree response is, of course, an assertion of personal competence; and these responses constitute a majority in every case except responses to item 1 in the 1957 survey. On the other hand, it is rather surprising that a significant part of the legislature does admit having feelings of incompetence as indicated by the frequency of "agree" and "tend to agree" responses.

There is also a trend. The frequency of "agree" responses to every item falls from 1957 to 1969 with the greatest change occurring in responses to the first item. Evidently, legislators in 1969 felt

TABLE 6.18

Responses to Items Concerning Personal Competence of
Legislators, 1957 and 1969 Surveys
(in percent)

Responses (N)	1		2		3	
	1957 (156)	1969 (51)	1957 (159)	1969 (51)	1957 (162)	1969 (51)
Agree	36	10	15	4	15	4
Tend to agree	33	29	28	33	25	24
Undecided	1	0	1	0	0	6
Tend to disagree	17	35	25	37	37	37
Disagree	12	25	31	25	22	29

Source: Compiled by the author.

263

time pressures much less than had legislators in 1959. They seem also to have felt more able to comprehend details and technicalities and to handle competing group pressures. In general, feelings of competence seem to have increased.

The three items relating to competence and morale that appeared in the 1968 and 1969 surveys are shown below. The first two deal with competence, but, unlike the three items just discussed, they deal with the competence of the legislature and not with feelings of personal competence. The third item measures morale as demonstrated by willingness to return. Questions and the range of responses are as follows:

1. With regard to the legislature itself, how do you think it has handled the problems of the state during the present session?

_____Very Well _____Well _____Not Very Well _____Poorly

2. How do you think the legislature has done with regard to solving the problems of the state during the present session?

_____Very Well _____Well _____Not Very Well _____Poorly

3. Would you be willing to serve in three or more sessions after this one?

_____Yes _____No _____Undecided

Results to the first two questions dealing with competence appear in Table 6.19. The data show that in 1968 most legislators thought the legislature had done a good job of handling bills with the majority Republicans being better satisfied than the minority Democrats. ("Good job" is measured by summing the frequency of "well" and "very well" responses.) Furthermore, nearly all the Republicans thought the legislature had done a good job in solving the problems of the state; and nearly half of the opposition Democrats agreed. At this point in time, legislators were ascribing considerable competence to the legislature which had, of course, moved substantially toward professionalization in the 1967-68 session.

In 1969, however, the picture is different. Most of the Democrats thought the legislature had not even done a good job in handling bills much less solve the problems of the state. The frequency of Republican "very well" responses plunges with regard to the more processing of bills, and the same thing is true with regard to solution of the problems of the state. Many short-run factors may have contributed to these relatively low marks, but the significant point would be that Ohio's professionalizing legislature does not necessarily score well with its own members with regard to internal operations (processing of bills) and to substantive achievement (solving the problems of the state).

TABLE 6.19

Responses to Items Concerning Competence,
1968 and 1969 Surveys
(in percent)

	1				2			
	1968		1969		1968		1969	
Responses	D	R	D	R	D	R	D	R
(N)	(25)	(35)	(18)	(33)	(25)	(35)	(18)	(35)
Very well	8	43	0	18	0	46	0	6
Well	72	54	28	67	48	51	17	67
Not very well	12	0	61	3	36	0	39	15
Poorly	4	3	11	12	12	3	44	12
NA	4	0	0	0	4	0	0	0

Source: Compiled by the author.

TABLE 6.20

Willingness of Legislators to Serve Three or More
Additional Terms, 1968 and 1969 Surveys
(in percent)

	1968		1969	
Responses	D	R	D	R
(N)	(25)	(35)	(18)	(33)
High	60	49	78	54
Medium	20	14	11	15
Low	20	34	11	30
NA	0	3	0	0

Legend: High   = "Yes" response to item
         Medium = "Undecided" response to item
         Low   = "No" response to item
         NA   = No answer

Source: Compiled by the author.

The third item in the 1968-69 set had to do with willingness to return, which is taken to be an indicator of morale. Results appear in Table 6.20.

A majority of the legislature is quite clearly willing to seek extended service, and the number who flatly reject that prospect is relatively low. Interestingly, Democrats, although a minority, are more willing to continue in the legislature than are the Republicans. The reason may be that Republicans more than Democrats view legislative service as but a step in a longer career rather than as a stopping point.

The data also show that willingness to return increased from 1968 to 1969 among Democrats to a significant extent but not among Republicans. Given this large party differential, it is hard to assert a trend for the entire legislature. It does seem clear, however, that morale as measured by willingness to continue legislative service was fairly high in both the 1967-68 session and the 1969-70 session.

The other item in the 1968 and 1969 surveys to be considered here had to do with party caucuses. The question and possible responses are:

We realize that most members of the legislature will support their party after a caucus decision has been made. We would like to know, however, how often you have been in agreement with the decisions of your caucus in the present session.
_____Always   _____Nearly Always   _____Usually

_____Sometimes   _____Seldom

The reason for taking this to be a measure of morale is that a member is not likely to be either comfortable or effective in the legislature if he is not comfortable in his party caucus since the caucus and party cohesion are conspicuous parts of the legislative process in Ohio. Replies to this question are summarized in Table 6.21

What appears is that the vast majority of legislators usually agree with their party. In 1968, Republicans were obviously more in accord with caucus decisions than were Democrats. In 1969, however, Republican satisfaction with caucus decisions seems to have declined slightly while Democratic satisfaction increased. It is hard to divine a general trend in these contrasting movements, but it is fair to say that legislative morale seems fairly high as measured by agreement with caucus decisions.

In summary, a feeling of personal competence has been the majority position in the legislature through the period 1957-69 although a substantial minority has not shared the feeling of the majority. More important, the trend has been to a feeling of greater

TABLE 6.21

Frequency of Agreement with Caucus,
1968 and 1969 Surveys
(in percent)

Responses	1968		1969	
	D	R	D	R
(N)	(25)	(35)	(18)	(33)
Always	8	3	6	6
Nearly always	28	63	50	52
Usually	48	29	33	30
Sometimes	12	3	6	3
Seldom	4	3	0	6
NA	0	0	6	3

Source: Compiled by the author.

personal competence. Judgments by legislators concerning the competence of the legislature as a whole vary greatly with party with the majority Republicans rating the legislative performance much higher than the minority Democrats. But there is a drop in the evaluation of the legislature in both parties from 1968 to 1969. Morale seems to be high as indicated by several measures and may also be rising. With regard to the developmental hypothesis, the findings are somewhat mixed, but they tend to confirm it with reference to feelings of personal competence and morale.

Partisanship

In the earlier stipulation of legislative models, high partisanship was associated with the citizen legislature and lower partisanship with the professional. If these assumptions are correct and if the developmental hypothesis is also correct, then partisanship should be declining in the Ohio legislature. Whether or not partisanship is, in fact, declining can be measured in a variety of ways on the basis of existing data. One way involves the use of four items involving attitudes toward parties that were included in the 1957 survey and repeated exactly in the 1969 survey. A second way involves use of three items involving loyalty to party that were included in the 1963, 1968, and 1969 surveys. A third way involves consideration of social patterns within the legislature, and there is a relevant item in the 1963, 1968, and 1969 surveys. And, of course, the partisan character of a legislative body may be analyzed by examining roll call votes. All these methods will be used here.

The four items used in the 1957 and 1969 surveys are:

1. If a bill is important for his party's record, a member should vote with his party even if it costs him some support in his district.

2. The two parties should take clear-cut, opposing stands on the important state issues in order to encourage party responsibility.

3. Under our form of government, every individual should take an interest in government directly, not through a political party.

4. The best interests of the people would be better served if legislators were elected without party labels.

Response opportunities were agree, tend to agree, undecided, tend to disagree, and disagree. Results are shown in Table 6.22.

The first two items relate quite clearly to party responsibility. Agree answers constitute endorsement of the principle, and disagree answers constitute disavowal. With regard to item 1, there is a majority support for it in both 1957 and 1969, but support in 1969 is weaker than in the earlier year. With regard to item 2, the desirability of party conflict, there is considerable opposition in both sessions with opposition being stronger in the more recent session.

TABLE 6.22

Legislator Attitudes Toward Parties,
1957 and 1969 Surveys
(in percent)

Response (N)	1		2		3		4	
	1957 (156)	1969 (51)	1957 (160)	1969 (49)	1957 (153)	1969 (51)	1957 (162)	1969 (51)
Agree	26	8	13	2	24	2	4	0
Tend to agree	37	45	20	18	14	10	4	8
Undecided	2	12	1	4	1	4	1	2
Tend to disagree	17	22	32	41	26	47	27	31
Disagree	19	14	34	35	38	37	65	59

Failure of column totals to equal 100 is due to rounding.

Source: Compiled by the author.

Insofar as a movement away from the notion of party responsibility indicates a reduction of partisanship, there appears to be some decline in partisanship.

The second two items have to do with parties as vehicles for political participation or expression. Agreement would suggest a negative view of political parties from this point of view, and disagreement would suggest a positive view. Interestingly, disagreement with items 3 and 4 is overwhelming; and there is very little change from 1957 to 1969. Insofar as these items measure partisanship, it does not change in the period covered.

Items relating to legislator attitudes on party loyalty in the 1963, 1968, and 1969 surveys are:

1. A legislator should support the plans and programs of a governor belonging to his own party whether or not the governor can impose rewards and punishments.

2. A legislator should vote with the majority of his own party in the legislature whenever the majority of one party opposes the majority of another, and he should do this as a matter of principle and not merely as a matter of self-interest.

3. To get ahead in the legislature, a member must support the stands taken by a majority of his own party.
Responses to these questions are shown in Table 6.23.

With regard to item 1 concerning gubernatorial support, the data show that there never has been majority support for this proposition except among the Republicans in 1968, support being measured by the sum of agree and tend to agree responses. That may have been owing to the fact that Republican Governor James Rhodes won a smashing victory in 1966 and asserted strong leadership in the legislative session that followed. In general, the response of legislators to item 1 is to assert a position of legislative independence that the link of party does not overcome, at least, at this verbal level.

Trends may be measured by summing agree responses and tend to agree responses. Democratic acceptance of the position asserted in the item declines from 1963 to 1968 but rises again in 1969. Republican acceptance rises from 1963 to 1966, but declines in 1969. Hence, there is no clear trend; and, as measured here, no change in partisanship.

Accounting for interparty differences and differences from time to time is not required in this analysis since concern is with the appearance of expected changes with the passage of time; however, the differences that appear in the data arouse curiosity. The explanation likely to occur to observers of Ohio politics is that legislative attitudes toward executive leadership depend on the recent experiences of legislators with governors of their own or of the opposition party and on what they think the future might hold.

TABLE 6.23

Legislator Attitudes Toward Parties, by Party,
1963, 1968, and 1969 Surveys

	1					
	1963		1968		1969	
Response	D	R	D	R	D	R
(N)	(35)	(64)	(25)	(35)	(18)	(33)
Agree	14	12	4	0	0	9
Tend to agree	23	27	24	54	39	27
Undecided	0	2	4	0	0	18
Tend to disagree	17	17	20	17	17	30
Disagree	43	36	48	29	44	12
NA	3	6	0	0	0	3

	2					
	1963		1968		1969	
Response	D	R	D	R	D	R
(N)	(35)	(64)	(25)	(35)	(18)	(33)
Agree	20	27	16	9	6	24
Tend to agree	17	33	20	29	22	33
Undecided	9	5	8	3	6	6
Tend to disagree	11	11	32	40	17	18
Disagree	40	20	20	17	50	15
NA	3	5	4	3	0	3

	3					
	1963		1968		1969	
Response	D	R	D	R	D	R
(N)	(35)	(64)	(25)	(35)	(18)	(33)
Agree	29	22	4	14	28	21
Tend to agree	14	38	32	40	33	42
Undecided	0	2	16	11	6	12
Tend to disagree	17	14	24	20	29	6
Disagree	37	17	20	14	6	12
NA	3	8	4	0	0	6

Failure of column totals to equal 100 is due to rounding.

Source: Compiled by the author.

Item 2 in the table states the norm that a legislator should support his own party on floor votes. Majority support (the sum of agree and tend to agree responses) for this norm is given by the Republicans in both 1963 and 1969, while Democratic support in these years was substantially less. In 1968, Republican support for the item 2 norm was down to about what seems typical among Democrats. There is no clear trend in either party with regard to majority support for the proposition that a member should vote with his party nor in partisanship as measured by responses to this item.

The preceding two items in this set of three have to do with norms and roles involving political parties. Item 3 in the set has to do with role sanctions; in particular, whether support for party is sanctioned. Republicans give majority support to the proposition in each of the three surveys and even the Democrats give majority support in 1969.* Among Republicans there is a trend to greater support of the view that to get ahead, you go along with your party. There is a similar trend among Democrats. So it would appear that members see an increase in the efficacy of sanctions directed to support of party, that is, no decline of partisanship.

Respondents in the 1963, 1968, and 1969 surveys also answered a question concerning the party affiliation of their friends in the legislature. The question was, "How many of your closest friends in the legislature belong to your party?" Available answers were all, most, some, few, none, and don't know. Results are shown in Table 6.24.

Interpreting the data can be a little confusing because the number of respondents not answering the question was much higher in 1963 than in the later surveys.† Consequently, 1963 data are not precisely comparable to later data. However, this may be remedied by thinking of answers given by 1963 respondents as percentages of those answering the question. For example, 51 percent of the Republicans said that most of their closest friends in the legislature belonged to their party; and 26 percent did not answer the question. Thus, from the three-fourths who did answer, about two-thirds said most of their closest legislator friends were Republicans (50 percent being two-thirds of 75 percent).

What the data show is that friendship patterns tend to have partisan boundaries although these are not insurmountable, and this is

-----

*The existence of interparty differences tempts speculation. One thought is that the Republicans are expressing a majority party point of view and the Democrats a minority party point of view. Somewhat less support by Democrats for the proposition in item 3 may once again be a reflection of a minority rather than majority party view.

†This is probably attributable to the format of the 1963 questionnaire.

TABLE 6.24

Percent of Friends in the Legislature Belonging to
Same Party, by Session and by Party,
1963, 1968, and 1969 Surveys

Response	1963		1968		1969	
	D	R	D	R	D	R
(N)	(35)	(64)	(25)	(35)	(18)	(33)
All	3	3	0	9	0	3
Most	34	51	56	71	44	61
Some	26	9	44	17	39	30
Few	0	2	0	0	6	0
None	6	3	0	0	6	0
Don't Know	9	5	0	0	0	3
NA	23	26	0	3	6	3

Source: Compiled by the author.

more true on the Republican side than the Democratic. Insofar as trends are concerned, there may be some weakening in the pattern in the 1969 session. For example, 56 percent of the Democrats give an "all" or "most" response in 1968 and only 44 percent in 1969. The comparable figures for the Republicans are 80 percent and 64 percent. These data do suggest a weakening of partisanship.

This analysis of trends in partisanship up to this point has been in terms of legislator attitudes and in terms of social patterns. Another aspect of partisanship is the behavior of legislators on roll-call votes with reference to the parties. To determine that, all "controversial roll calls"* from 1957 through 1969 were examined. The number of party votes[†] was counted, and indexes of cohesion and likeness were computed for each roll call.[10]

Some of the data generated by this roll-call analysis are shown in Table 6.25.

---

*The definition of controversial or contested roll call is that suggested by Kenneth Janda: "A contested roll call vote is defined as any vote on which at least 10% of the membership of the chamber is recorded voting 'yes' and at least 10% is recorded voting 'no.'"[9]

[†]Party votes are those on which a majority of one party opposes the majority of the other.

High partisanship on roll calls is evident. The modal number of controversial roll calls in the Senate is more than 200 per session, and the modal frequency of party votes is greater than 70 percent. The modal number of controversial roll calls in the House is even higher than in the Senate, but the frequency of party votes is less. Calculations from the preceding table reveal that there are, on the average in the period covered, 139 party votes per Senate session and 148 in the House.

Not only are party divisions common in Ohio, the parties are cohesive on these votes. The modal index of cohesion for Republicans

TABLE 6.25

Frequency of Party Votes as a Percent of All Controversial
Roll Calls, Number of Controversial Roll Calls, Mean
Index of Cohesion, and Mean Index of Likeness by
Party on Party Votes, Ohio General
Assembly, 1957-69

Session	Frequency of Party Votes	Number of Controversial Roll Calls	Party Votes Mean Index of Cohesion		Mean Index of Likeness
			R	D	
Senate					
1957	49	57	72	80	24
1959	75	279	72	84	22
1961	70	240	85	83	16
1963	79	258	95	91	7
1965	75	251	82	90	14
1967	76	135	84	70	23
1969	66	107	71	64	33
			R	D	
House					
1957	41	152	49	54	48
1959	61	392	61	65	37
1961	46	277	70	53	39
1963	57	274	72	61	33
1965	43	271	61	57	43
1967	49	387	71	69	30
1969	49	308	59	60	41

Source: Compiled by the author.

in the Senate on party votes is 82, and the comparable figure for the Democrats is 83. Indexes around 80 are produced by parties voting 90 percent to 10 percent on an issue. Modal indexes for the House are a little lower being 61 for the Republicans and 60 for the Democrats. Indexes around 60 are produced by 80-20 divisions within a party. Since all indexes of cohesion tend to be high for each party in each house of the legislature, indexes of likeness are necessarily low. The general picture is frequent party conflict with each party being united in its opposition to the other.

Fluctuations do occur, and some are rather clearly traceable to majority party policy. In 1957, the Republicans had just recovered the governorship and had continued their control of the legislature. Furthermore, 1958 was to see the election of the state's first four-year-term governor. Republican strategy was to prepare for the reelection of their incumbent governor by having a short, quiet legislative session. Conflict was suppressed, but 1958 turned out to be a Democratic year. Policy of the exultant Democrats was to press for enactment of programs long stymied in the legislature with the consequence that conflict was very frequent.

Although fluctuations appear, trends are not readily apparent. The number of controversial roll calls in the Senate declines in 1967 and 1969 as do the frequency of party votes, but no such movement occurs in the House. In the short run, at least, roll-call behavior does not seem to have changed much with regard to partisanship despite formal change in the direction of a professional legislature.

Thus, a number of attempts to measure partisanship have been made. The first was in terms of the principle of party responsibility. It was assumed that rising levels of support for the principle would indicate increasing partisanship and vice versa. It was found that support for party responsibility was apparently declining if anything; hence, partisanship was presumably decreasing. Another test involved an attempt to measure attitudes toward political parties as vehicles for participation and expression. A positive view of parties in this role would indicate partisanship, and increasingly positive views would indicate increasing partisanship. It was found that the vast majority of legislators did view parties as suitable vehicles for participation and expression and that there was no trend.

Another test involved executive leadership. It was felt that increasing support for the notion that a member should support a governor of his own party would indicate rising partisanship and vice versa. No trend was discovered. Members were also asked if they thought they should support a majority of their own party as a matter of principle. Increasing support for this idea would indicate increasing partisanship and vice versa. Once again there was no trend. Members were also asked whether they thought party loyalty was sanctioned.

Greater acceptance of this belief over a period of time would certainly indicate rising partisanship and vice versa; and there was, in fact, increasing belief that party loyalty was sanctioned. Partisanship was, therefore, presumably increasing.

Study of friendship patterns suggested on the other hand that partisanship might be declining, but study of roll-call votes suggested that there was no readily apparent change in partisanship. The general conclusion is that there may be some changes in the partisan character of the legislature underway but as yet no clear increase or decrease in partisanship.

CONCLUSION

As was stated in the beginning, advocates of structural change do not push these changes merely for their own sake. Rather, they expect them to be associated with other changes that will have an impact on performance. The association may be causal in nature or it may be expected to occur because structural change and other changes spring from some common underlying factor or factors. Or the association may be perhaps inexplicitly normative; that is, structural change and other associated changes may be both expressions of some common norm.

And broadly speaking, reformers hope for a move from a citizen legislature to a professional legislature. Distinguishing the formal characteristics of these two types is not hard since it is only a matter of noting some accepted definitions. But the informal characteristics to be ascribed to each model are hardly ever articulated; so their statement is conjectural. So what appears are two models of the legislature whose formal arrangements are definable and whose associated informal arrangements are conjectural.

For the purpose of analysis, it was postulated that there was a development in progress marked by a change from citizen legislatures to professional legislatures. This was the developmental hypothesis. The first step then in the actual analysis was to look for changes in relevant formal arrangements, if any; and the second step was to see whether informal arrangements associated with structural change were appearing.

Two results were sought. One was simply to discover whether expected developments were occurring. The other was somewhat more complex and involved possible correction of, at least, the professional model. That is, if expected formal changes were appearing without presumably associated informal changes, the model might be altered to eliminate and alter expectations with regard to the association of its formal and informal elements.

What has been found in the case of Ohio is that the general assembly has moved very clearly toward the professional model with regard to its formal arrangements. So to that extent the developmental hypothesis is clearly confirmed.

With regard to informal arrangements, the picture is much less clear. The first condition associated with a professional rather than citizen legislature was a broadly open recruitment process. Data were drawn mainly from the 1966 survey of nominations for the first reapportioned legislature, and they showed the process to be very heavily influenced by major political party organizations. Data from the 1969 study suggested there might be some opening of the process, but the suggestion was a weak one indeed.

A second condition associated with increasing professionalization was rising occupational status in the membership of the legislature. There did seem to be some small increase in the proportion of legislators drawn from professional occupational categories. Whether this by itself would indicate rising occupational status is doubtful, but the possibility must be counted.

It was thought that a more professional legislature would be one with more high-tenure members. However, movement in and out of the legislature, which has been high in the past, remains high. The verdict is no trend, and as was indicated, this is perhaps what should be expected as a consequence of reapportionment.

A fourth looked-for change associated with growing professionalization was a shift in representational roles from delegate to trustee and of representational focus from local to state. Contrary to expectations, there is not only no movement in the hypothesized direction but possibly an increase in the relative frequency of the delegate role and perhaps of a local focus.

Purposive roles were also considered, and an increase in the so-called inventor role and a decline in ritualist and tribune roles was the expected pattern of development. With considerable caution generated by methodological problems, it did appear that the expected pattern was appearing in the period from roughly 1957 to the present with the complicating factor that a reversal in trend evidently occurred between 1968 and 1969.

A sixth condition associated with a professional rather than a citizen legislature was greater distance between legislator and interest group representatives and activity. It was found that reliance on interest groups for technical services, e.g., the drafting of bills, had declined and that the belief that interest groups were too strong had increased somewhat. Legislators were also a bit less likely to see the role of interest groups in the legislative process as positive. All this would seem to be consistent with what would be expected given the increasing professionalization of the legislature.

Another development associated with a professionalized legislature was an increasing willingness to support governmental activity. For whatever reason, this has certainly occurred on the level of attitude and verbal expression.

An eighth condition associated with increasing professionalization was the growth of specialization. Surveys toward the end of the 1960s showed a legislature in which specialization was not valued very highly; and, in fact, there was a somewhat lower appreciation for specialization in the 1969 legislature than in the 1968. All this is contrary to expectation.

Still another condition associated with the change from a citizen legislature to a professional legislature is an increasing sense of competence and morale. The evidence is that feelings of individual competence did increase from 1957 to 1969. On the other hand, evaluations by legislators of total legislative performance were not necessarily high at the end of the 1960s. It seemed fair to infer that the sense of personal competence was increasing concurrently with professionalization but that evaluations of total legislative performance were likely to be the function of short-run factors. Morale was measured in several ways, and was counted as fairly high.

The tenth informal change anticipated as a concomitant to rising professionalism was a decline in partisanship. A variety of measures were used to try to detect a trend. Findings were changes away from partisanship in some cases, movement toward it in others, and no change elsewhere. The general conclusion was that there might be some change in the pattern of partisanship but no net reduction in its strength.

So in the net, what informal conditions associated with formal changes to a professional legislature have emerged in Ohio? The answer is a few. They are an increase of the purposive role of inventor, greater distance from interest group and by extension interest group politics, more support for state government activity, a heightened sense of personal competence among legislators, and fairly high morale. Some other possible developments have been noted, but they are only possibilities at best.

What then should be said? One answer is that adoption of the arrangements said by reformers to constitute a professional legislature is associated with only a few other changes that are rather easily predictable. Are they important enough to justify the effort and expense of professionalizing? The answer to that may be "yes," but that leads to other conjectures and other studies.

Another response to the outcome of this attempt to detect the informal changes associated with the professional model of the legislature is to say that some expected conditions seem to be present and that with regard to other possibilities it is too soon to know. The right phrase with which to summarize this reaction would be "not yet." That too leads to other studies, particularly to ones that would continue the longitudinal dimensions that were traced with varying degrees of uncertainty in this study.

But, leaving the "not yet" position for future inquiry, it may be said that the transition from citizen to professional legislature means some new formal arrangements and a short list of concommitants: growth of inventor roles, removal from interest group politics, more support for state government action, heightened sense of competence, and good morale. This then would be the corrected model of the professional legislature; and when it is urged, it may be said that this is what is being discussed and not some other not specified set of wider ramifications.

NOTES

1. John C. Wahlke, Heinz Eulau, William Buchanan, and Leroy C. Ferguson, The Legislative System: Explorations in Legislative Behavior (New York: John Wiley, 1962).

2. Thomas A. Flinn and Frederick M. Wirt, "Local Party Leaders: Groups of Like Minded Men," Midwest Journal of Political Science, February 1965, pp. 77-98, esp. pp. 97-98.

3. For a thoughtful discussion of this innovation in staffing, see the article by C. W. Chance and Higdon C. Roberts, "Staffing Legislative Standing Committees: The Ohio Experience," State Government, Winter 1970, pp. 31-38.

4. The concepts are those of Wahlke et al., The Legislative System, especially chap. 12 and 13.

5. Items are those used by Kenneth Janda, with some small adaptation, in an unpublished paper.

6. Wahlke, et al., The Legislative System, chap. 11.

7. Ibid., p. 256.

8. Ibid., p. 259.

9. Janda, Data Processing, p. 229.

10. These indexes are those of Stuart Rice, which are described in a number of places. One is Lee F. Anderson, Meredith W. Watts, Jr., and Allen R. Wilcox, Legislative Roll-Call Analysis (Evanston, Ill.: Northwestern University Press, 1966), pp. 33-35, 44-45.

JAMES J. BEST is a member of the faculty of the University of Washington. After graduating from the University of Chicago, he studied at Tufts University and the University of North Carolina. In addition to his studies of state legislative phenomena, Dr. Best has published research on communications media and public opinion.

THOMAS A. FLINN has been regarded for many years as one of the leading specialists on Ohio politics and a significant contributor to literature on state political behavior. He taught political science at Oberlin College from 1955 until 1967, during which time he served a term as mayor of Oberlin. After three years on the faculty of The Ohio State University, he assumed the chairmanship of the Department of Political Science at Cleveland State University.

DOUGLAS S. GATLIN is Professor of Political Science at Florida Atlantic University. He is known for his studies of southern politics, especially in the states of North Carolina and Florida. He has also edited a text on political parties and political behavior that is widely used in U.S. colleges and universities.

SAMUEL K. GOVE has been on the faculty of the University of Illinois for more than two decades. Throughout virtually all this time he has been affiliated with the Institute of Government and Public Affairs, of which he became director in 1967. From such a vantage point he has been close to Illinois government, from which experience he has written several valuable articles, monographs, and books on state politics.

JAMES A. ROBINSON, who edited this volume, is Professor of Political Science and President of Macalester College. His interests as a political scientist include conditions for innovation in legislatures and the role of representative institutions in government. He is a former Congressional Fellow of the American Political Science Association.

ALAN ROSENTHAL has been associated with the Eagleton Institute of Politics, Douglass College, Rutgers University, since 1966. His works include special studies of several state legislatures as well as of the U.S. Congress. He was formerly a Congressional Fellow of the American Political Science Association.

ALAN J. WYNER is a member of the faculty of the University of California, Santa Barbara. Formerly he taught at The Ohio State University and directed a comparative study of fourteen state governorships under the auspices of the National Center for Education in Politics.

STATE LEGISLATURES: An Evaluation of
Their Effectiveness

The Complete Report by the Citizens
Conference on State Legislatures

STATE ENVIRONMENTAL MANAGEMENT:
A Nine-State Survey and Handbook

Elizabeth H. Haskell and
Victoria S. Price

GOVERNING URBAN AMERICA IN THE 1970s

edited by Werner Z. Hirsch and
Sidney Sonenblum

EDUCATIONAL POLICY-MAKING AND THE
STATE LEGISLATURE: The New York Experience

Mike M. Milstein and Robert E. Jennings